THE BEST WAY TO WALK

THE BEST WAY TO WALK
The CHIC MURRAY Story
Andrew Yule

Chick and Maidie with young Douglas, Rothesay 1951.

MAINSTREAM
PUBLISHING

This edition 1995

First published in Great Britain in 1989
by Mainstream Publishing Co (Edinburgh) Ltd
7 Albany Street, Edinburgh EH1 3UG

ISBN 1 85158 782 9

A catalogue record for this book is available from the British Library

Typeset by C. R. Barber & Partners (Highlands) Ltd,
Fort William, Scotland
Printed and bound in Great Britain by
Butler & Tanner Ltd, Frome and London

This book is dedicated with much love to Maidie Murray.
It would not have been possible without her personal reminiscences,
good offices, good soup and wonderful, generous nature.

Acknowledgments

My thanks to the following for granting interviews: Jack and Tom Alexander, Johnnie Beattie, Joe Beltrami, Nat Berlin, Andy Cameron, Alex Clark, Ian Christie, Billy Connolly, Iain Cuthbertson, Rikki Fulton, Jack Gibson, Barbara and Murray Grigor, Jimmy Hepburn, Jack House, Bill Jenkinson, Kathy Kay, Israel Kaye, Jimmy Logan, Ben Lyons, Alexander Mackinnon, Billy Marsh, Archie McCulloch, Neil McNeil, Father Joseph Mills, Jack and Mary Milroy, Liz Moriarty, Spike Milligan, Alex Norton, Bill Peterson, Bill Reid, John Tate, Tom Walsh, Jenny Wells, Lilian Welsh, Wullie Woodburn, Anna Young—and especially Annabelle, Douglas Sr., Douglas Jr., Deanna and Nana.

A special 'thank you' for their tremendous support on the project to Eunice Sweenie, Hattie Forrest, Harry Shaw, Eric Fung—and Alasdair Marshall and George McKechnie.

Contents

Foreword

[by Billy Connolly]

It must have been around 1960, that I was sitting in the living room of a Bearsden house belonging to the parents of my friend Billy McKinnell. Billy's father was a builder with his own business, and relatively well off, which was reflected in the classy furnishings of the house. Mrs McKinnell had recently been shopping in town and had purchased a rather fancy sofa suite—Sanderson I do believe, covered in a heavy embroidered material, with a basic colour of canary yellow. In order, I imagine, to preserve the sunshiny yellowness of this suite she had had the whole thing fitted with polythene covers, which, while rendering the whole thing a bit tacky to say the least, did perform the function of preserving the original colour.

It was on this suite that I sat, on the couch to be precise, secretly fearing that she might sneak up behind and cover me in polythene as well if I should drop off while waiting for my friend Billy. He did eventually get ready and came downstairs to meet me, and we were about to leave when a voice from the television in the corner said, 'Ladies and Gentlemen, Chic Murray and Maidie'. We both turned to watch this couple, a big man with a tartan bunnet balanced on his head and a little blonde woman standing in front of him, almost, it would appear, leaning on him, and playing a huge accordion. Every now and then she would look up and back, giving him a loving glance, which he would return, but as soon as she turned away, he would draw her the dirtiest look imaginable. The audience were in fits of laughter; so were Billy and I. I think I can say without any fear of contradiction I had never seen anything so funny before, but the best was yet to come.

At the end of the song, *China Doll* if memory serves me, Maidie took a back seat and Chic stepped forward to tell a story. He started with a few one-liners that had us howling—weird observations like, 'I always use the door handle, it saves you putting your hand through the letter box.'

9

Then he started on a lengthy story about two friends who wanted to emigrate to America together, their names were Semit and Drawers. There was a part of the story, quite near the beginning, when Drawers is talking to his father, and bidding him a fond farewell when his father sagely gives him the advice, 'Never let the Drawers down!' I remember nothing else of the story, because it was at this point that my limp, out-of-control body slid right off the polythene covers and landed in a shuddering heap on the floor, another helpless victim of the Murray Magic.

Until then I had been toying with the idea of comedy as a career, but on that night, like a blinding flash on the road to Damascus, I knew that there was nothing else for me, that nothing else would do. As the years rolled by, when I had indeed taken up comedy as my livelihood, I was lucky enough to befriend Chic, whose partnership with Maidie had then ended, and I had many a laugh over a pint or at dinner with this most clever and witty man.

Possibly the most impressive thing about Chic as far as I am concerned was the abstract form of his humour. It had a surreal feel about it that nothing else I had ever heard resembled or compared with. As he got older, with this side of his humour still developing, goodness knows where it might have led if we had only been given a few more years of his genius.

He was by far the funniest man I ever heard, and one of the nicest people I ever had the privilege of knowing. Chic was a Comic Legend in his own time.

Billy Connolly
February 1989

I

Star Turn

'I'm living with my aunt here in town. Well, it's not really my aunt. You always say you're living with your auntie and it's never really your auntie, you know. In this case I know it's not my auntie, it's my uncle. *He just likes to be* called *auntie!'*

'Stirling can have seen few more picturesque sights,' said Chic as he surveyed himself in his dressing room while awaiting the cue for his part in a television recording at the town's University. He was indeed resplendent in a navy suit, dashingly embellished by the addition of a pink carnation in the buttonhole of his lapel and the tartan bunnet perched on his head. The young driver, who had brought him from the BBC's headquarters in Glasgow to the University campus, was creased with laughter, as he had been at all of Chic's asides on the journey.

Over the intercom they could hear the show's compère, Danny Street, serenade the audience with his latest song, 'The World is a Circle'. 'And I'm so square,' Chic cracked. 'What do I think of Danny? Oh, he's not *bad*—but a bit *pedestrian*, if you ask me. He should consider a name change—look how it did wonders for Engelbert Humperdinck. Something with *impact*, something arresting, something like *Sauchiehall* Street would do it!'

Now they could hear Danny introduce Chic with 'My next guest — well, he never seems to know whether he's coming or going—but wherever he goes, laughter is always around. Here he is, ladies and gentlemen—the Tall Droll, Chic Murray!'

As conductor Brian Fahey struck up his fanfare with 'Sweet Georgia Brown', Chic walked on, alternately smiling and wincing at the applause from the audience and the band's unbridled enthusiasm. He was indeed a tall, fairly stout figure, who seemed to test the ground first before each tentative step, allowing his feet to hover—like mine detectors—over each proposed landing area before actually making contact. As arranged, the band relentlessly continued its ebullient fanfare while Chic tried to make himself heard, until Brian was firmly instructed to cease and desist. '*Half* of that would have done me!' Chic admonished. 'What are you after, a knighthood or something?'

The preliminaries over, and with the audience already amused and intrigued, he drew their attention to his buttonhole carnation in well-modulated, genteel tones that would have done credit to an extremely refined Edinburgh librarian, banker—or landlady.

'You might be wondering why this Eiffel Tower's in my Whistle and Flute,' he said. 'Well, I put it in for a wedding—just in case you thought it had been thrown by some careless maiden in Stirling. So I went to the wedding—a nice wedding—in Blackpool—nice wedding, well—just the *usual* type of wedding—a *man* and a *woman* getting married, that was *all*. That was all that was in it as far as *I* could see. Eight times married, I didn't know that, but the fellow sat beside me, he knew that. Eight times married he said—in a whisper that carried all over the church! And then I realised it myself as soon as I heard the organist. He didn't play "Here Comes The Bride", he played "Here We Are Again!"'

'And an incident happened which I didn't mean to mention, but it's *out now*. There was a woman there with the longest nose I've ever seen. Now I've nothing *against* long noses. We have them in our family. They *run* in our family. But she had a real beaut—you could have touched it. I didn't, but you *could* have touched it. And I thought—if things don't liven up, I'll touch her nose! But what attracted me to it—speaking in the neutral gender of course—was the way she used it to turn the pages of the hymn book.' Here Chic bemusedly and hilariously demonstrated to much laughter from the audience.

'And then she said to me—*sotto voce*—she went "Sniff! Sniff!" and said, "There's someone cooking cabbage in Manchester!" So we left the church after the ceremony and we made our way to the hall adjacent to the church—which they must have paid for, because there was no difficulty in getting in. And then the wedding cake was brought in—oh, a beautiful cake with candles on it and I was completely *intrigued*, so much so that I sort of lost control and I pointed at the cake and said, "There's candles on the cake!" And someone said, "Yes, there is. It's the bride's birthday. It's a dual-purpose cake." Well—I don't know what age she was, but the heat was *desperate*!

'And this woman with the long nose was seated opposite me and I was trying to ignore her without being rude—because it's so easy to be rude, but I was *fascinated* with her nose—and what she could *do* with it! Why, I watched her pick up a bun from the floor!

'And then it *all happened*. *Someone*, inadvertently I suppose, nodded to her. And as she nodded back she cut the cake! Of course the bride was in tears—so was the cake. So, as we left the church, you know the

tramlines which run in Blackpool—well, *they* don't run in Blackpool, but
they allow the *trams* to run in Blackpool—we crossed the tramlines—oh,
an interesting ceremony—and this long-nosed woman was at my back. I
knew that because of the constant prodding I was getting—at least I was
hoping it was her.

   'And then she slipped—and as she slipped, she *fell*. Fortunately I was
leaning forward at the time—otherwise I would have been *dissected*! And
she fell face downwards and straight as a die she made for the tramlines.
And her nose *lodged* in the aperture of the line—the aperture, which
allows the wheel to run freely to Fleetwood or—well, I've never gone the

other way, I don't know where it goes! Anyway, we took a chance and a few of us bent down. We tugged and pulled but we couldn't dislodge her nose and someone beside me, an engineer from Motherwell or somewhere, said, "It's the heat of her nose and the cold of the steel doing this." I said, "Oh, *no!*"' At this Chic grimaced and shook his head at the memory.

'We ended up picking her up by the legs and wheeling her along to the depot, and *someone* phoned the mayor and he took the salute at the North Pier—did it very well, I must say. But she was *frightened*. I didn't know that until she whispered out the side of her mouth, she said, "Could I be *electrocuted?*" Well, I hadn't thought of that and I dropped her leg *immediately*. "No, I don't think so," I replied, "Not unless you throw your other leg over the top wire!"'

Chic went off to thunderous applause, still walking as if on hot coals and with one arm held out to the side and a pinky elegantly extended. From the moment he had walked on to the stage until the moment he had left it, he had carried the audience in the palm of his hand. His timing was uncanny and apparently effortless, with every nuance of meaning wrung from his tale and milked for all it was worth. He looked completely at ease and the total professional to the audience, who recognised him in 1974 as a comedian whose unique style was acknowledged throughout Britain—and much farther afield as well.

*   *   *

Chic, two years old.

Isabella and William Murray's wee boy had come only a short distance geographically from the Clydeside town of Greenock—but a long, long way professionally. His parents, William Murray and Isabella McKinnon, had become engaged just before William left for the Western Front. He had been badly gassed during the Battle of the Somme in 1916 and invalided home, his lungs so badly damaged that he was permanently disabled. Before the war he had been a foreman with the Glasgow & Western Railway and it was a year before he could resume work and before he and Isabella could marry. Their only child was a boy, Charles Thomas McKinnon Murray, born on 6 November 1919. It was a grim time for Greenock, the immediate post-war boom being quickly followed by a slump, depression and widespread unemployment with all the attendant hardship and misery for the town's families.

TIVOLI
THEATRE OF VARIETIES
ABERDEEN

Programme

Licensee & General Manager G.W. BOLTON

2

Growing Up in Greenock

'This friend of mine had a terrible upbringing. When his mother lifted him up to feed him, his father rented the pram out. Then when they came into money later his mother hired a woman to push the pram—and he's been pushed for money every since! I asked him once what his ambition was and he replied it was to have an ambition. In the end tragedy struck—as he lay on his death-bed he confessed to three murders. Then he got better.'

Fifteen hundred men who had left Greenock to fight for king and country were never to return. For those who did survive, some measure of post-war prosperity might have been expected; instead the majority of the returning ex-servicemen found themselves the forgotten generation. With a population of 81,000 to support, Greenock's main sources of employment foundered with the slump in the shipbuilding and sugar industries.

In 1920 a married man could expect to earn only a scant one shilling per hour, reducing to seven pence for single men, and it was not until the mid-1920s that prospects would brighten again, if only briefly. Scott's and Kincaid's experienced a brief revival in shipbuilding demand, this time for motor ships. With the American Stock Market crash of 1929 even this petered out although a revival of trade did take place in sugar refining, which had been hard hit by imports from the USA and Cuba. As a result of the down-turn in worldwide demand, these imports fell, enabling several sugar refineries to reopen locally. It was a fragile recovery, based on the lowest-ever price to the customer, but a welcome respite amid the prevailing gloom. Bitterness overflowed as a means test was introduced where the unemployment benefit of the house was reduced according to the earnings of the rest of the family. Many families were split up as employed sons and daughters were forced to leave home. In 1929, when the Town Council refused to meet a deputation from the Labour and Trades Association, 4000 demonstrators ran riot in the town. A year later a second deputation of unemployed men was again refused a hearing, but a committee was employed to interview them. Their central demand—that the scale of relief be raised—was turned down, but certain of the unemployed who had been taken off the relief list were restored to it for the fortnight covering Christmas and the New Year.

A Royal Commission report of the time read: 'The majority of the families at present occupying houses in the central area of Greenock are living in conditions of great poverty.' A later report summarised: 'Everyone suffered in that depression. There were splendid journeymen of every trade walking the streets unemployed.' Was this what fifteen hundred men—and millions more all over the country—had laid down their lives for?

At least William Irvine Murray, with his steady job on the railway, did not have to suffer the indignity and hardship of unemployment, but he had his own legacy of the war to contend with in his growing infirmity. He turned to evangelism with the formation of the Burning Bush Society in Greenock. When young Chic (Isabella having formed the abbreviation of 'Charles' and her family name of 'McKinnon') was only seven, he was drafted in by his father to play the organ at the society's meetings. To Chic's accompaniment a selection of gospel songs would be sung, always preceded by their introductory, 'We are the members of the Burning Bush Society', for the benefit of anyone listening who might have been in any doubt. The collection was taken up to the tune of 'John Brown's Body', but the lyrics ran, 'When the plate is passed around, put half-a-crown in'. If any member felt that one of the public was holding back on the stipulated donation, the words would be yelled out for greater emphasis in an attempt to shame the miserly into producing the full amount.

After the singing was over the assembly would head for the nearest green patch and proceed to select their 'burning bush' of the evening. The local fire station invoiced for their services in those days, resulting in all sorts of complications for the society from aggrieved landowners, who reckoned that having their bushes burned was bad enough without being charged for having the conflagration extinguished.

Isabella McKinnon was a handsome woman, with a sunny disposition and an air of serenity. She stood exactly six feet tall, the same height as William. Her easy-going nature hid a keen intelligence, for as an avid reader Isabella was a match for anyone and the walls at their Bank Street home were lined with bookshelves containing volumes on every subject. Her favourites were historical novels, the poetry of Robert Burns and anything on astronomy. She would often leave annotated passages for Chic's benefit when she passed a book on to him and through them he was able to travel the world and take himself far away from the grey streets of Greenock.

William took Chic on fishing trips and country rambles, where there was ample opportunity to talk to his son on his own wide range of subjects, everything from world affairs to ornithology, William's speciality. Chic did well enough at school in every subject save one—but his overall understanding of the world and how it worked probably exceeded that of his contemporaries thanks to his parents' subtler, but no less effective educational approach.

Isabella grieved for her husband as his infirmity increased and comforted him to the best of her ability, referring to him fondly as 'my poor bonnie laddie'. In the evening she would frequently read aloud to father and son, favouring them with declamatory excerpts from her current book, and acting out all the parts for their benefit. Chic would sit enrapt at these performances, taking it all in as he listened to his mother's voice, while marvelling at the pictures the words conjured up.

Her husband's Burning Bush Society was regarded by Isabella with tolerance and understanding as a therapeutic aberration, realising that it sustained him in some small degree as his health continued to fail and chronic bronchitis began to set in. Isabella herself was a devout member of Greenock's 'Wee Frees' church, giving Chic a foot in both camps, since he was obliged to attend church with his mother and his father's meetings on top. He had no complaints. 'I was helping Dad and being close to him. I knew instinctively it wasn't going to last forever, so I did it while I could. He drew in a lot of the eccentrics and worthies of the town, many of them marvellous characters that I've never forgotten.'

As William's condition deteriorated and his recurring respiratory difficulties became more prolonged, he found he could no longer attend his beloved society's meetings. Sinking into despair in spite of his wife's tenderest ministrations, he turned to the bottle after a lifetime of abstinence. He drank to ease his pain, but even in drink remained a caring husband and loving father. Chic was shattered when William was admitted to hospital and Isabella was warned that her husband's condition was hopeless and that it was only a matter of time. William would often write to Chic from hospital with lists of subjects he wanted him to study, describing his hopes for his son's future. There would be two or three pages of great detail, then the letter would finish vaguely, as if a curtain had come down. Towards the end he continued to write, with many touching, whimsical observations of life from his hospital bed. These were letters that Chic would always treasure, for to him they were the very essence of his father. One of his favourites read:

My dear Chic,
There was a great fight last Monday morning outside my window, about six o'clock. Mr and Mrs Sparrow (Stumpy and his wife) had started putting their house in order on Saturday and had it nearly finished. A Mr and Mrs Starling, on the lookout for a family residence, noticed the Sparrows' villa nearly ready and attempted by force to take advantage of the work done by Stumpy and his good lady.

Stumpy would have none of it and guarded the nest against the attack of the Starlings, winking at his wife, who flew off for help. The Starlings were proving too much for poor Stumpy, whose home was being badly torn. He was panting sore and on the point of collapse when from round the corner swooped about fifty sparrows, led by Stumpy's angry wife. The Starlings got more than they bargained for and after being pecked, slapped and buffeted, they gave in and flew off, one of them bleeding. They came back again on Tuesday, but did not offer to renew the fight. Stumpy and his wife are now quite safe.

Love, Daddy

With the help of William and Isabella the world and its limitless possibilities had been opened up for their son, but for William these possibilities were ending. A fervent believer all his days in the shining hour, for him it was now rapidly passing on this earth. The end came on Chic's fourteenth birthday. Having arranged for several of her son's pals to come round in the evening for a small celebration, Isabella found herself summoned that morning to the hospital to be told that William was dying.

'He passed away soon after we arrived in the middle of that cold, sunny November morning,' Chic recalled. 'I'll never forget that blank, timeless moment when Mum and I stood in the room alone. The tears wouldn't come and I kept repeating dumbly "Dad's gone . . .".'

On their return home a postcard lay behind the front door, addressed to Master C. Murray. Isabella picked it up and handed it slowly to Chic. It was from William and read:

My dear Chic,
Fourteen years ago today you came into the world and made a great big noise. You have not been a bad boy thro' all these years. I wish you every good wish and hope you have a jolly party tonight.

Daddy

This time there was no stopping the tears as Chic broke down and cried in Isabella's arms.

*   *   *

Before William's death Isabella had invited her brother Tom to move in with them. Like William, Tom in his own way was a victim of the First World War, having been taken prisoner in Salonika and held in a camp for two years before his eventual escape and return home. He had been presumed dead and found that his childhood sweetheart, to whom he had been engaged, had married another.

Isabella saw the terrible change the incarceration had made on Tom. Physically he was a wreck, down from eleven to eight stone, but a more dramatic change had taken place inside him. He was morose and fretful, as if all the joy of living had gone, leaving just a wounded shell. Although his health recovered enough to enable him to take up his old job on the railway, he kept to himself outside of work.

Before William's death Tom was very much a background figure in the Murray household, and in this role Chic could accept him. He was sorry for his uncle and went out of his way to get on with him, but this was to change when it emerged that Tom saw himself as the new head of the house. Young as he was, Chic would have none of it, but their falling-out intensified over the ownership of William's gold watch, with Tom claiming that William had intended it for him. Chic never forgave him for this.

The organ lessons which had made Chic a natural for his father's Burning Bush Society had been provided by a Miss Brown, whom Chic remembered with great affection. 'We didn't have a piano at home then, just this enormous American organ, so the dear lady started me off on that instead. My speciality was Handel's Largo in G which I played so often I even began to like it. I practised for hours. It took me out of myself, although I won't say where it took me.'

Chic was also able to find a piano eventually at a friend's house. His mother insisted he practise the organ for at least an hour after school whatever happened and only after this could he get out to play with his pals. His great delight was to play football in the streets, although this was a punishable offence in Greenock in those days. An old school friend, Bill Jenkinson, recalled the two of them being fined half-a-crown each the first time they were caught: 'This made a very deep impression on him. So much so that the next time the police came along in their "Wee Huey" as we called their tiny patrol car, he immediately left goal and tagged on alongside a passing woman shopper, marching in step beside her. I was left to pay a five-bob fine for my second offence, while he walked off scot-free.'

Bill also gave an impression of the Murray household as it appeared to a schoolboy: 'I didn't see much of his father. He was there, but he wasn't there, if you know what I mean. Mrs Murray was a cut above. She always kept a plate of Kemp's chocolate caramel wafer biscuits and offered them along with her own marvellous baking. The biscuits were a penny each, which was a hell of a lot of money in those days. Aye, but she offered them, mind you, not Chic! We thought she was a toff. Chic was the limit. He'd play her up all the time, but she was a match for him.'

A second impression was given by another pal, tall, serious Neil McNeil, or Big Neilie as he was known: 'She was the best respected, nicest and cleverest woman in all of Greenock. I've never seen anything upset her. She had the most wonderfully placid nature. In the Thirties you could see her out getting the messages, trailing her shopper behind her. Nowadays everyone's got one, but I reckon Mrs Murray was the first. She had rigged it up herself from a walking stick, a basket and a set of wheels.'

Many years later Chic would recall his first day at school—and his first meeting with some new school friends. 'There was Sammy Cruickshanks, a real character, who distinguished himself when the teacher was taking us through an early "get to know you" session—oh, Greenock was very far ahead in those days, very far ahead. When Sammy was asked what his mother and father did, he replied that he didn't have a mother and father. Was he an orphan, then? No, Sammy replied, he was his auntie's bairn by the lodger!

'Then there was Gooey Scott. I'd known him for a year or two and we all accepted that was his name, but this didn't satisfy the teacher, who insisted, "No, Gooey, that must be your nickname, son, what's your real name?" He insisted indignantly that Gooey was his real name, so the teacher asked him to spell it. He handed her a piece of paper with "Guy" written on it. It seemed that when his mother had been expecting Gooey she had come across "Guy" in a book and thought that would be a lovely name for her son. Unfortunately she thought it was pronounced Gooey—so Gooey to us he always remained. Sammy, Gooey and I were always thick as thieves after that, with another friend of mine who lived close by, Jimmy Gorman. Neilie and Bill I met later.'

Chic became renowned for his erratic timekeeping at school, and the increasingly fantastic explanations he advanced when he turned up late. His classmates would be in stitches at his involved stories—'I was pressganged by a bunch of landscape gardeners,' was one excuse—while even his teachers began to look forward to his latest tale, which would invariably be delivered with absolute conviction, no matter how unlikely.

Chic's front door was a dozen steps up from the street and in his hurry to get out to play football one day he skidded down them, chipping several bones in his left ankle. This affected his walking for the rest of his days and largely contributed to the famous stage walk, for thereafter he always contrived to land first on his toes to protect his ankles.

As the eldest daughter of 14 children, it was to one of her brothers, Chic's Uncle Alex, that Isabella turned when her son began to get very bad reports from school after William had been admitted to hospital. Chic seemed to be innumerate, for when he took him on Alexander McKinnon found that his nephew had difficulty in adding even two and two: 'He would go into a dwam sometimes even with me, but he would get a skelp on the lug for his pains. It went against the grain because basically all Chic wanted to do was play the organ and kick a ball! His father wasn't much help at the end. Chic worshipped him, but William shut up shop a wee while before he died and that boy suffered with him in his last months.'

As well as becoming highly proficient on piano and organ, Chic dabbled on the banjo, mandolin and guitar. He developed a melodic singing voice and had the rare ability to yodel in harmony. As he approached school-leaving age he put his name down for a five-year apprenticeship in marine engineering in Kincaid's. His timing could not have been better, for at last prospects on the Clyde were looking brighter. Unemployment in Greenock dropped below 10,000 in 1934 for the first time in years, while Scott's, the local barometer of forward business, had a busy season, launching two destroyers, fitting out a cruiser and with a submarine on the stocks. Rearmament was the saviour, for soon Scott's would have a full order book of naval vessels, necessitating the employment of 2500 craftsmen. Kincaid's fortunes rose in line, as they turned out engines and boilers to cope with the new demand.

When Chic was accepted and began his term at 15 he knew he was in for years of hard work and sweat, often in cramped and dangerous surroundings. It wasn't what he wanted to do, but it did bring 8s 3d per week to the household, helping to augment Isabella's pension from the railway. He knew he could look forward to an improver's wage only when his apprenticeship was finished, but what sustained him was the prospect of the overseas travel that might come with the job. Chic had an insatiable fascination with foreign places that never faded and he would often sit rolling their exotic names around his tongue.

This helped to keep him reconciled to the long years of apprenticeship stretching ahead, but on its own it wasn't enough. He decided he simply had to use his musical ability in some way and began to accept an occasional engagement playing piano at parties. More often than not the reward for this was only a jeely piece or two, but in the 1930s even that was not to be sniffed at. Being Chic, however, he was not content to leave it at that and soon afterwards the idea of forming a group was born.

Big Neilie McNeil, who lived just round the corner from the Murrays, had also been picking up amateur gigs playing banjo, and together the two boys decided to form a hill-billy group. Neilie would play the banjo and guitar and Chic the pedal organ. Together they would vocalise, more often than not with Chic singing the lead and Neilie harmonising. After many discussions on a suitable name for the group, Chic decided to borrow from the Whinhill at the head of the town adjacent to Greenock's golf course—thus they became the Whinhillbillies. 'That should fool them,' he explained to his baffled partner.

As his apprenticeship at Kincaid's proceeded so did the part-time amateur career of the Whinhillbillies. They had themselves decked out in false beards, checked shirts and brown bib overalls to look the part. When Chic belted out 'I'm Gonna Drink My Coffee From An Old Tin Can' Neilie covered for him through any rough spots with a well-timed 'Ya-hoo!'. Later a bit of business was born when Chic came on stage dragging a small toy horse on wheels by a rope. He always got a laugh with the entrance as he pretended to struggle when the horse fought back, then when he managed to get it to centre stage he would make a big thing of tethering it to the leg of the piano before launching into his first number. The idea grew until later in the act, after the horse had been dragged off again, he would take a brush and shovel and mime sweeping up the dung left behind. Once he had everything gathered up, he would hurl the imaginary contents over the front stalls. This always got a tremendous response, so Chic decided he had to take things a step further. Without telling Neilie what he was up to, he acquired a bag of tiny, very wrinkled potatoes. When it came to the sweeping up of the imaginary horse manure at the end of the act, he surreptitiously loaded two dozen or so of the potatoes on to the shovel, then without further ado unceremoniously flung the lot over the smiling faces of the unfortunates in the first half-dozen rows. As the little spuds landed, the patrons really thought they had been pelted with dung and there was uproar. Instead of stopping to take a bow Chic found himself running for his life, with a bewildered Neilie close behind asking, 'What happened?'

Neilie was in his early twenties at this time and worked on the buses. Newly married, he was altogether a more responsible and sober type than the harum-scarum Chic and continually lectured his partner about punctuality. It was to no avail, because all the lectures in the world could never induce Chic to change his ways. He seemed to be incapable of either turning up on time, or indeed of ending the act on schedule. When some of their amateur shows finished there was a scramble for the theatre bar before closing time. The people who ran the shows relied on the business they got from the bars and would despair as Chic would merrily sail on, coaxing Neilie with 'Hey, it's going great. Let's give them "Tin Can" again.' Not for the first time Chic would hear a manager cry, 'What are you playing at? You've buggered my bars, you lanky bastard!' Then, as later, it made no impression. Neilie remembers, 'He'd cheek back to the manager with a broad grin on his face, "What did you call me—lanky?!" He would say to me, "Here we are—properly endeavouring to be entertainers and these characters treat us like licensed grocers!"' Chic was indeed long and lanky by this time, having grown to a slim six foot three inches, overtaking even 'Big' Neilie.

At Kincaid's, where he was not considered an entertainer, his time-keeping was equally erratic, but he worked hard and was well thought of when he did turn up. By the late 1930s the duo were starting to make a name for themselves, but Chic resented the fact that certain organisations asked them back frequently, then paid them only in dinners or with profuse thanks. 'Oh, we're popular all right,' he would tell Neilie, 'but from now on we're charging. No more of this bloody "cup of tea and bun" nonsense. These folk must think we've come up the Clyde in a banana boat.'

Neilie fretted that Chic's new stance would frighten off many potential customers, but was lost in admiration for him as deal after deal was struck. They were still amateurs, but were no longer paid just in meals. It was one more step up the ladder, and for Chic it was a turning-point. Getting paid, or even getting their expenses covered, was one thing, but equally important was the knowledge that they merited it.

With the outbreak of the Second World War Chic awaited his call-up papers while continuing to build up the act. He would often join Neilie in the cab of his bus, sitting alongside him on the fuse box. As Neilie waltzed the double-decker up and down the steep, twisting braes of Greenock, the two of them would chat and pass the time. Always the sobersides, Neilie was embarrassed when Chic would suddenly shout, 'Stop the bus! Look at that wee bird—what a stoater! I wouldnae mind giving her a skelpit erse!' Neilie would say, 'Chic, I'm a married man!' to which the response would be, 'Does that mean you've lost your eyesight?'

Neilie was exempt from army service thanks to his job on the buses, but in due course Chic's call-up papers arrived. Although Neilie commiserated with him, Chic played up the drama for all he was worth—it was goodbye to the act, he lamented. His histrionics were soon ended when he was turned down after a medical examination because he had flat feet. 'Hasn't everybody?' Chic asked. He still claimed that he felt grounded and restless at being left out of the war effort, but worse was to come when he was given a wartime job with Fairey Aviation as a riveter, which he loathed.

Bad as his timekeeping in the past had been, it now became deplorable. He would not turn up at all often for days on end, although he left home supposedly to go to work. When Isabella heard of his absences she tried to reason with him, firmly pointing out that everyone had to work in wartime, especially those excused military service. She already had a compromise solution in mind, however, with which she approached the authorities and soon—at her behest—Chic found himself posted for a spell to Fairey Aviation's plant at Hayes in Middlesex. He was to stay with his Aunt Tizzie, another member of the large and far-flung McKinnon family, who lived near the plant and was serving as a Warrant Officer in the Army Catering Corps. She was a large, kindly woman constantly threatening to burst out of her uniform. Before signing up, Tizzie had been employed as a cook by the blonde film star, Madeleine Carroll. Her madcap sense of humour appealed to Chic enormously and he was intrigued also by her work as a medium and the contacts she claimed to have with the spirit world. The details of these exploits, together with her one brush with showbusiness in the Carroll household, enthralled the impressionable youth. As always with Chic, he made friends easily and after one foray with his pals from Fairey's, he returned with a small bluebird tattooed on the back of his left hand, just below the thumb. Tizzie took one look at it and chuckled. 'Chic,' she said, 'I'll make this prediction now—that's one bird that'll never leave you!'

His stay in Hayes brought him into direct contact with the war: 'For someone medically unsuitable I had some narrow escapes and saw a fair bit of action down south. Once I was around when a stick of three bombs was dropped by a dive-bomber. The men with me were blown over like ninepins and I got up to find the front of my jacket ripped off. We were all lucky to be alive. My eyes were damaged by the bomb blast and for a time there was a risk of blindness, which passed. Just as well—there wasn't much call for a blind marine engineer.' After this incident Chic was posted back to Greenock to recover and was to remain there for the rest of the war. Although he had spent only six months with Tizzie, the visit had made a lasting impression on him.

On his first day back he was visited by Neilie, now a proud father. Excitedly they talked about the resumption of their musical careers. Gooey and Jimmy Gorman were still in town finishing their apprenticeship at Kincaid's and had approached Neilie to coax Chic into making the group a foursome—led, of course, by Chic. He was all in favour and suggested a change in emphasis from purely country music to skiffle. The Whinhillbillies became Chic and His Chicks, with Chic on piano/organ, Jimmy on guitar, Gooey on washboard and Neilie on banjo. Rehearsals were soon under way. When Chic found himself reinstated at Kincaid's for the duration of the war, his cup overflowed.

Chic and Neilie performed most of the vocals for the new group between them, retaining their biggest numbers such as 'Tin Can' and adding 'China Doll'—where Chic would get in his yodelling—together with standards such as 'Steamboat Bill'. If Gooey had his way, the repertoire would also have included 'Someday My Prince Will Come', but much to his annoyance Chic vetoed the song, patiently explaining that it was meant to be sung by a woman and would drag the pace of the act. Gooey's reply was, 'It's better than some of that garbage you're spewing out,' but Chic was unpersuaded by Gooey's advocacy and ended the discussion with a conciliatory, 'Christ, what are you—a music critic suddenly? Gooey Lombardo? Let me put it to you this way, Gooey—belt up!'

At the first gig of the new outfit Gooey had his revenge. As Chic was in full flight with 'China Doll' the audience started laughing heartily. It wasn't meant to be a comedy song and Chic quickly had a look to make sure his trousers hadn't fallen down. No, they hadn't, so what was breaking the audience up? Looking behind him for the answer, which Neilie could see but was powerless to do anything about, Chic was just in time to catch the bold Gooey holding his nose and pulling in the air at an imaginary chain. He froze when he saw Chic and the audience laughed louder than ever.

When the act was over Gooey raced off stage, hotly pursued by Chic. 'Here, you chanty wrestler,' Chic yelled. 'Who's a right little smart arse, then?' 'I didn't mean any harm by it,' pleaded Gooey piteously as Neilie and Jimmy looked up, sweating and awaiting the outcome. To their relief and amazement Chic's reply was, 'It didn't *do* any harm. Lucky for you, the audience loved it—we'll keep it in!'

The new group were off to a tremendous start and Chic had begun by negotiating their fees as he meant to finish. They still agreed to do some genuine charity shows for the proverbial 'cup of tea and a bun' but these gigs were few and far between. 'Let's see the bawbees!' was the rallying cry for Chic and His Chicks, although after the war Chic would piously state in an interview, 'At Forces concerts we usually played for nothing, but if anyone was silly enough to book us for a private dance or function, we didn't mind accepting the odd guinea. After a time we even became well known and popular—our popularity arising, I am sure, from the fact we still very often worked for nothing. Our satisfaction was in providing at least some sort of entertainment in a very grim part of wartime Scotland.'

The effects of the war were everywhere in evidence before Greenock itself became the bombers' target. Isabella found herself appointed Welfare Officer for the town. Barricades were built around the mouths of closes, and air raid shelters and civil defence centres established, from which wardens, rescue services and first-aid units would operate. The establishment by the Air Ministry of a 'decoy town' behind Loch Thom occasioned much hilarity in Greenock, as well as complaints of wasted public money. The 'town' consisted of a large area where mounds of inflammable material had been assembled and could be set alight from one control spot.

Tram lines were lifted and iron railings sacrificed in the drive for scrap metal to aid the war effort. Gas masks were standard issue and sent many a shiver down the spines of families—including the Murrays—whose loved ones had been affected by the deadly attacks in the First World War.

At first the most visible sign of war for the Greenock populace was the constant procession of bombed and torpedoed Allied ships admitted to the local yards for repair, but the town did not have long to wait for more tangible—and deadly—contact with the enemy. In July 1940, a few German planes flew over the town and dropped single sticks of bombs. One of them scored a direct hit, destroying one house completely and killing the father and daughter inside. March 1941 brought a further skirmish and more casualties, but on this occasion the real target was Clydebank, where the German Pathfinder Force KG100 struck at dusk and devastated the town. Just seven houses were left intact out of 12,000, 528 people were killed and over 1,000 seriously injured. The blitz had arrived on Clydebank—and it was to be Greenock's turn next.

The first night's bombing took place on 6 May 1941, the air-raid sirens sounding just after midnight. Fifty aircraft blitzed the town indiscriminately for two hours from the east end to the west end, causing widespread damage and losses. Worst hit were the East Crawfurd Street area and Bellville Street, but the largest single number of casualties was sustained in a tenement building on the corner of South Street and Robertson Street, where the tenants sheltering in the basement were the victims of a direct hit.

The following night the sirens again sounded just after midnight, only this time there were between 250 and 300 aircraft, which attacked in three waves, the first ringing the town with incendiary bombs. The second wave carried both incendiaries and high-explosive bombs, concentrating on the east end and town centre and scoring a direct hit on a whisky distillery in Ingleston Street. The flaming river pouring down the hill was ideal for the Germans' purpose, acting as it did like a gigantic beacon and illuminating much of the town. Full advantage was taken of this and the buildings in the distillery's vicinity were mercilessly bombarded.

The third wave of bombers swept over Greenock shortly after 2 a.m., this time carrying deadly parachute land-mines and heavy high-explosives. Long after the all-clear was sounded at 3.30 a.m., fires raged throughout the town until morning when the full extent of the damage could be assessed: 280 people killed, more than 1,300 injured, and more than 1,000 houses completely destroyed. Still the damage could have been worse, had it not been for the Air Ministry's much-maligned 'decoy town' which had been set alight after the first wave of aircraft had done its work on the second night of the bombing. Next day, scores of huge bomb craters were found in the area. Had these bombs fallen on the town itself, they could undoubtedly have doubled the devastation.

Bank Street escaped the bombing, but Chic kept the memory forever of the two nights spent in an air-raid shelter with his mother, Uncle Tom and their neighbours. When he emerged after the second night it was to scenes of havoc he had never imagined possible. 'It was numbing,' he recalled, 'There were mountains of rubble everywhere, whole houses wrecked, walls scorched. Rows of bodies were laid out in the streets, covered with white sheets and tarpaulin. I spent the rest of the night and most of the following day helping exhausted firemen—the last blaze was put out by early afternoon, but it was days before the town lost its scorched smell.'

The bombing of Greenock, and the destruction caused further up-river at Clydebank, could reasonably have been considered successful assaults by the Germans, who were determined to stamp out the war effort on the Clyde. Unfortunately for them, not a single bomb had fallen inside the main target of John Brown's Shipyard in Clydebank, where work was almost back to normal within a few days of the embattled workforce emerging from the rubble of the town.

Greenock's yards were not to be let off so lightly, Scott's head office being burnt to the ground in the blitz, with the loss of all records, models and documents. Their engine works suffered heavy damage also, although the Herculean efforts of the workforce had them rebuilt and re-equipped within six months. During the second raid a destroyer, its hull fully plated and approaching the launching stage, was blown off its keel blocks at Scott's and had to be taken apart and rebuilt. A submarine occupying the next berth was blasted bodily some inches off its blocks, but was miraculously undamaged. Another bomb came through the west boundary wall, just missing a destroyer in dry dock, while yet another bomb burst under the stern of a cruiser on its building berth. Although it blew some cast iron keel blocks through the roof of the plating shed 30 yards away, the ship itself escaped damage.

As the town dragged itself back to normal, Chic and His Chicks found themselves in great demand, with their venues ranging from drill halls to army gun sites up and down the coast. One such army engagement was at a gun site in Greenock and with minutes to go there was no sign of Chic. Frantically Neilie arranged for another act to go on first, then conferred with the lieutenant in charge. 'What are we going to do?' Start the show without him,' suggested the officer. 'It's not possible,' protested Neilie. 'We're not just a collection of songs, one after the other. It's all timed and built around Chic.' A jeep was duly dispatched to Bank Street and 20 anxious minutes later Neilie watched as the vehicle made its way up the steep hill to the gun site. There in the passenger seat was Chic, beaming and waving magisterially, his long, gangling legs bunched up. 'He looked like bloody Lord Muck,' Neilie laughed as he recalled the scene, 'and when I asked him where he'd been he just shrugged nonchalantly. "I got the date wrong," he explained. There he was, as cool, calm and collected as you please—and me reduced to a greasy spot!'

Winter Garden
Rothesay

G. B. BOWIE

presents

The

Rothesay Entertainers

of

1951

6-45   TWICE NIGHTLY   9-00

BOOKING OFFICE OPEN DAILY
10 a.m.

Programme   .   .   2d

3

A Gorgeous Wee Bird

'There's a lovely blonde I met the other day who took my eye. I don't mean she really took it, for I need it, it's one of a set.'

After much coaxing by friends, and no coaxing at all by Chic, Isabella decided to attend one of her son's shows for the first time—without letting him know, in case it made him nervous. As the act proceeded she sat open-mouthed in astonishment. 'Make him nervous?' she said later. 'I must have been daft! I knew he could be a cheeky devil at home right enough, but on stage he's got the nerve of ten people!'

One evening in 1943 as Chic and Neilie were practising together in the parlour, they heard a knock on the door. 'Mother!' yelled Chic. 'Can you get that? Neilie and I have come to a critical bit.' When Isabella answered the door she found two exhausted girls, who turned out to be soubrettes booked to appear in variety at Greenock's Empire theatre. (Soubrettes? Basically singers, soubrette being the term used in the theatre at that time. The dictionary defines a soubrette as a pert, coquettish, intriguing maid-servant in comedy; a singer of light songs of a similar character.) They had been referred to Isabella in her capacity as a wartime Welfare Officer to help them in their search for digs.

Maidie Dickson and Lilian Gaye were two attractive brunettes, although neither one of them looked her best as they stood there. They had been obliged to lug their suitcases—and in Maidie's case her accordion as well—up the steep climb to Bank Street in a downpour.

Lilian was from a theatrical family of sorts, as was her cousin Ann Doell, the show-business strain in the family stemming from the girls' two aunts, known professionally as the Ember Sisters. 'No talent at all,' had been the rather cruel summing-up for this song-and-dance duo, resulting in their nickname, the 'Dying Embers'. The family's real name was Larkins, the sane members of the family running a highly successful umbrella and leather goods store in Glasgow.

At 21, Maidie Dickson was a veteran of the Scottish theatrical circuit. She had hardly ever known any other life since her first professional appearance on stage, dancing and singing at the tender age of four at the Capitol Theatre, Leith, in her home city of Edinburgh. According to her mother: 'She was a tremendous dancer at a time when tap was not widely known in this country—over here it had been referred to as "buck dancing". On her first show at Leith Maidie opened with a dance, then launched into her repertoire of songs, which numbered about a dozen. Unfortunately we hadn't told her there were only two or three required and she proceeded all down her list before she was unceremoniously yanked off! Apart from that, she got a terrific reception.'

Mrs Dickson then obtained a position for Maidie, when she was six, with Gilroy's Entertainers, a travelling troupe. By the time she was booked to appear on a bill with the hugely popular Will Fyffe at Burntisland, accordion playing had been added to her accomplishments. After the run was over the famous comedian was impressed enough to hand her a ten-shilling note on which was written: 'To a very clever wee lassie. Yours aye, Will Fyffe'.

In the mid-1930s, when she was 12, Maidie was booked for an eight-week winter season at Portobello, near Edinburgh, with Andre Letta's Entertainers, a group that was a legend in its own lifetime at the Showplace in Bath Street. The holiday-makers who crammed into the popular seaside resort formed the bulk of the audience.

Letta's main rivals were housed in the Prom Palace, run by the Demarco show-business and ice-cream empire. A son, Umberto Demarco, went on to make a considerable name for himself as a singer, as did an aspiring crooner with whom Maidie appeared at the Prom Palace, a pawky-faced youngster known as Donald Peers. This was a few years after her apprenticeship with the enterprising Andre, however, for while she was with the Entertainers she was not allowed to even *look* in the direction of the Prom Palace and the Demarcos.

Maidie was the bairn of Letta's troupe and found herself adopted during the summer season, when she was allowed by law to work full-time during the school holidays. Andre's wife was singer Peggy Desmond—a formidable lady who retained a patrician air even while singing the daftest songs of the day. Maidie was completely in awe of Peggy and her majestic ways. Andre also had his individual trademarks—a fresh pink carnation in his lapel buttonhole and a full set of enormous teeth, with correspondingly large gaps between them. Maidie was dispatched to the florist daily for his carnation, while Peggy would gently tease Andre on his extraordinary choppers. After a steak meal, Maidie observed Peggy gazing at the gleaming mouthful, while Andre smiled beatifically. 'God, Andre,' Peggy declared, 'I could make a pot of soup with the meat stuck in there!'

IMPERSONATION OF VESTA TILLY.
BY DAINTY MAIDIE.

Maidie about 12 years of age, with accordion.

In 1935 Maidie was one of the cast of Jack Mulford's 'Vaudeville Parade' which toured Scotland. She was billed as 'The Discovery Of The Year!' and the programme announced: 'She's the artist with that "Something" that others haven't got!' In the same show were the Carson Sisters ('In Peppy Song and Dance'), Archie Shield ('The Yodelling Guitarist') and Jack Purves ('The Master Magician who will amaze you'). Her sweet, melodic voice had made her a firm favourite by this time and the fact that she could also play the accordion and tap-dance was a considerable extra attraction, enhanced further by her sonsie good looks.

The rest of the 1930s were spent touring theatres, town halls and seaside pavilions the length and breadth of Scotland, with the occasional foray into Newcastle and the surrounding area of Geordieland, where she made such a favourable impression that for a charity concert in 1936 at the Regent in Edinburgh's Abbeymount, she was billed as 'The Newcastle Pantomime Star'. Sharing this bill—in aid of the May Island

Disaster Fund—were Neil Douglas ('The Debonair Aristocrat'), Don Pablo and his Borsinian Accordion Band, Ina Forbes ('The Scottish Nightingale') and Jock McKendrick ('Scotch Character Comedian of BBC and Gramophone Recording Fame').

Two years later—at the same venue—Maidie shared the bill with Dr Walford Bodie, who was listed then simply as an 'Entertainer'. In his day the tall, saturnine Bodie, who sported jet-black hair and a pointed moustache, had claimed to be one of the highest paid performers of all time. He toured with the Electric Magic Show, under his full title 'The Great Walford Bodie, MD'. Electric currents crackled from his fingertips as he practised hypnotism. Crutches, draped all over the stage, were claimed to be mementoes left by cripples he had 'cured'. All sorts of weird stories were fed to Maidie by the other members of the cast, with the result that even before she set eyes on the 'doctor', she was already petrified of him. When he tried to put her at her ease with an outstretched hand and a greeting of 'Hallo, little girl', Maidie's reaction was to turn on her heel and flee in terror to her dressing-room. The devil himself could have been on her heels, indeed when Bodie was finally challenged in court as to the MD after his name, his teeth bared in an unapologetic smile. 'Merry Devil,' he clarified.

By 1938 she was fully grown at a petite five feet and affectionately known as 'Dainty Maidie' to her fellow performers. She toured the north of Scotland in that year and continued to please audiences with her renditions of 'I Double Dare You' and 'Let Us Be Sweethearts', while her medley of 'auld Scots songs' was a consistent favourite. The fellow members of her cast on a Stonehaven booking included comedian Ken Wood ('I Ken you will like him'), Joan Davis ('A Yorkshire Lass who'll cause the most sobersides to relax'), Robert Dinwoodie ('The Musical Director of our Show and a good one at that') and Jean Hamilton ('Possessed of a rich soprano voice she knows how to use!'). About Maidie the handout declared: 'This talented little lady, although young in years, has had a varied experience in concert party and theatrical work. The owner of a nice singing voice, she can put over numbers in a telling way and her dancing and accordion playing will be a feature of the show!' Sustenance for the entire troupe at Stonehaven was fish and chips from Zaccarini's nearby Valencia Fish Restaurant, which Maidie, being the youngest member of the troupe, was invariably selected to fetch. The succulent cod was fresh daily from the North Sea, cocooned in Zaccarini's inimitable crisp batter, topped with salt and vinegar and accompanied by golden-brown chips from locally grown potatoes. On high days and holidays, cartons of Duncan's ice-cream finished off this treat.

The last time Maidie saw Andre Letta was during a visit many years later to Patrick Thomson's store (PT's as it was known to one and all) on the North Bridge in Edinburgh. Underneath the wig and whiskers of the store Santa Claus, Maidie spotted the unmistakable Letta choppers. The marriage to Peggy was over and he had sold up all his show-business interests. The Santa job was just for pin money, he explained. Maidie promised to come back and see him again during the season, but when she did there was a wee note pinned to the grotto that left her not knowing whether to laugh or cry. It read, 'Santa Gone To Tea.'

Peggy was last seen by Maidie in another chance encounter in the restaurant of Jenners the fashionable Princes Street store, taking tea and cakes in the Desmond manner of old. She was still every inch a lady and a performer to her fingertips, although her style had long since peaked. Peggy was tolerating her enforced retirement, while waiting for the call back on the boards that would never come.

Charity called Maidie back again to Stonehaven just a few weeks before the outbreak of the Second World War. This time the concert was in aid of the Aberdeen Girder Accident Fund, and Maidie would again beat the well-worn path to the Valencia after the show. 'You should get a commission,' Zaccarini told her. 'Or a medal,' said Maidie. When her mother phoned soon after it was with the news that Hugh, Maidie's father, had been called up.

With the advent of the war, forces concerts were quickly organised and early in 1940 Maidie found herself reunited in Edinburgh with Will Fyffe at the Theatre Royal in the army review, *Jock's Box Varieties*. Later in the year, by public demand, she was booked for a whole series of concerts at the same theatre. Topping the bill was Jack Anthony, billed as 'Edinburgh's Favourite Comedian', while Maidie was described as 'A Treat for the Eye and Ear'. ('Add a nose and you could open a hospital,' Anthony cracked.) Also on the bill were the Henderson Twins, introducing Dick (the late Dickie Henderson's first stage appearance), Berta Ricardo, a regular on Jack's bill who eventually managed his Dunbar hotel, Cicely Hullett ('The Essence of Comedy') and Bob and Alf Pearson ('My Brother and I—Bringing you Melodies from out of the Sky'). Not much had changed—except the now statutory air-raid warnings displayed everywhere. 'In the event of an air-raid warning,' the notice read, 'the audience will be informed verbally from the stage. *This does not necessarily mean that a raid will take place.* Anyone who desires to leave the theatre may do so, but the performances will continue and members are advised in their own interests to remain in the building, where they would be safer than in the streets.' One thing that never changed was A. J. 'Bumper' Wark, the Theatre Royal's handsome, imposing figure of a manager. He was never seen by the public other than in top hat, white tie and tails, his aristocratic presence adding a real touch of class to the theatre.

After the show there were several local venues of special interest to the players—for a drink there was Kelman's Bar opposite the theatre, serving the tastiest ham sandwiches in Edinburgh, or for a full meal there was the Auld Reekie Grill and Café, serving after-theatre suppers of tripe and onions with cream sauce and mashed potatoes for eightpence. If one had no desire even to cross the street, there was the Horseshoe Bar right next door to the theatre, where proprietor John Muir guaranteed 'Good Cheer and the Finest Beer'. For appetites of a different kind there were always the Rose Street and Leith Walk girls, angels of the night who often took their clients to the notorious Imperial Hotel, where it was said the sound of creaking mattress springs drowned out the traffic noise from the street, while genteel Edinburgh looked the other way. Sailors especially patronised Leith Walk's girls, if they failed to get a lumber at Fairley's dance hall, half-way down the street.

Although Maidie had carved a well-deserved niche for herself in her profession, she never had a chance to draw back and take stock of where her personal life was going. There had been little time for romance, apart from the occasional teenage crush which she had been sensible enough to recognise for what they were. All that was to change with the fateful booking at the Greenock Empire in 1943.

*   *   *

By the time the two girls arrived at Bank Street it was too late for Isabella to find them digs, but she did not have the heart to turn them away. Darkness was already falling and it was a wet, chilly night, so she made them a cup of tea and left them sipping it while she went away to confer with Chic.

'Mother, can't you see we're rehearsing?' he bellowed as she entered the room. Neilie had been astounded the first time he had heard Chic address his mother in this manner, but by now he knew better, for they were like a well-rehearsed double-act that knew just how much would be allowed. Isabella was more than a match for him and nothing that Chic said, or the manner in which he said it, could upset his supremely placid mother. For the next few minutes the only change would be for Chic to be addressed by his 'Sunday' name. 'Be quiet, you'll only get high blood pressure, Charles,' she replied. 'Now you listen to me. Two wee dears have come to the door looking for digs and I haven't the heart to turn them away. I thought they could share the spare bedroom overlooking the back green.' 'Where am I going to put my model railway?' Chic wanted to know, looking around distractedly. 'Well, you could pack it away for the time being,' Isabella replied serenely, already on the way to tell the girls the good news. She turned at the door. 'If you could just clear all your stuff out now while the girls are having their tea, that would be grand—the model railway included, of course. It's high time you were out of that now, anyway!'

That night the girls were in the parlour tucking in with some gusto to the substantial supper Isabella had conjured up out of her ration allowance, when they heard the clatter of the front door and the sound of heavy footsteps tramping down the hall—Chic had arrived home with big Neilie, Sammy, Gooey, Jimmy and Bill Jenkinson. Having completely forgotten about the girls his mother was putting up, his first thought as he saw Maidie was, 'Who's the gorgeous wee bird?'

Maidie stopped in mid-bite as she took in the tall, dark young man who had just stepped in through the door. She remembers wondering, 'Who's the gorgeous big guy?' then resolving to assume a little more ladylike decorum in the way she would dispose of the rest of her supper. As Isabella prepared to introduce the group to the girls, she saw Chic and Maidie furtively looking and smiling at each other, then looking away shyly, then looking back again. She had never before seen Chic stopped in his tracks by a girl.

At six foot three, Isabella's 'wee son' towered over Maidie. One of her first practical thoughts was that she would need to be several steps higher on the landing to be able to kiss him properly when the time came. Chic, now 24, was dark, slim and possessed of matinée-idol good looks accentuated by a dashing pencil moustache. 'Pleased to meet you,' she heard him say in a rather posh accent. Isabella beamed knowingly— the two were clearly smitten. When the rest of the introductions had been made, she retired to let the young folks have a blether. Chic and Maidie's eyes never left each other. He wanted to know all about her. 'I'm in show-business too,' he confided, adding a bit dreamily, 'I dare say everyone's in the business to some extent, whether they know it or not. You should see some of the unconscious comedians in the yards.'

Gaiety

PROGRAMME 2d.

4

For Better, For Worse

'I rang the bell of a small bed-and-breakfast place, whereupon a lady appeared at an outside window. "What do you want?" she asked. "I want to stay here," I replied. "Well, stay there then!" she said and banged the window shut.'

Chic attended both houses of the first night's show at the Empire, then collected Maidie at the stage door and walked her home. 'I thought you were great,' he told her later, 'the best in the show. You ought to be on the stage, you know. Oh, you're on the stage already, that's right. Well, you ought to be in pictures.'

Maidie laughed, 'So should you. Silent pictures! Your head's full of wee battleships, Chic. Nice ones, though.'

The following night Chic and His Chicks had been booked for a Royal Navy dance, to which Chic invited her once the Empire's second house was finished. She was delighted to accept and turned up in a stunning gold lamé dress and matching sling-backs. It was the first time she had seen Chic perform and she was tremendously impressed. When they danced together later, he felt all eyes upon them, for he knew he was dancing with the belle of the ball.

When the Chicks were announced again, Maidie suggested that she join them in a couple of numbers. 'I'm Gonna Drink My Coffee From An Old Tin Can' had never sounded so good, while 'Steam Boat Bill' took on a completely new lease of life, this time without Gooey's antics. Maidie was a smash—both with the dancers, and with Chic.

At home later they kissed goodnight and made for their rooms. Maidie lay dreamily for a few minutes, then sat up again with a start as she heard Chic tuning up the American organ in his room. A moment later a melody was struck up and Chic began yelling out the lyrics:

Two lovers they were strolling down a coalmine,
The girl had been a female from her birth,
Give me back the ring I never gave you,
For this has been my second time on earth.
Ten weary years have passed in fifteen minutes,
So wipe the cobwebs from your eyes,
And always think of m-o-t-h-e-r,
And the Dublin Fusiliers!

Each time he sang it he gave a different treatment to the various lines, but each time the result was the same—Maidie dissolved in helpless laughter. Next day she asked Isabella about the origin of the masterpiece. 'Och, that's one of Chic's own daft things. What a racket he made with it last night! He's been singing that on and off for years. I keep telling him it doesn't scan and he keeps defiantly trying to do just that. There's wiser folks locked up!'

The days that followed were exciting and romantic ones. For Maidie, however, after years of discipline in the theatre, it still had to be 'business as usual'. The day after the dance she had an early-morning band call, then the rest of her time was taken up with costume fittings, new lighting cues and rehearsals for the following week's show. Although she was in Greenock for an eight-week season, a complete change of act every Monday was necessary if the public were to be kept coming back again and again. Maidie's first sighting of Uncle Tom came as she was walking through the hall and noticed his bedroom door ajar, prior to a foray to the bathroom. As soon as he saw Maidie the door was slammed shut again. 'That's Mum's brother, Uncle Tom,' Chic explained later. 'I call him the "Ghost". He keeps himself to himself—and in his case that's the best way.' Maidie was curious. Was that the lot, she wanted to know, or were any other denizens hidden away she had yet to meet? Looking about him as if to make sure no one was overhearing his words, he declared, 'Well, there's only two more and you'll be hearing more about them soon enough—that's Woolchester and Mrs Pollock.'

Maidie couldn't keep her face straight. 'Woolchester? Come on, Chic,' she said.

'Woolchester Cowperthwaite, to give him his full name,' Chic insisted.

'Not Woolchester X. Cowperthwaite?' Maidie wanted to know.

'No,' Chic replied. 'No X. At least, none that *I* have been informed of.' With this he almost smiled; he was thinking to himself as he looked appreciatively at Maidie, 'This one's fully up to me.'

'And what about Mrs Pollock?' was Maidie's next question. 'Where do you keep her—in the airing cupboard?'

'Mrs Pollock,' promised Chic, 'you will most certainly be hearing more about.'

Maidie in local concert party, Edinburgh *circa* 1937.

If this was Maidie's first encounter with Chic the story-teller, she did not have to wait long for the next occasion. One night when she got back from the theatre she found him holding court around the fire with an enthralled audience of the Chicks and a few of Isabella's friends. Maidie could make neither head nor tail of the story he was telling, but it was breaking up the fireside audience. When Chic was finished he left the room and the next they heard was the peal of the organ and Chic yelling, 'This one's for the "Ghost"!' before he launched into the inevitable 'Dublin Fusiliers'. Isabella smilingly shook her head as she passed coffee and sandwiches around the room. 'I fear for the boy's sanity,' she declared to one and all.

Maidie's plan was to finish the last show on Saturday night, then turn in early and be up at the crack of dawn to catch the early train. She seldom passed a weekend without visiting her home in Edinburgh, although she always had to be back at the theatre on Monday morning for band-call. When Chic heard about this he announced he would see Maidie to the station. Unfortunately Chic's definition of 'crack of dawn' did not coincide with Maidie's and it was mid-morning before they approached Greenock Central. A disconcerted Maidie half ran alongside Chic as he took his giant strides, then when she turned to take her suitcase, Chic carried doggedly on and entered the station.

'But Chic,' Maidie protested, 'you need a platform ticket.'

'No, I don't,' Chic replied smiling, 'I'll see you as far as Glasgow Central, it's the least I can do after keeping you waiting this morning.'

'What about your work, though?' the conscientious Maidie asked. 'Aren't you supposed to be doing overtime at Kincaid's this morning? I don't want you to get into more trouble.'

'My pal Pete's covering for me, doing my clocking in and that,' he explained. Maidie was horrified, for she had never missed a show in her life.

'Oh, Chic,' she said. 'That's cheating.'

'No, it's not,' protested Chic. 'I'd do the same for Pete!'

Maidie wouldn't be stilled. 'You know that's not what I meant,' she insisted. 'It's Kincaid's that's losing out.'

Chic rocked back on his heels in mock horror. 'OK, OK, I'll send them an anonymous donation—if you've got an envelope and one and sixpence we can maybe get it posted off before the train's due.'

As they sat down in the carriage, Maidie shook her head and looked reprovingly at her companion. 'You,' she asserted, 'are one cheeky devil!'

When they arrived at Glasgow Central, Chic declared that there was just no question of Maidie carrying her own case to Queen Street station where she was due to catch the connection to Edinburgh. As Chic proceeded to board the Edinburgh train with her as well she realised that he had all along intended to accompany her home. She was touched and proud, but concerned about the return journey he would have to undertake on his own. 'Not to worry,' he said. 'It'll give me time to dream up what I'm going to say to Wullie on Monday. It'll also give the "Ghost" the chance of a good dander round the house.' Together they walked to her house, dallying for a while on the doorstep and reluctant to part, until Chic explained that he had to get back for a concert with the group. Maidie was relieved, for she hadn't wanted to ask him in to meet her mother just yet, preferring to break the news gently. After all, he was hardly someone to be sprung cold on anyone.

However, it was no more than a few weekends before the meeting did take place and Chic had his feet planted securely under the table. Maidie's father, Hugh, was serving in the Royal Navy, but Chic took an immediate liking to Anne Dickson, who was equally taken with him.

Soon Maidie's run at the local Empire was over, although her next engagement was only a ferry ride away at Millport. Chic promised to visit at every opportunity and was as good as his word—so much so that, less than 24 hours after their tearful farewell, he pushed his time off from work to the limit. He claimed he had sailed over in a canoe and anchored the boat half a mile from the theatre before walking there in his wellington boots. Maidie spotted him marching relentlessly along the front in his wellies, head held high and swinging his arms in exaggerated military style. 'The man's an idiot, but I love him,' she thought happily.

When she later asked why he hadn't taken the ferry over like everyone else, he replied, 'It's cheaper—I got the boat for nothing from a pal.

Mind you, it's not entirely free. There's the wear and tear on clothes in the rowing to be taken into account.'

She was in Hawick in the middle of a Borders tour, when Chic's first letter arrived in a small, peculiar square envelope. Its size and shape were not her primary concern, however, and she eagerly read his letter over and over again. He had written:

My dear Maidie,

How are you? I am fine. I worked on Sunday morning this weekend and bumped into my foreman, who seemed very pleased and a wee bit surprised to see me. I think my visit brought a bit of sunshine into his life. I often wonder what's at the root of his carnaptiousness. I was a few minutes late, but I explained that I'd been set upon by hundreds of mice and he seemed happy enough with this.

Nothing doing in the afternoon so I gave the organ big licks until Mum came to get me for tea. I wasn't hungry and could only manage two platefuls of cottage pie; I must be unwell. As usual the pie was a stotter. Mrs Pollock had evidently dropped in for a chat, but I had missed her. By the bye, Mum has won some sort of national newspaper competition for the best review of *Gone With The Wind*. I hope it doesn't go to her head, me being so modest and that, but I always did say there was talent in this family. She sends her warmest regards. Take good care of yourself. Here's a kiss and love from,

Chic.

P.S. Write soon.

The letter brought a lump to Maidie's throat—the only thing that puzzled her was the mention of Mrs Pollock again, but she had no time to dwell on that. As she penned her reply she could feel her heart beat faster—she loved him so much and it seemed that the big galoot loved her too.

Some weeks later Maidie let Chic know she would be able to visit him soon while appearing at the Victory Theatre in nearby Paisley. This rated fairly low on the list of Maidie's touring venues, largely because of the grim state of the dressing-rooms, where she was obliged to share with every other female member of the cast a dark and unheated room, lit only by two naked bulbs that bobbed and danced from the ceiling as the performers went through their paces on the stage above. The river that flowed on the other side of the sweating brick walls constantly threatened to flood the room and since the manager faithfully switched out the lights for economy reasons as they left for the stage, Maidie returned at the end of the show more than once to find the floor covered in several inches of water, and the room in total darkness. Someone—usually Maidie—then had to wade through the water to reach the light switch at the far end of the room.

When she arrived in Paisley on this particular occasion, she made sure she was first in with the band-call, then rushed off to catch the bus for Greenock—at least this time she was not humping an accordion, as she had been when first making her way to the Murray household. All set for a glorious romantic reunion with Chic, she eagerly rang the bell at Bank Street.

On receiving no reply, she noticed that the door was off the latch and pushed it open. There was Chic striding down the hall, yelling at the top of his voice, 'Send for Mrs Pollock! Send for Mrs Pollock!' His hands were held high in the air and he waved them gospel-style (shades of his Dad's Burning Bush Society), while his mother followed close behind. She was shaking her head and saying, 'You must calm down, Chic. You'll get high blood pressure if you carry on like that.'

Just then the 'Ghost' opened his door, and caught sight of a perplexed-looking Maidie at the door in the hall. 'This place is a bloody madhouse,' he declared, breaking his silence for once, before slamming the door shut again. 'Hallo, Maidie,' Chic greeted her, 'come on in. You're not Mrs Pollock, but you'll do.' From inside the 'Ghost's' door they heard a muffled 'Fuck Mrs Pollock!' When the dust had settled, Maidie asked Isabella who was the mysterious Mrs Pollock. Chic's Mum replied that she had no idea, except that for some reason it was the name that Chic gave to an imaginary cleaning woman who always kept the house spick and span. 'Whenever he feels I'm not getting tore into the housekeeping sufficiently I get Mrs Pollock flung at me!' Isabella explained.

Since she handled the whole thing with her usual serenity and aplomb that was the end of the matter. For his part Chic was not in the slightest put out by Maidie arriving in the middle of the stramash. He never did fully explain the origin of Mrs Pollock to Maidie, his mother, or to anyone else. It was as if the whole thing was a matter of the most irreducible logic and as such an explanation was superfluous.

That very night in the parlour, with Isabella in an armchair immersed in her latest novel, Chic proposed to Maidie as they held hands across the table. 'Maidie, let's tie the knot,' were the words he used. 'Oh, Chic,' Maidie replied, 'are you sure?' Over in the armchair Isabella turned a page and smiled. 'He's sure,' she said, then got up to give Maidie a cuddle. 'I couldn't be more pleased,' she whispered. 'You're such a wee cracker.' 'Hold on a minute,' said Chic. 'The "wee cracker" hasn't said "yes" yet.' 'Yes, I have,' whispered Maidie. 'Over and over again. I don't mind taking you in out of the rain, you big dope. Someone's got to do it!'

Chic beamed at her, then at his mother, before his expression turned serious. 'Of course,' he said, studying his fingernails and with eyebrows raised, 'there's the small matter of the dowry to be settled first.' At this

Isabella gave him a cuddle as well. 'Oh, Charles,' she scolded happily, 'you and your jokes!' Maidie's mother was delighted also when asked to give her blessing, Chic's somewhat persistent dowry cracks notwithstanding.

For Maidie's part she had to work throughout the spring of 1945 until the week before the wedding on 28 April and wherever she went, the peculiar square envelopes would follow. They were the source of much amusement to the rest of her troupe, for they recognised them for what they were—'pay pokes' from the shipyards which Chic was using instead of purchasing proper stationery.

Someone noticed that Maidie had taken to wearing a necklace with a single gold charm on it. This seemed to be in the form of a Chinese character, but Maidie demonstrated that when you twirled it round, it read 'I love you'. One of the chorus girls was lost in admiration. 'Did your man buy you that?' she asked, to which the ever-honest Maidie replied, 'No, I bought it myself.'

Chic left Maidie to shop around to select her own engagement ring, which would then be set aside for his approval. Although Maidie had chosen well—a beautiful antique ring with a diamond and sapphire setting—and within the price limits they had discussed, Chic turned several shades paler when he heard the actual price. As Maidie was getting to know, Chic liked to go through all the reactions of shock, horror and dismay as a matter of routine. The difficulty lay in trying to discern when he was faking it and when his response was genuine. It was a little guessing game he liked to play with people, as if he never wanted anyone to feel entirely sure of themselves when he was around, for in this way his reaction could never be taken for granted. As Neilie had discovered earlier, Chic and Chic alone had to be the one 'calling the shots'. In this case, however, his adverse reaction was short-lived, although he made a token protest, explaining to Maidie's consternation that it was not even a new ring—it was, after all, second-hand.

The couple planned the trip to Edinburgh to buy the ring, stopping off first at Chic's bank in Greenock to collect the money for the purchase. 'Do you want to come in with me?' he asked her as they stood outside the bank. 'No, I'll just wait outside,' Maidie replied. Chic looked at her long and hard, then said, 'Well, if it's all the same I'd rather you came in. Banks make me nervous and it's better if you're there to bring me round when—I mean *if* I collapse. Oddly enough, I only get like this when I'm taking money out.'

Maidie decided it was best to humour him and together they entered the bank, joining the small queue for a teller. When Chic's turn came and he was asked by the fellow how he could help, Chic stared at him as if hypnotised. Clearing his throat finally, he explained, 'I'd like to draw some money out from my account.' As he spoke he licked his lips nervously and stared about him as if suffering from acute claustrophobia. 'Certainly, sir,' replied the teller. 'Could I have your name, please?' To Maidie's astonishment Chic stammered, 'M-my n-name? Well—as a matter of fact, I don't like to say!' The teller began to lose patience. 'Look, sir,' he pointed out. 'If you want the money, I must have your name.' Chic looked behind him furtively to check if anyone in the queue could hear. Next he stared glassily at Maidie, then at the teller before replying, 'Oh, very well. It's Tighthole. Timothy Tighthole!' The teller and Maidie looked at him in blank amazement, as Chic went on to explain. 'That's why I don't like to say it. As a matter of fact I'm thinking of having it changed. What do you think of *Charlie* Tighthole?'

By this time the manager of the bank had picked up on the conversation and broke in to greet Chic. 'Is it a withdrawal, Mr Murray?' he asked. 'Well,' Chic replied, laughing nervously. 'If it isn't, I've certainly got all the symptoms!' The required amount was duly handed over by a very unamused teller, and with the money in his pocket Chic escorted Maidie to Edinburgh to purchase the ring.

Despite his performance at the bank—or maybe because of it—Chic seemed in good spirits as the money was handed over and the transaction completed. 'At least,' he said to Maidie as he lovingly placed the ring on her finger, 'I've got something to show for it. By the way, did you notice something funny about that jeweller? He's the first man I've ever seen who wears his sideburns behind his ears. And parts his teeth in the middle.'

'A gag merchant,' said Maidie, 'I'm marrying a gag merchant.'

Maidie's mother had arranged for the wedding to take place in fine style in the historic Moray Aisle of St Giles' Cathedral in Edinburgh and for the service to be conducted by the minister, Dr Charles L. Warr, whom Isabella had known in Greenock when he was minister of St Paul's Parish Church there just after the First World War. The evening before the wedding, while Chic was *en route* to his stag night with the gang, Isabella surprised Maidie by asking her to make a promise. She took her hands in hers and looked at Maidie directly in the glow from the hearth. 'Promise me you'll never leave Chic,' she asked. Maidie's eyes widened, for she genuinely could not conceive of such a thing ever happening. She readily gave her promise, convinced that when two people loved each other as much as they did, any difficulty could be overcome.

'He can be a bullying devil sometimes, and he'll push you as far as he can,' Isabella cautioned, 'but it doesn't last and he's good-hearted. You'll have to adjust to some of his funny little ways—like giving that organ laldie for hours on end—but I've never seen Chic as taken with anyone before, so already you're half-way there!'

Earlier Chic had been sorting out two problems of his own. He was in

28 April 1945.

the habit of sleeping in the nude, but felt that he should appear before his bride, at least initially, clad in a natty pair of pyjamas—first impressions being so important. He did not want to buy a pair, reasoning that after a couple of nights he probably would have no further use for them, so he began to think from whom they could be borrowed. He seemed to remember his Uncle Alex sporting the articles during some of his maths lessons, so made his way to Alex's house. Having ascertained that his uncle did indeed have a new pair, he explained the situation. Alex promptly agreed that he could borrow them, leaving just one more request—could Alex lend him some clothing coupons so he could buy a new pair of shoes for the wedding? After a quick check of the coupons left in the household, Chic went on his way rejoicing.

The wedding went beautifully, the only tiny hitch coming from the groom's entry into the hushed cathedral. Uncle Alex permitted himself a smile as the noise of a dozen mice apparently among the pews coincided with Chic's appearance. It was the amplified sound of his brand-new shoes, squeaking loudly with every step he took up the aisle.

At the reception afterwards Chic tried to divide his time up between friends and relations. Faithful Neilie attended, and there was a joyous reunion with Aunt Tizzie. Uncle Tommy had not been invited on the grounds that even if he had, he wouldn't have come and if he had come he wouldn't have been wanted—as Chic put it. This was one rift that would never be healed.

After the wedding the couple left for a weekend in Dundee and their honeymoon quarters, for another of Isabella's sisters, Auntie Marion, had let them have her house for the occasion. Shortly after they arrived Chic discovered a pedal organ in the front parlour and began to tinker with it. When Maidie asked if he was hungry, Chic looked up after blowing some dust off the keys. 'Maidie,' he replied, 'sometimes I take a terrible notion for a plate of custard.' As she prepared a great panful of the stuff she heard Chic strike up a tune, then repeat it over and over again. She smiled as she stirred the custard, for she recognised the melody Chic kept playing . It was 'In The Mood', and with each rendition the tempo increased and the key was raised. As Chic finished the custard, he sat back like a contented cat and licked his lips. 'Maidie, that was great,' he said appreciatively, then added, eyes twinkling, 'but anything after it is bound to be a complete anti-climax!'

All too soon the idyll was over. ('I could get used to this. It's like playing houses, and doctors and nurses, both at the same time,' Chic declared.) Maidie had to catch a train to her old stamping ground of Stonehaven to begin a series of East Coast concerts, while Chic reluctantly made his way back to Kincaid's. Their tearful farewell was leavened only by the knowledge that they would be reunited the following weekend. They would have something else to celebrate by then, for Victory in Europe was about to be declared.

DUNDEE
PALACE

Proprietors .... DUNDEE VARIETIES, LTD.

Managing Director .... J. G. TURNER

Resident Manager and Licensee .... ERIC PAGE

Assistant Manager .... NORMAN ASH

Stage Manager .... MATT BROWN

PRICE —— THREEPENCE

PROGRAMME

5

Wines and Spirits

'I was once approached by this rather inquisitive young lady who wanted to know the age-old secret. She said, "Pardon me Mr Murray, but my friends and I would like to know what is worn under your kilt?" I indignantly replied, "Madam nothing's worn. Everything is in perfect working order."'

Chalmers Wood organised six summer shows in 1945, in venues as far apart as Perth and Carlisle, pinning down whatever talent they could lay their hands on—and it was considerable. Alec Finlay starred in *Great Scot!* at Gourock's Cragburn Pavilion; *Joy Parade* featured Dave Bruce at the Cosy Corner, Dunoon; Perth's Theatre had Bobby Telford; and at Carlisle Her Majesty's starred Tommy Hope in *What's Cookin!* Maidie found herself booked again in Millport for the Chalmers Wood show, *Lucky Strike*, headlined by Jimmy Wallace and Jimmy Vincent, the bill also featuring the Royal Caledonians ('Eight Feet in Rhythm'), Peggy Maxwell ('At the Piano'), Cissie Glen ('Our Lively Lump of Fun') and Irene Campbell (variously 'The Blonde Bombshell' and 'Scotland's Betty Hutton').

As the season came to a close—and with it the end of the Second World War—Maidie was booked to appear in a charity concert at the Usher Hall, Edinburgh. When she overheard the organiser mention that they were short of just one musical double-act, she did some fast talking. Chic slumped into a seat when the news was broken to him of the one-night-only reformation of the Whinhillbillies, but his was a calm reaction compared to Neilie's unbridled panic. 'I'm not cut out for show-business. It's not for me,' he insisted, but in the end Chic persuaded him to take part in the concert as the one last gig the Whinhillbillies would accept. 'We'll call it your farewell tour,' he explained.

The occasion was stamped indelibly on Neilie's memory: 'I was petrified, but Chic acted as if nothing was happening. He chatted away to billtopper Leslie (Hutch) Hutchison as if he were an old friend, not someone he'd just met. He was in his element, whereas I was in misery—just wanting to get it over with. Sure enough, 15 minutes before we were due on, Chic dropped out of sight. I tracked him down eventually to the toilet and had to nearly shout myself hoarse before he'd come out. He was fixing his hair, he said. We just made it to the wings as we were being announced.

'The Whinhillbillies went down really well—we were the only amateurs on the bill, thanks to Maidie—and at the end of it the curtain closed on our act. They were big, heavy things and came in at a helluva lick. No one had warned us. Chic got out of the way in time, but they caught me off-balance and knocked me sideways. That was my exit from show-business—on my arse, with applause ringing in my ears—not a bad way to go. I knew all along Chic would make it on his own. He had all the nerve in the world. Anything we achieved was through him, but boy, he really put you through the mangle!'

Maidie eagerly greeted them backstage after the show. Chic had easily passed his audition, for his wife had more in mind than just the Usher Hall date. Her plan was a bold one, but to her entirely logical. Chic was already a top-flight amateur entertainer, so the step to turning professional should not be too difficult.

When she put the idea of forming a double-act to him, Chic was filled with self-doubt. 'What exactly would I do?' he agonised. Maidie's reply was to take a piece of paper and pen and compose this list:

1   Act opens, first song I sing and play, you harmonise.
2   Second song, we duet.
3   You tell your jokes.
4   We finish with another couple of songs.

'Oh, I see,' said Chic, smiling wanly, 'just like that?' At the end of the discussion Chic decided that the gamble was on, although he was adamant that initially he should appear unbilled. Maidie agreed, since it would be easier to get a booking just under her own name until they were established. 'You're not coming along just to carry my accordion, though,' she declared, without realising her perspicacity. 'You're a full partner and that's that—and we'll get the billing sorted out soon enough.'

A week after the partnership decision was made the couple had something else to celebrate, as Maidie discovered that she was pregnant. They were both thrilled at the prospect of a family, but with the first theatrical booking for the new team fixed for only weeks after the birth, Chic confessed, 'Yes, I'm tickled. But there's so much going on—chucking in my job, our first season to face and now this. I don't know if I'm having a shit or a haircut, or both at the same time!'

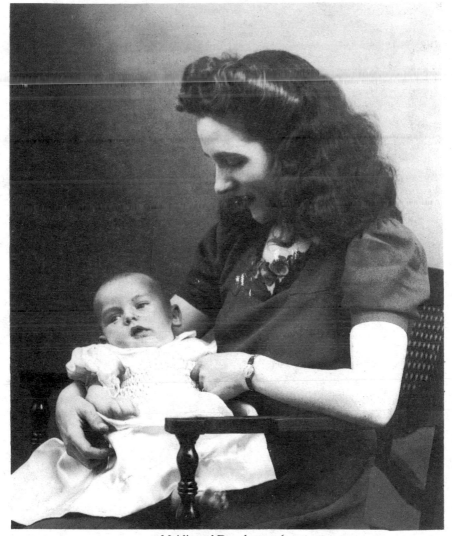

Maidie and Douglas, 1946.

Their son Douglas arrived on his expected date, a year to the day after their wedding. Their first night was just two weeks away at the Links Pavilion, Carnoustie, impresario Archie McCulloch, together with his young assistant, Eric Morley, having arranged the booking for Maidie to do her usual act. The theatre had asked for an accordionist, so they were already ahead with a singer and tap-dancer as well. They had no idea, however, just what else they were getting.

Douglas was to be left with Maidie's parents while the couple stayed

in digs in the holiday town—promptly dubbed 'Carsnootie' by Chic—
for the summer season. When Maidie first informed the show's producer
that her husband would be appearing with her, Jack Barton protested
that they were expecting only a solo act. 'Look,' she replied, 'you can
pay extra for him if you want to, but we're not asking for that yet. We
want to prove ourselves as a double, at no risk to you. We'll share my
salary until he makes his mark.'

'If he ever does,' came the dubious reply.

More of Chic's doubts set in as the first formal rehearsals approached.
He had a dozen jokes to tell and he had six minutes to tell them in.
Maidie couldn't see the problem. 'I've heard them all before,' wailed
Chic. 'Everybody's heard them all before,' retorted Maidie. 'There's no
such thing as a new joke, just old jokes dressed up differently. Don't
worry, you'll be fine.'

'I don't know so much,' groaned Chic, as his doubts increased about
the wisdom of walking out on Kincaid's. Maybe they would take him
back, he thought desperately—after all, he was well qualified—but even
as the thought entered his head he knew there was no possibility of that
happening. He could never go back now, for he felt the pull of the stage
and instinctively knew it was right for him, despite his declared
misgivings.

Rehearsals proved a chance for Maidie to introduce Chic to fellow
members of their Carnoustie extravaganza, *Back in Civvies*, where the
chief comic was Billy McLeod. Phil Wood ('Oor Heilan' Sinatra'), Mae
Milby ('Mae Will Bring You Memories') and Moira Kaye ('Sweetly
Sophisticated') all said 'hallo', then they repaired to Fred Dubber's 19th
Hole for a light refreshment—a sandwich and a half-pint of shandy—
before returning for afternoon rehearsal. The only thing to break Chic's
deepening moroseness was a sign in Dubber's bar which took his fancy.
It read 'Patrons over 90, accompanied by their grandparents, can have
their requirements free!'

Rehearsals were soon over and nothing in them provided any element
of reassurance. The jokes sounded tired and flat and as Chic heard them
echo around the empty theatre he felt what little confidence he had
mustered drain away. He agonised over what could be done to improve
and was deaf to Maidie's reassurance that the live, paying audience
would make all the difference. 'Come on, Chic, let's get back for a meal,'
Maidie entreated as everyone started to leave. It had been a long
Saturday and already it was getting dark outside. 'I want to hang about
for a while,' Chic replied. 'You go on and eat for me. I've got to sort
something out here.'

Maidie did not protest, wisely accepting that her husband needed time
on his own. With light from a single bulb behind him, he sat forlornly
on a rickety stool and watched his long shadow spilling across the stage.

As he looked out beyond the orchestra pit to the rows of stalls beyond, he felt the challenge of generations of stage acts that had preceded his, many of which this venerable old theatre had seen. 'I've got to make my mark,' he said to himself over and over again. 'I'm not a jokes man, but I do want to make people laugh. What the hell am I — what's the answer?' Some other members of the cast already saw him as nothing more than a box-boy for Maidie, but this certainly wasn't the answer he was looking for.

He thought back over his past life. The theatre was dark and still, with only the night watchman occasionally shuffling past, contentedly puffing away at his clay pipe. Chic thought of Isabella's selections from her favourite books, recounted to his father and himself by a blazing fire. His mind roamed again to his father and their country walks, then to the letters William had written while in hospital. He thought of his Aunt Tizzie and her wildly improbable spirit world and show-business stories. He thought of Maidie and her faith in him, then of Big Neilie as he had wished them luck at Carnoustie—good old Neilie, his old pal.

Still the question remained—what was he going to do? When at last he left and the night watchman had locked up after him, Chic stood in front of the theatre and surveyed the billing. It read:

Chalmers Wood presents
BACK In CIVVIES
with
BILLY McLEOD
& full supporting cast
(*change of programme every Monday and Thursday*)

By the light of the lamppost Chic looked at the jokes he had scribbled down on a piece of paper. He stared at them until the words were blurred and he could no longer make them out. What was wrong with them? he kept asking himself. They were reasonably good jokes and he knew how to tell a joke, so what was the big deal? All right, the act would not be a sensation, but neither would it die the death.

He could hardly bring himself to leave the pool of light he stood in, for it was quiet, peaceful and comforting. Into his mind came the memory of his story-telling days at school and work, where the only challenge had been to invent a new excuse every time he was late. He had let his imagination wander then, and the results had always got him off the hook.

Spotting a bar on the corner, he went into the busy snug and ordered a large rum, smiling at the memory ('Pressganged by landscape gardeners', indeed!). He sat and stared at the tipple for almost an hour, trying to put into words what he knew was inside him.

Another half-hour passed while he scribbled away on the back of a succession of beer mats, then the inside of a Woodbine packet. Only when he had finished did he begin to sip his rum. He re-read what he'd written. It tickled him, but would it tickle anyone else? Finishing his drink, he memorised the whole thing and repeated it silently to himself. He moved his lips soundlessly and ran through all the facial changes of expression from annoyance to outrage and bafflement. One of the crowd opposite him laughed and nudged his neighbour, while nodding in his direction. My first audience for the new patter, Chic thought wryly. But the real test would be on Monday night on the stage—until then he vowed to keep it to himself.

For the first show, Maidie had agreed to do a musical spot on her own as the second act ('A Breath o' the Heather frae Maidie'), then later re-emerge as 'Maidie Dickson' with Chic in tow. The unannounced double-act was to start off with 'There's a Blue Ridge Round My Heart', 'Virginia', a straight duet, followed by 'I'll Get By' with Chic providing the harmony to Maidie's lead, and a yodelling section for him in the middle. Chic's comedy spot was next, then a final two numbers, during which the accordion would be unbuckled and there would be a little tap-dancing. Maidie knew all of Chic's jokes backwards for that first show and was all set to prompt him if he dried up.

As they waited in the wings she looked at him, all dressed up in his Sunday-best tweed suit, topped off by a tartan bunnet he had insisted on wearing at the last minute. He seemed not at all nervous after the anxiety he had shown before, but she knew instinctively that something had changed in him since that final rehearsal.

The musical numbers went well, eliciting warm audience response. They were already familiar with Maidie, and her husband's harmony and yodelling enhanced the act nicely. As the applause faded after 'I'll Get By', Maidie gave Chic centre stage, at which he positively leapt in front of the microphone, quickly jacking it up to his level before the applause died away completely.

'I got up this morning,' he began. 'I like to get up in the morning; it gives me the rest of the day to myself.' The blood drained from Maidie's face—this wasn't in the script. Where were the jokes? She felt her head whirling as Chic continued, 'So I dressed. I always dress. I like to be different, but I think undressed you're a bit *too* different. I went down the street, went down the front—oh, you can go down the front, there's no law against it—and I was walking in my usual way, one foot in front of the other, oh, that's the best way—I've tried various methods. I remember once I tried a series of jumps, I heard someone say, "Look at that Australian!" I didn't answer, just wagged my tail.'

Maidie began to feel as if Chic had been talking for about an hour. In place of the yawning silence that had greeted him initially there were

now growing sounds of unrest among the audience. She prayed for him
to stop, she'd sing their wrap-up number and they'd be off, but no—
Chic was going on, intoning his story without let nor hindrance.

'Then I met someone. I knew him, otherwise I'd never have spoken to
him. He was sitting on top of a horse with a brief-case, bowler hat and
wellington boots. I said, "What are you doing on top of that horse?" He
said, "I thought you'd say that." I could have cut my tongue out; I
wished I'd never mentioned it. I thought—if I'd only just said "Hallo"
and never mentioned he was on a horse—or "Fanny's your aunt", or
anything. I should just have passed him as if it were an everyday
occurrence.'

By this time the audience were beginning to show their impatience in
the form of stamping feet and muffled boos, until one worthy yelled,
'Get off. You're rubbish. Give us Maidie.' Chic glared down briefly in
the approximate direction of this remark, while Maidie stood there, her
mouth gone completely dry. Chic took another breath and carried on,
'Then he said, "As soon as I saw you, I said to myself—*he'll* say what
are you doing up on that horse?" I was awfully embarrassed—and to
hide my embarrassment, I patted the horse. I said, "This horse has a flat
head." He said, "You're facing the wrong way".' Chic grimaced. 'I
wondered why it had refused the sugar lump!'

This time he was interrupted by some genuine laughter. The theatre
wasn't shaken to its foundations, but it was a beginning. Maidie started
to breathe again. There was no stopping Chic now; he seemed positively
hell-bent on telling his story. 'I gave the horse a thump on the rump and
it reared up. He looked down and said, "If you're coming up beside me,
I'm getting off," and slid over the horse's neck and landed on his head.
Luckily the pavement broke his fall.' This produced a little more
laughter—and one loud raspberry—from the audience. 'Oh, Chic,' Maidie
thought, 'finish it quick, for the love of God, while you're ahead.'

'So I hung about till he recovered,' Chic went on. 'It was the least I
could do. After all, I was the last one to talk to him. So when he came to
I said, "That was a dreadful thing that happened just now." He said,
"Just now! It's happened five times already this morning!" I said,
"What are you doing on the horse in the first place?" He said, "That's
another thing that's annoying me, I don't know." I said, "You don't
know? How's that?" He said, "I can't get my brief-case open to find
out." I said, "I'll have to go now, half the summer's gone in already
talking to you." He stalked off, leading the horse to a wall where he
could mount it. I said, "Now, now, don't get on your high horse!"'

This time there was considerable laughter, so Maidie took advantage
of the break and cued the conductor straight into 'Painting the Clouds
with Sunshine'. She heard Chic behind her mutter, 'I hadn't finished
yet!' She thought, 'You'd finished all right! And nearly finished me!'

When they got back to their dressing-room Chic smiled broadly at Maidie. 'Well, what do you think?' he asked. 'They seemed to like it OK.' Maidie could hardly find the words. 'Why didn't you stick to the jokes?' she said at last. 'And where on earth did that awful story come from?' Chic bridled a little, a bit in keeping with his horse talk. 'Maidie, the jokes were crap. I chucked them away on Saturday night and wrote my wee story in the pub. I didn't want to mention it to you in case you worried and, well, it went OK in the end, didn't it?'

Just then Jack Barton popped his head round the door. 'What the hell was that all about?' he asked. 'Just giving the customers what they want,' Chic replied coolly. Jack smiled at his cheek. 'Try modulating it a bit, then,' he advised.

On thinking this over before the next show, Maidie asked Chic to see the written version of his 'story'. 'He had put it down just the way he had read it,' she recalls, 'without punctuation marks of any kind. I read and re-read it, then inserted "ha ha" where I felt Chic should pause and give the audience a few seconds to realise that a funny bit had been reached and let it sink in. Chic agreed it was much better and said he would read it that way at the second house.' This time he started out his monologue as before. 'I got up this morning. I like to get up in the morning; it gives me the rest of the day to myself.' Then he inserted a dry, sardonic 'ha ha' and shook his shoulders up and down.

Maidie wished the floor would swallow her up when she heard this— Chic was obviously going to enunciate every 'ha ha' she had written down. Then an odd thing happened. Within a few seconds of the first 'ha ha' the audience started laughing. Chic carried on, 'So I dressed. I always dress. I like to be different but I think undressed you're a bit *too* different. Ha ha.'

Again it seemed that Chic had delivered the cue the audience were waiting for. It was as if everything he'd written was now funnier, but still in a different way from what variety audiences were used to, as Chic's amused yet dry 'ha ha' seemed to make them re-examine what had just been said and see the humour of it. Maidie couldn't believe her ears—Chic was actually leading the audience with him. Half-way through the story he left out an odd 'ha ha' and still got a laugh, just by pausing. Where Maidie had cut in before, she let him go on this time after the 'high horse' line.

'He was mad,' Chic continued, now in full spate. 'I just left and then I saw the producers of this show. I wasn't surprised the type of luck I was having. I thought—I'll dodge them, but they saw me and I heard them calling, "Chip, Chip"—they've never got my name right yet! Ha ha! "Chip, you're coming with us." I said, "Where are you going?" They said, "We're going out in a fishing smack." Well, you should have seen how the two of them were dressed—one had a yachting cap and a pair of water wings—I nearly choked on my seasick pill. The other one had a red tammy, a fisherman's jersey, shorts and plimsoles. I said, "What are you walking like that for?" He said, "It's a sailor's roll, walking the decks, laddie, a sailor's roll." I said, "It looks more like a ham roll to me!"'

This time Chic himself cued the pit orchestra and Maidie hastily came back to centre stage while her husband beamingly acknowledged the enthusiastic applause. Maidie was content—Chic had survived the baptism of fire in his own way, telling his own funny stuff, if with a modicum of help from his experienced partner.

Unknown to them both, Alex Watkins, the theatre manager, summoned Jack Barton to his office. 'What the hell's going on?' he demanded. 'We book Maidie for her usual stuff and we get her half-baked husband as well.'

'I didn't think he was all that bad,' Jack replied.

'Didn't you? Well, I did! Furthermore—Archie McCulloch's going to hear about this,' Watkins declared, picking up the phone. 'How's the show going?' asked Archie breezily as the call was put through. 'Terrible,' was the reply. 'I booked Maidie Dickson and I get her husband wandering on in the middle telling daft stories.' Archie got right to the heart of the matter as he asked, 'Did he get any laughs?' 'Well, yes, a few,' Watkins conceded. 'What's the problem then?' Archie asked. 'Keep him on—you're getting him for nothing—and I hear you're getting full value from Maidie in a Scots medley as well. What does Jack think of Maidie's husband?' 'He thinks he's got the makings,' Watkins was forced to admit. 'Well, then,' said Archie, 'let him run. Why not?' 'I ought to have my head examined,' declared Watkins wearily. 'Cheerio, Archie. Jeez, next time I ask for a monkey you'll send me an elephant!'

As they sat quietly in their flat later, unaware of the carfuffle they had caused, Maidie asked Chic how the monologue had emerged. He shrugged. 'I don't know,' he replied. 'It just came to me, it's the sort of patter I used to spring at school. I just let my imagination wander.' Maidie's next question almost floored him. 'Will it wander some more in time for the change of programme on Thursday night?' Chic's jaw dropped. 'Holy God, I'd forgotten about that,' he replied distractedly. 'Two a week for the next ten weeks!'

'That's right,' said Maidie, 'but make them all good and you can repeat them the length and breadth of Scotland in the next year. You'll get your full use out of them.'

Chic turned pensive and looked at Maidie fondly. 'There's just one more thing I think we could do to make the act a bit more seamless. It's something Gooey used to do behind my back on the stage. It's all right if you don't mind being the butt of the joke.'

'I always knew I'd end up a comic's labourer,' Maidie sighed.

Gradually the act settled in as the engagement continued. After each audience's initial bafflement had passed, they began to respond to Chic's humour. Alex Watkins himself often sat in the stalls and confessed to being pulled into what he called Chic's 'daft stories', until he too was laughing helplessly. 'Are the buggers just glad to see us go?' Chic quipped merrily one night, as they left to cheers. A new double-act had been born—and a new type of comedian.

A reporter from the *Evening Citizen* called in to see the new act during the run. Ramsden Craig had written glowingly of Maidie before as a solo act and picked her out as a future major star. This time his review was not to be favourable. 'You've made a mistake, Maidie,' he told her bluntly. 'OK, you've married the man, but did you have to take him on the stage with you?'

'He's got to have a chance to prove himself,' Maidie retorted. 'Gag merchants are ten a penny. Great comics are rare.'

Craig choked. 'Great comics?' he replied. 'Great comics? Maidie, he's not even a comic, he's just a blether. I'll bet he won't last beyond this season.'

'You're wrong,' Maidie replied. 'I know you mean well, Ramsden, but you're wrong. And he'll prove you wrong.'

'If he does,' Craig replied, 'I'll be the first to eat my words. Good luck, Maidie, you'll need it.'

As he left, Chic entered the dressing-room. 'Who's the gadje?' he asked.

'A man from the *Citizen*,' Maidie replied. 'He's given me some nice write-ups in the past. He's been a friend before and he will be again.'

Gradually Chic familiarised himself with the stage lingo. 'Can you open and close in one?' Jack wanted to know. 'No problems,' replied Maidie. 'What's that?' asked Chic, warily. 'We open with the curtains closed after the previous act,' explained Maidie. 'Then while we're singing our first song the stagehands move the previous dropcloth away and give us one of our own. This time I've asked for dark blue to show off my new light blue satin dress. Then for our final number they close the tabs again (Chic: 'Tabs? What's tabs?' Maidie: 'Curtains.') and we do our last song in front of them while they take our dark blue away and fix up the dropcloth for the next act.'

Chic immediately feigned indignation. 'Why should we open and close in one?' he demanded. 'Because,' Maidie smilingly retorted, 'I've been doing it for ages and until a few seconds ago you didn't know any different. So can it!'

'No wife of mine,' Chic insisted magisterially, 'should have to open and close in one!'

As usually happened in cases like this Maidie ended up unsure whether Chic was being entirely serious or merely being Chic, so she later explained to him that once they worked their way out of the 'wines and spirits' (Chic: 'What's that?' Maidie: 'Bottom half of the bill.'), then they might have more clout and not have to open and close in one. 'Now collect our dots and we'll be off,' she said to the immediate query, 'Dots?' 'Music,' she replied.

After two weeks of non-stop effort and continual changes, Jack Barton strode up one day to Chic and handed him a piece of paper. 'What's that?' asked Chic, 'My jotters?'

'Read it,' said Jack, 'it's a draft of next week's programme.' To Chic's astonishment and delight, the billing after Maidie's solo was now down as Chick and Maidie. 'You've misspelled my name,' said Chic, deadpan, then he grabbed Jack's hand and shook it warmly. 'Is this what they call making it?' he asked, beaming.

EMPIRE
Theatre · Belfast

"The Home of Good Entertainment"

Proprietors - - - The Belfast Empire Theatre of Varieties Ltd.
Resident Manager - - - - - - - - - Frank E. Reynolds

PROGRAMME

PRICE THREEPENCE
BOX OFFICE OPEN DAILY 11 A.M. TILL 8 P.M.
Phone 24833

ADMISSION (including Tax) :
Box Seats 6/9, Front Stalls 4/6, Circle 3/6, Back Stalls 3/- (*All Bookable*)
Gallery 1/3

6

Squealin' Annie

'I got up and crossed the landing and went down stairs. Mind you, if there had been no stairs there I wouldn't even have attempted it.'

Maidie was left to attend to all their future bookings and despite their eventual good reception at Carnoustie, it was hard to find theatres prepared to take on and pay for a double act, with full billing—especially one that was still untested as far as they were concerned. In between engagements Maidie haunted the offices of the William R. Galt Agency at 13 Sauchiehall Street, Glasgow. She would ring the bell to get the attention of Willie's chief booker, a wee wire of a woman named Nellie Sutherland. 'Anything for me this week?' Maidie would inquire, as Nellie pulled up her window. Shifting her Woolworth spectacles further up her nose, Nellie would reply in her somewhat melancholy nasal tones, 'Nothing today,' before sharply banging the window back down again. At other times her reply might be, 'There's something in Paisley. Come inside and we'll talk terms.' Maidie would then be allowed into the inner sanctum of the Agency. The man himself would hardly ever be seen and many would have questioned his existence were it not for the distinctive spidery scrawl on a contract. Others maintained that the redoubtable Nellie was really Willie in drag.

During her pregnancy Maidie continued to appear with Chic at a string of small-time dates she finally managed to fix up through Nellie, until eventually she had another auspicious booking—in a maternity ward in May 1947, where their second child, Annabelle, was born.

Chic frequently appeared without billing despite his achievement at Carnoustie and the duo's summer show of 1947, presented by Archie McCulloch at the Town Hall, St Andrews, was one such occasion. Here the top comics were Johnny Rae and Bert Williams, whose big sketch was 'Black Market Clothes'. Also featured were John Cumming ('Don Juan of Song') and the May Moxon Lovelies.

Although the show ran for ten weeks with programme changes twice weekly, Chic never received billing recognition. Maidie put it to him that it was all for the best, as they would be allowed to build the act up slowly, away from the glare of the limelight. Chic had no complaints, for he was having the time of his life. He enjoyed the travelling, although for the moment it was confined to Scotland. While theatrical digs held no charms for Maidie, to Chic they were still a novelty and all part of the fun.

Again he was unbilled at the Roxy Theatre in Falkirk where they were booked by G. B. Bowie in October 1947. Chic promptly dubbed musical director Jimmy Running 'Running Wild, Lost Control' as he struggled manfully with the Roxy orchestra. *Down Mexico Way* billed 'Maida' Dickson twice, with and without her accordion. Johnnie Rae again provided the comedy supported by Vicki Lester ('Scotland's Judy Garland') and George Rex ('In Popular Songs').

Dunfermline's Opera House helped out with a booking in their *Christmas Fare* show of 1947 with 'Madie' Dickson billed first on her own, then the double as 'Dickson and Murray' ('With Popular Songs'). Tommy Conran was top comic while a versatile double-act, Carr and Vonnie, was also featured. This duo had 'been the roonds' several times and were already seasoned veterans of the circuit. Vonnie was an Irish colleen who could switch accents from Irish to Scots at the drop of a shillelagh, while Jimmy Carr had an unmistakable high-voiced Glasgow accent. They sang, danced, clowned and, when times were thin, appeared as the front and rear legs of a pantomime horse—nothing daunted, all-in-the-game true professionals. With Christmas gone the same cast were featured in a brand new show, *The Sleeping Beauty Pantomime*.

They next found themselves quickly rebooked at Falkirk, this time as 'Chic and Maidie—The Lank and The Lady', and with their confidence in the act considerably enhanced by the enthusiastic reception they were receiving. Chic had continued to come up with a string of funny yarns which were increasingly surrealistic and involved. His delivery of them was improving all the time and he was learning to differentiate between first- and second-house reactions, having found that for the first house there were more women than men in attendance and that generally the crowd seemed less sophisticated. His face-pulling à la Gooey behind Maidie was only partially successful for this house, since many of the women would yell out, 'Stop that!' or 'Look at him, he's just making a bloody fool of her!' The second house took it all in good part and roared as Maidie almost caught Chic out. He followed Jack Barton's advice to modulate the act depending on the house, then gradually even between weekday and weekend performances. He was learning.

Maidie arranged for her parents to travel through from Edinburgh to see the double-act for the first time on their opening night at Falkirk.

On the Monday morning the producer ominously stood with a stop-watch as each act went through its paces. Chic and Maidie had put together their smoothest-running act yet, with a couple of changes of song, a yodelling solo for Chic, and a very accurate Al Jolson impersonation he had perfected.

When the break came for lunch, the two of them repaired to a nearby bar for a pie and half-pint. Chic said, 'Did you see that wee bachle with the stop-watch? I thought being a licensed grocer was bad, now they've got us down as flaming sprinters!' Nothing could deflate Maidie on this occasion however, for the thought of her parents' visit filled her with a warm glow. Her mother would be so proud, she thought. As for her father, Hugh had never seen her on stage since she was a teenager, having spent the war years as a Petty Officer in the Royal Navy, so the Roxy date assumed even greater significance.

They eagerly trooped back to the theatre in time to see the star comic, Billy Wallace from Kilmarnock, finish his act, again being clocked by an increasingly worried-looking producer. The reason for the anxiety became all too clear as he gathered the whole cast together on stage. As they stood around in a semicircle the wee bulbous-nosed man pushed his comical bowler hat back on his head and stuck his thumbs down the side of his braces. Chic remembers a sense of foreboding as he began to address the company: 'I'm sorry to tell you this, but the show's running over, and badly. We need the bars at the end of the second house, so I've got a choice of cutting each act a little or just giving one act the chop—only for tonight. Tomorrow or Wednesday we can sort something else out for the rest of the run.' Here he looked toward Chic and Maidie, not exactly at either one, more somewhere in the middle between the two. 'You're the act for the chop tonight,' he announced. 'Take the night off—go to the pictures or something. Tomorrow we'll rehearse again.'

Maidie burst into tears, while Chic felt the blood drain from his face. 'Why us?' he asked tersely. The producer rocked back and forth on his heels. 'We've overbooked and I think we're top heavy on the comedy side,' he replied. 'Besides—I don't have to justify myself to you. Billy's the lead, he's the one everyone's coming to see. You're out. Right?'

Chic grabbed Maidie's hand and together, they walked into the wings. Back in the dressing-room neither could speak, until Maidie determinedly brushed away her tears and blew her nose. 'Chic,' she said, 'I can't see my Mum and Dad disappointed like this. I'm going to go and plead with him. He's got to let us go on.' Chic took her hand in his and felt it tremble. He swallowed hard. 'It's not on, Maidie,' he replied. 'You're just going to demean yourself. And me.'

Maidie looked at her husband for the longest moment before getting up and walking toward the door. He heard the click-click of her high heels as she walked the short distance down the corridor towards the producer's office. Her expression when she returned 15 minutes later told him all he needed to know. Maidie had even telephoned Galt's in front of the producer and tried to get them to change the man's mind, but it had been a wasted effort. He was adamant—they were out and that was that.

Maidie went off disconsolately to have her hair done at Davidson's in the main street–offering new 'machineless permanent waving'–while Chic went off to have a dauner round Falkirk on his own before meeting Hugh and Anne Dickson at Grahamston station.

When they were all united the situation was explained. Their disappointment was evident, but they saw that there was nothing to be done, so off they went to the hotel where Chic had reserved a table for dinner. To Maidie's surprise it turned out to be the top hotel in Falkirk, where an excellent table had been reserved near the floor of the small dance area, close to a wee man doing his best on a light classical selection at the piano. Chic proved to be the life and soul of the party, and Maidie gradually felt the knot in her stomach relax and her disappointment begin to ease a little. As they were sipping their coffee, the pianist finished his selection and stood up, bowing to the polite applause. He cleared his throat and addressed the diners.

'Thank you for your warm appreciation,' he began, 'and now I'd like to point out that we have a pair of real professionals with us tonight. You've all heard of Maidie Dickson—well, she's teamed up with her husband, Chic. They're enjoying a rare night off this evening, and in the very special company of Maidie's parents, but I wonder if I could prevail upon them on your behalf to do a short turn for you?' Maidie looked at Chic in blank amazement. He shrugged his shoulders and rolled his eyes innocently, whispering, 'It's the price of fame,' as the diners applauded them on to the dance floor. 'But I haven't got my accordion,' Maidie protested. 'Yes, you have,' Chic assured her as the pianist carried it in, 'and I've got his manky old piano.'

Maidie looked at Chic, then at the expression of delight on her parents' faces. 'Bend down,' she ordered, which Chic did immediately, receiving for his pains a lingering kiss, to cheers from the assembly. 'Now let's give them all we've got,' said Maidie. Chic was all compliance. 'OK, captain,' he agreed.

For the next 20 minutes the couple went through an extended version of their latest act, ending to rapturous applause as they made their way back to their table. As Maidie's parents got up to hug them both, a waiter appeared as if on cue, and asked if they would accept a bottle of champagne, courtesy of a group of diners. 'Bring it over,' said Chic, 'we'll see what we can do,' giving the group a cheery wave of thanks. The wine proved the perfect finale to the evening, then it was time to escort Maidie's parents back to the station in time to catch the last train to Edinburgh.

Anne Dickson hugged Chic and kissed him on the cheek. 'I don't know how you managed it, but by God, you did us proud,' she told him. 'Well done son,' said Hugh, pumping Chic's hand.

With her parents safely waved off Maidie asked him how the whole thing had come about. 'Oh, I just wanted to show you I could manage a booking myself,' Chic replied. 'I went round to the hotel to reserve a table to take our minds off the disappointment and suggested that since we had a night off we might be persuaded to do a turn for the locals. I was introduced to the hotel manager and he agreed with the dinner thrown in as well.'

Maidie remembered vaguely someone telling her that with Chic she would never know poverty, although the remark had not really been meant in a kindly way. It should have been, she thought, as her eyes misted over at the remembrance of the evening they had just enjoyed. All trace of the disappointment had been wiped away. 'OK, no more mucking about, back to the flat for a spot of heavy breathing,' Chic declared with a grin. Maidie put her arm around his waist and squeezed as hard as she could. 'Chance would be a fine thing,' she replied.

*   *   *

The couple now had a gap between engagements that was embarrassingly wide. In desperation, Maidie turned up almost daily at Galt's in Glasgow until one day Nellie Sutherland came up with something for them. 'Well, Maidie,' she droned, adjusting her specs. 'I do have one week I could give the pair of you. It's a wee bit unusual, but it'll certainly suit that man of yours. Glasgow Corporation have asked us to put together a bill to tour their five mental institutions, one a night, Monday to Friday, starting off at Gartcosh. It's not much, but it's all I can offer you before Easter.' 'We'll take it,' said Maidie without hesitation, but her mind was racing. What would Chic say?

When he heard the news his response was to go into a diatribe on the frailties of the human condition that threatened to blister the paint off the doors, but then he relented, commenting, 'I only hope they can sort the entertainers from the inmates at the end of it all.' Maidie referred to the booking as a 'three half-crowns job', but it was a booking, and would at least give the wolf at the door a smell of food, if not an actual nibble, as Chic put it. In the event it turned out to be a salutary experience for him, as he recalled 25 years later.

'The tour confirmed for me the fine line that separates sanity from madness. I was used to shipyard humour, but during those five days I got my first taste of mental home humour. Although it was new to my ears a lot of it sounded familiar, almost as if I'd been there before. I talked to many of the patients before and after the shows, visited their canteens and took my meals with them. Let me tell you, there was a lot

of perception and insight there and I felt strangely at home and comfortable with their rather odd, elliptical way of looking at things.

'One of the inmates was convinced that the whole troupe of us were really doctors in disguise, sent to spy on them. As our conjuror did his bit, changing green water in a bottle to red and back to green again, one of them yelled, "See, he's a doctor. That's the medicine he's getting ready for us." Well, of course, the fact is that we were there as therapy for them so they were not that far wrong. Then when the conjuror made rabbits vanish, that caused a commotion as they maintained that they would get the blame for their disappearance.

'When Maidie and I asked them to join in one of our choruses, they reckoned this was proof positive that we were from the authorities. This way we were finding out who was co-operating and who wasn't. I think, mind, I eventually persuaded them that we were not doctors, or from the authorities, because after hearing my patter I heard one of them shout, "Christ, they're dafter than us!" Meantime one of them asked if our act was a punishment of some kind for their bad behaviour. Very flattering—calculated to bring anyone down to earth with a thud.

'They expressed colourful opinions of the medical staff in the institution, stating unreservedly that, "They're off their heids. There's saner folk locked up." After the show a couple of patients came up and shook our hands. "Hallo. How're you doing? All right? Cheerio, then!"

they said, then walked off giggling. As they left, someone—who turned out to be the Welfare Officer—popped his head round the door and repeated what we'd just heard, which was his apparently standard greeting of, "Hallo. How're you doing? All right? Cheerio, then!" One of the patients turned to me and said, "Hear that? Call him a Welfare Officer? That's all we ever see of him. He's more like a fuckin' Farewell Officer!"'

Chic was somewhat disconcerted to find that he shared many of the patients' insights and attitudes, and even more so when he found himself inadvertently locked in with the group considered to be dangerously disturbed. An orderly had closed the door behind him, thinking there was no one there from the visiting party. After a while Maidie began to wonder where Chic had got to and raised the alarm. A search was organised, but it was a full hour before anyone thought of checking the restricted compound into which Chic had wandered.

As they opened up the heavy metal door, they saw a dozen or so of the inmates squatting in a group in the middle of the floor. At the centre was Chic, engrossed in a game of dominoes. He looked up distractedly as the orderlies approached to take him out. 'Give me another five minutes,' he pleaded, 'these buggers are beating me hands down!'

Since their wedding the couple had lived out of suitcases, either with Maidie's parents in Edinburgh, Chic's Mum in Greenock, one or other of the McKinnons in Glasgow or Dundee, or at theatrical digs. Staying with relatives wherever possible saved a little money, but Chic still noted that they never seemed to get ahead of themselves financially.

They ate well, both preferring simple food, although Chic did like rather a lot of it. Maidie would ask landladies' permission to use their kitchens to make the thick lentil soup and Scotch broth he relished for she was only too aware of the high standards he had been used to in Greenock. For a main course nothing pleased him more than a heaped plate of sausage and mash, or mince and tatties—unless it was two heaped plates. Maidie watched his weight go from the skinny ten and a half stone he had been when they met, to a more comfortable twelve stone, and climbing.

An unexpected booking suddenly arose at the Greenock Empire and the two happily boarded the train at Glasgow Central to take them to Chic's home town, where they would be staying with Isabella. On the way through Chic reminded Maidie that he had appeared at the Empire before—as an amateur one night on a bill with Ma and Pa Short, Jimmy Logan's parents. Young Jimmy himself had been there on piano, not yet in his teens, years before he had branched into comedy.

'Did you ever come across Squealin' Annie?' Maidie asked. Chic grinned at the reference to the well-known comedians' Nemesis. He had never encountered the lady in full flight, he was glad to report. 'I did,'

Maidie told him. She was the theatre-goer that every comedian
dreaded—a somewhat eccentric old lady who turned up regularly at the
Greenock Empire. Apart from her wild applause and her jigging in the
aisle between the acts, she got her name from the ear-splitting howl she
let out at the end of comics' jokes. Nothing wrong with that—except she
never waited until the punch line was over, but always timed her squeal
to coincide with the last line, drowning it out for everyone else. 'I don't
know how she did it,' said Maidie. 'It must have taken years of practice,
but she always knew the exact, precise moment to let rip! It was a kind
of gift, I suppose.'

As it happened Chic had other problems to cope with during his week
in Greenock, such as remembering which side of the stage to exit from,
for the layout of the theatre was such that there was no actual 'backstage',
merely a brick wall covered with a velvet curtain. One side of the stage
contained the men's dressing-rooms, the other the ladies'. Chic found
himself pressed into service in a sketch before his own spot, in which he
played the 'heid of the hoose' in a Glasgow household. He was required
to sit up in bed wearing pyjamas and a nightcap, issuing orders to one
and all. As this scene was being set up in front of the velvet-covered
brick wall, the previous act was appearing in front of the tabs.

The act in question was known as 'Master Joe Peterson', although Joe
was one Mary O'Rourke, whose speciality had for years been dressing up
as the 'young master', her hair Eton-cropped and topped with a
schoolboy's cap to look the part. Mary's high piping voice did indeed
sound like that of a young boy, hence the act had become her very
successful stock in trade, to the extent of frequent gramophone records
being issued under the Master Joe Peterson appellation.

On this particular night both Chic and Master Joe were suffering
from heavy colds, but whereas Chic was doctoring himself up with
aspirins and pastilles, Joe's cure was a half-bottle of whisky downed
before taking the stage. As a result of this Master Joe was rather the
worse for wear and began to give somewhat inspirational versions of her
song selections. With the frantic pit pianist trying to keep up with her
meanderings, Chic sat behind the tabs, propped up in bed, awaiting
release from the torture of Master Joe's lilting tones.

As Master Joe's last song was sung, the conductor handed her a
bouquet of flowers from an admirer in the audience. Overcome by
emotion—and whisky—at this gesture, Master Joe began a speech that
became more and more maudlin and slurred as she praised the donator
of the flowers, the theatre, the people of Greenock—the list went on and
on. Meantime, Chic sat in bed waiting impatiently for her to finish so
the sketch, and the show, could restart.

Master Joe, however, was not about to stop, until the conductor had a
wonderful idea. The cue music for the sketch was 'There's No Place

Like Home', so he struck up the tune. Master Joe, still overcome by emotion, took this as a cue for an encore only too fitting for the occasion, and started to join in—as the curtain parted to reveal Chic, the bed and the Glasgow household scene.

As Master Joe faltered, an exasperated Chic muttered in a stage whisper, 'Get off!' Master Joe turned to look at him disdainfully, and a bit unsteadily, as Chic repeated his request, somewhat louder this time. Master Joe staggered towards him, the flowers still in her hand, then turned back to the audience, 'See him!' she slurred. 'That's not a well man there. Not a well man. He shouldnae be here the night.' Pointing now at the conductor she scolded, 'And you! You're not helping much either!' By this time Chic was almost choking and he made no attempt to moderate his tones as he yelled at her—with a volume that not even Squealin' Annie could have topped—'Get *fuckin' off*!'

At this even the bold Master Joe felt that something was amiss and it began to dawn on her that possibly she had overstayed her welcome. Quickly she made for the side of the stage, still clutching her bouquet—only one thought in mind now, to escape Chic's obvious wrath. Unfortunately she picked the side with the men's dressing-rooms. How to get back with dignity? Chic's sketch was in full progress as Master Joe edged herself along behind the velvet curtain, scrabbling furiously as she made her way to the other side of the stage. Chic turned to watch as the velvet billowed. 'How the hell do I follow this?' he was thinking, for the audience was rolling about the aisles by this time. 'Jees, all I need is Squealin' Annie!' Luckily he was spared this, and it was a shaken Master Joe who emerged from the velvet curtains, cap missing from her head and still holding on to the tattered remains of her bouquet. Her courage had failed her. 'Do you think that man of yours was angry with me?' she asked Maidie, who had watched the whole performance. 'Angry?' came the reply. 'If I was you, Mary, I'd be on the early bus back to Glasgow!'

One day Chic came back to Bank Street looking decidedly shaken, carrying a copy of the *Glasgow Herald*. 'Dukinfield's dead,' he announced. 'Who?' asked Maidie. 'Dukinfield—oh, you knew him as Woolchester Cowperthwaite, remember? Our landlord here at Bank Street.' 'But you don't have a landlord,' replied Maidie, puzzled, 'your Mum owns the house.' 'That's just the point,' Chic agreed. Still perplexed, but determined to get to the bottom of this, Maidie asked, 'You mean he had two names—this landlord of yours?' 'A lot more than that,' Chic replied. 'But his real name was Dukinfield. Oh, his stage name was W. C. Fields, but he was also known as E. Whipsnade Larson, Ambrose Wolfinger and Elmer Prettywillie, among others. Now he's dead. He'll be a terrible miss.'

Maidie reflected for a moment on the way Chic's mind functioned.

He had never mentioned W. C. Fields' name to her once before—
Woolchester Cowperthwaite yes, but never W. C. Fields—yet here he
was, clearly moved by the comedian's passing. At this rate, she thought,
even Mrs Pollock's origin might one day be revealed.

7

Tall Droll, Small Doll

'My wife went to the beauty parlour and got a mud pack. For two days she looked nice, then the mud fell off. She's a classy girl, though, at least all her tattoos are spelt right.'

Maidie began to long for a place of their own, even though she knew their time spent anywhere would be limited. While visiting her Mum and Dad after Annabelle was born she had spotted an apartment for sale two floors above her parents' own flat in Montague Street. Chic had no wish to disappoint her, but gently pointed out that they didn't even have the money for a deposit.

'Suppose we could raise it, wouldn't it be an idea to find out what sort of mortgage we could expect to get?' Maidie asked. Chic agreed and an appointment was made with a building society. When he returned from the meeting he had a more-than-usually baffled look on his face. 'Tell the story,' Maidie said.

'Well,' Chic began, 'Did you know that we're classed as vagrants? That's what I've just been told—we're showbiz folk of no fixed abode and no security.'

Maidie was thunderstruck. 'No mortgage, then?'

'No,' Chic replied, 'not until we can put a big lump of cash down, anyway. But at least one thing's come out of it—the fact that we know now how we're classed. I don't know how that strikes you, Maidie, but it tickles me. I think I've always felt an affinity with the gentlemen of the road.'

Maidie looked dumped. 'Good for you,' she said, 'but we're temporarily off the road for the moment—something of an enforced lay-off. The dates aren't exactly flooding in.'

'They'll pick up,' Chic assured her, cheerfully. 'Then we can go back to playing tramps.'

After their journeys all over Scotland, everywhere except the cities, a

booking in Edinburgh was a major achievement. 'Big city,' beamed
Maidie. 'Small theatre,' moaned Chic. 'But a wee beauty,' Maidie
countered, the 'beauty' in question being the Gaiety, Leith, which was
to feature them in the 1948 Summer Show. Jimmy Donoghue and
Jimmy Ramsay were the star comics and although the two were partners,
there was obviously no love lost between them. Irish comic Billy Stutt
was making one of his first appearances, while Hector Nicol was making
his non-comic début with his musical partner of the time, Sonny Allen
('Music for the Moderns'). Sonny Farrar ('Five Feet of Fun and a
Banjo') was also featured, Chic teasing his partner with 'You and he
would be like a pair of bookends', while the bill was completed by Grace
Calvert ('The Whistling Songstress') and—to Maidie's delight—her
erstwhile mentor from Portobello, Peggy Desmond.

Maidie had started a scrapbook of the odd favourable mention they
got in the press, but their best notice yet now came from the Edinburgh
Evening News: 'We all know Maidie,' the review ran, 'and she's always
been a favourite. But take a listen to her very funny husband, Chic. He's
not a "Scots" comic, he doesn't tell jokes in the ordinary sense, but he's
starting to tickle audiences with his daft stories, which are cleverer than
they sound. Maidie's obviously taking a relative back-seat to give her
husband's talent a chance to come through. I think this act could go
places.'

Again the redoubtable Nellie turned up trumps for them as they were
booked into the Empire Theatre, Motherwell, for their annual Christmas
show. Heading the bill was Edinburgh comedian Johnny Victory. He
was a great admirer of Sir Harry Lauder and ran one of Sir Harry's old
cars, but his humour could not have been further removed from that of
his idol, for Victory favoured monologues in a variety of accents and
often featured what appeared to be Maurice Chevalier impersonations.
Despite the fact that he was not considered a top-flight comic, he had a
winning personality and generosity of spirit. He helped many unknowns
through their first, faltering steps on stage and was one of the three
popular stalwarts of manager Dan Campbell's doughty Edinburgh
Palladium, along with Lex McLean and Billy Rusk.

At Motherwell the billing was 'Maidie Dickson and Chic' and the bill
was rounded off by Sally Fay ('Personality Girl') and Sadie Stevens
('Delightful Soprano'). Johnny ('Your Favourite Comedian') Victory
carried on in triumph at the theatre with much the same cast and crew—
Chic and Maidie included—in the 1949 New Year review *Down to the
Sea in Ships*, featuring two additional acts, Archie Roy ('You Will Like
Him') and Jakie Connell ('The Yodelling Cowboy').

Two months later it was through to Glasgow and the Empress
Playhouse for a one-week engagement that brought much relief to Chic,
for he had been convinced that somehow Glasgow would be a jinx for

him, possibly because it was too close to home. Here they were 'Chic and Maidie—A Large and Small Scotch' and it was not long before Chic's fears were put to rest as John Worth, the theatre manager, approached them both after the show. 'That was a treat,' he told them. 'I haven't laughed so much for ages.'

One memorably evening they had both come on stage blacked up for a Jolson selection. Maidie had daubed her hands and face and Chic his face only, since he had a brand-new pair of white gloves for the occasion. On this particular night Isabella was in attendance on one of her rare visits to Glasgow as the couple bounced on, singing 'Toot Toot Tootsie, Goodbye' at full pitch. After a couple of bars Maidie turned to Chic and whispered, 'You've forgotten the gloves.' Instantly Chic glanced down with horror at his hands to verify this statement. 'Christ,' he said, and promptly fled the stage, leaving Maidie to busk on as best she could while the conductor Alex Smith mouthed, 'Where the hell's he gone?' 'Upstairs to get his gloves,' Maidie mimed back obligingly.

Their dressing-room in the Empress was situated in the 'attic' of the theatre, a considerable climb from the stage. Maidie was beginning to despair of Chic's return before the end of the number, when a tremendous roar and thunderous applause greeted his appearance. With a huge smile on his face he danced on stage, waving his white-gloved hands above his head. 'We slaughtered them that night,' Maidie recalls. 'Chic could have scratched his nose and they would have laughed. They just responded to anything he cared to give them. But I'll never forget the re-entry with the white gloves. It was like the Hampden roar!'

They ended their act with another Jolson number as Chic announced, 'OK fans, so much for the funnies. Just because a guy forgets his gloves! Our last number is singularly appropriate tonight—if you're a university graduate that is. For the rest of us it's dead right, and you'll see what I mean when I tell you my Mum's with you in the audience.' As the band struck up 'Mammy' and Chic got down on his knees during the song, tears came to the eyes of many in the audience—and not this time of laughter, for Chic scored with his Jolson act by not exaggerating it as many others did. For him an accurate impersonation of someone he considered an all-time great was enough; the audience could sense this and responded accordingly. There in the middle of the stalls was Isabella, standing up and waving her own white-gloved hands in the air, her eyes wet.

That year the summer season was spent at Largs, a little 'doon the water' from Greenock, in G. B. Bowie's *Follies of 1949*. They found themselves billed third from the top, a considerable step up. Needless to say, Maidie featured as a solo artist early on as well in 'A Medley of Music', but it was 'Chic and Maidie—the Big Yin and the Wee Yin' that almost closed the show. Although the couple stayed with Isabella during

the entire engagement and were royally catered for as always, Chic confessed to being 'in and out of Nardini's Esplanade Café like a whitrick', unable to resist their renowned cream ices. It was a happy season for the couple and their family, presided over by proud Granny Murray.

A busy holiday resort in the season, Largs was not known for its sparkling night life the rest of the year round. One night Chic and Maidie were having a walk along the front after the show before going home to Isabella's. It was very much at the tail end of the season and already things were winding down. They walked for about an hour without hardly passing a soul before they decided to stop off at Nardini's for an ice cream. As Chic ordered their ices he saw that the woman behind the counter was struggling to recognise him. She knew he was 'somebody', but was not sure exactly who. Finally she got it and said, 'Oh, you're Chic Murray, aren't you? And that's Maidie.' They both smiled and nodded. 'What brings you out at this time of night?' she then asked. 'Well,' Chic replied, deadly serious, 'we're trying to find a bit of excitement and someone tipped us off there's going to be a chimney set on fire a bit later.' 'I see,' came the innocent reply. 'Can I have your autographs then, while you're waiting?'

Jimmy Logan's folks had packed him off to their chalet in the hills overlooking Largs, as he had been suffering from low blood-pressure. While he lay stretched out in the fresh air his pals ventured into town and bumped into Chic, who accepted their invitation to come back with them and visit Jimmy. The fresh air was doing young Logan a power of good and he was delighted when his pals appeared with Chic, whose progress he had heard about with interest. The two comedians' paths would continue to cross regularly throughout their careers.

Whether a good report from Johnny Victory had anything to do with it or not—and the couple swore that it did—their next Christmas season was at Dan Campbell's Palladium in Edinburgh. Dan was a man who recognised and cultivated talent when he saw it, for he had been through the mill himself and knew all the wrinkles. As a Glasgow Highlander, in the 9th Battalion, Highland Light Infantry, he had entertained his pals with comedy songs before switching to serious stuff, like his stirring baritone rendition of 'La Marseillaise', in full dress kilt and with a blood-stained bandage around his head for good measure.

He was invited to make some early recordings for the Beltona label, including 'The Skye Boat Song' and 'Scots Wha Hae', before touring the London suburbs with George West's Highland Company. On his return to Scotland he toured the Highlands before teaming up with Billy Lester to form a travelling pantomime company. Alec Finlay and his wife-to-be, Rita Andre, were also approached to join the company, for which financial disaster was forecast. Instead the hardy group registered solid success, making fellow promoters and performers alike sit up and take notice. Later Dan became more interested in the management side of the business and settled down to run the Palladium.

A shilling bought a circle seat for the show and half a crown secured a front-stalls view of the Murray's Palladium engagement, with the bill headed by the battling Jimmies, Donoghue and Ramsay (they were even billed as 'They Agree To Differ'). Among the 'wines and spirits' were 'Youthful Dancing Stars' Lionel and Joyce Blair. As Lionel revealed later, this was not a happy booking for the team.

Following a spell as a junior with the Royal Shakespeare Company in

Stratford-upon-Avon, Lionel Blair had made his solo début as a dancer at the Gaiety Theatre, Ayr, in the 1949 *Gaiety Whirl*, produced by the ubiquitous Jack Barton. Now accompanied by his 15-year-old sister, Joyce, the billing at Dan Campbell's Palladium ran the 'Yorkshire Dancing Duo'. Lionel was unimpressed with the modest Palladium after the glamour of the Gaiety, then his despondency deepened when he found he was required to appear with the rest of the cast—Chic and Maidie included—in comedy sketches with the jousting Jimmies. The season for Lionel and Joyce was cut short 'by mutual consent'. Following this rough ride, Lionel was booked for the *Five Past Eight* shows and things began to look up.

Despite their own lowly position on the bill, Chic and Maidie received a favourable notice in the *Scotsman*, whose critic picked them out as 'An act to watch. Their appeal baffles me, but they're loaded with it.'

'I think he meant that as a compliment,' said Maidie. 'Sounds to me as if he could write my material,' replied Chic. 'Maybe I should audition him!' The fact was that they were being noticed, and proof of this came from the BBC, who signed them for a series of radio broadcasts. Chic took readily to the new medium and sharpened his already powerful gift of using the silence between phrases to optimum effect.

Their very first broadcast was recorded at the BBC's Rutherglen Repertory Theatre where Chic first bumped into Iain Cuthbertson, an actor he much admired, as they stood side by side in the BBC urinal. 'I didn't know you did this sort of thing, being a serious actor and all that,' Chic remarked. 'D'you mean peeing in here or working for the Beeb?' Iain wanted to know. 'Listen, Chic, I've heard you and Maidie at rehearsals—I think you're a bloody scream. I'll be watching your progress with interest.' 'How do you know there'll be any?' Chic asked, somewhat unctuously. 'I mean progress—or interest?' 'There will be,' replied Iain. 'Both. Take it from me.'

As the money and bookings continued to improve Maidie pointed out to Chic that the flat above her parents was still unsold. With the aid of a loan from friends, they found the necessary deposit and moved in, arriving to a telegram from Galt's which ran, 'Contact us immediately. Chance of Rothesay summer season for the double. Attractive offer.' Chic looked at Maidie as she stood in the half-empty gloom of the flat, surrounded by trunks and bits of furniture. 'Should we bother to unpack, do you think?'

They had two more shows before Rothesay—in Inverness and at Paisley, and it was in Inverness that Chic made a lasting impression on a local doctor, Bob Freer. He had been temporarily posted to the town at the same time the couple were appearing in the Alf Johnstone Concert Party at the local Royal Theatre. Still being in the 'wines and spirits', the couple had been billeted at a bed-and-breakfast some way from the central hotel where Alf was staying.

Bob Freer found himself called out in the middle of the night to attend to the ailing Alf and later accompanied him to the hospital in an ambulance. 'No chance of making the show tonight, then, doc?' asked Alf. 'None at all.' 'Well, then, do me a favour, it's worth a couple of complimentaries to you. Nip round to Nevis Bank and tell Chic Murray to fill my spot until I'm back.' Bob agreed and will never forget the look of dismay Chic produced as he broke the news. 'What will I *do*?' he beseeched him. 'No good asking me,' Bob replied. 'I'm Mr Johnstone's doctor, just delivering his message.'

Naturally Maidie was next to hear the news. Alf had been in the habit of doing a few minutes of comedy between introducing the acts and it was this spot that Chic was being asked to fill. Armed with his 'compli' Bob went to see the show that night and was staggered at Chic's professionalism. 'His Jolson impersonation was uncanny—"Sonny Boy" brought the house down. He was a wonderful comedian, but that was only part of the man's talent. I couldn't believe it was the same rather startled guy I'd spoken to in the morning.'

And so they were off to Paisley and the Theatre, where the Logan family were in residence, presided over by Jack Short himself—Mum, Dad, Heather, Jimmy and Buddy (billed as 'Scotland's Ace Crooner'). Chic and Maidie were in their element as 'The Long and The Short Of It', but Chic's big beef about this engagement was that they were not featured in the following week's programme starring the family. The advertising slogan ran 'See The Big Election Scene' and the title was *Vote for Fanny*. 'Trust me to get left out of that,' he complained.

Before the Rothesay season, which represented a new peak in their earnings, Maidie broached the subject of a car purchase—since they were travelling everywhere in trains and buses, she pointed out that a car was not a luxury to them, but an investment. She had a modest Standard 10 in mind, which Chic pretended to agonise over for weeks on end. Secretly he was delighted, though he kept this to himself, leaving Maidie to shoulder the guilt if anything should go wrong with their purchase. Since Chic's sole ambition as a young man had been to own a car one day, he gave in to Maidie and allowed her to order the Standard 10 before they left for Rothesay. Here they were billed for the first time as 'The Tall Droll with the Small Doll'.

Metropole
GLASGOW

Controlled by ALEX FRUTIN   Licensee : HYMAN D. FRUTIN
General Manager : W. REEVES   Manager : S. ALLEN

PROGRAMME

3D=

ALL-STAR
VARIETY

8

Clairty, Clairty

On one occasion Chic wanted to visit a friend at Partick Cross—exactly one stop, or about 30 seconds away, from Hillhead subway. On reaching the platform he collared a guard. 'Excuse me,' he said, 'can you tell me if the next train has a buffet service on it?'

'No it hasn't,' came the reply.

'Oh, dear. What about the next one after that? Has that got a buffet service on it?'

The guard smiled, for he knew Chic only too well. 'Come on, Mr Murray,' he said, 'You know we don't have buffet cars on the Glasgow underground.'

Chic looked distraught. 'Oh, dear,' he exclaimed, 'What'll I do? I'll be famished by the time I get to Partick.'

At Rothesay Chic's timekeeping took another turn for the worse, with the whole company kept waiting for him on occasions. 'Chic, play fair,' Maidie pleaded. 'Rehearsals are just as important as anything else. Don't make me look a fool when I have to turn up on my own.' He was penitent for the moment. 'OK, captain,' he promised her.

On opening night a couple of dancing brothers, the Maiberts ('Poetry in Motion') was the act preceding theirs. As Chic and Maidie watched from the wings, the brothers went through their routine, enacting a scene set in Poosie Nancy's bar. A large framed picture of Rabbie Burns hung on the wall with one of the brothers, Davie, dressed up as Rabbie inside the frame. His brother Bert was to enter, look up at the picture, and exclaim vehemently, 'Oh, it's *yourself*, Rabbie!' This was Davie's signal to step out of the picture, 'come to life', and hold forth with 'To a Mouse' from centre stage. He began well enough with—

> Wee, sleekit, cowrin, tim'rous beastie,
> O, what a panic's in thy breastie!

Thou need na start awa sae hasty

—before suddenly freezing up. His brother, and Chic and Maidie from the wings, tried desperately to feed him the next line, but Davie couldn't hear them or understand their miming. Like the true professional he was, he instantly decided he had to press on regardless and improvised:

Oh, Graven o' the graven grouts,
Graven o' the grossets,
Grossin' o' the graven grouts
An' graven o' the grassets
Oh, grossen groosin graven grouts
An' graven o' the grossets . . .

By this time the hapless act—and Davie in particular—was getting a mixture of derisory boos and catcalls, but he continued to the bitter end before taking a quick, shamefaced bow and exiting. Before Chic started his monologue he gleefully announced, 'I'm warning you now, if you don't laugh at me tonight, I'll get that last act put on again!' The audience roared its appreciation, but the theatre manager almost bit his cigar in two. Maidie saw the furious expression on his face and thought, 'Oh, God, we'll be out on our necks. Sacked with a Standard 10 to keep up!' Later Chic was given a severe ticking off, his perennial late-coming listed together with his crack on stage at the Maiberts' expense as unprofessionalism. As he departed, Chic turned to Maidie and asked, 'Is he a *stagehand* or something?'

The dancing duo were next door, swotting away at 'To a Mouse' to get it right for the second house, as Chic yelled, 'Davie! Davie Maibert!' Seconds later, the Burns' book reluctantly put down, Davie pushed up his window and yelled back impatiently, 'Yes? What is it, Chic?' Maidie watched Chic hesitate for an instant, choke back a laugh, then recite:

Oh, Graven graven grussen grouts
An' grassen o' the grovetts,
The graven grossetts of the grassets,
An' grossen graven grouts o' grossen . . .

Through the cold night air Davie's reply could be heard loud and clear, '*Fuck off!*' As Chic pulled down the window he got a second ticking off—this time from Maidie, only she couldn't keep her face straight.

Prior to *Workers' Playtime* in 1950—in between what Chic referred to as 'but and ben chasing' in the wilds of Scotland—they received a memo from the BBC, asking them not to refer to the quality of the food in the workers' canteens. This had been somewhat overdone in previous broadcasts, it was pointed out, and several complaints had been made. This was a challenge Chic could not refuse.

'We're not going to talk about the food in the canteen,' he started off the broadcast, while Maidie cringed at the deviation from their agreed script. 'After all,' he continued, 'it's not worth talking about. I won't say the custard's hard enough to dance on, but I saw someone try it. They slipped and broke their ankle. I'll say this, though, about the mince they serve here, it looks the same coming up as it does going down. Never mind, the tea's excellent. It's the finest paint stripper I've ever come across. They tell me the cook recently came back from a holiday abroad. All I can say is they must be relaxing the quarantine laws.'

As they came off they were approached by a very harassed-looking producer. 'Didn't you get my memo about the food?' he wanted to know. 'I did,' replied Chic coolly, 'but what I said wasn't meant as criticism. The food in this canteen is in the finest tradition of food throughout the blackout, when no one could see what they were eating. It raised incompetence to the level of an art form. Timothy Tighthole himself could ask for nothing worse. The Huns failed to bring this great nation to its knees, but that's being accomplished now right here in this canteen.'

'But Mr Murray, you haven't actually eaten here yet, you only just arrived before the broadcast . . .'

Chic looked aghast at Maidie. 'Is this true?' he demanded to know. 'If it is, heads will roll.'

Early in 1951 the couple were booked by G. B. Bowie on a bill called *Music in the Air* at the Empire Theatre, Inverness, a hall owned by the Caledonian cinema circuit. Variously billed as 'Chic and Madie' (*sic*), 'Long and Short' and 'Just Daft', their fellow troupers on the bill, devised and produced by Jack Sutton, included Sutton's wife Jose Donelli. The energetic duo Amanda and Marc ('Terpsichorean Tit-Bits') were recalled by Maidie as two adagio dancers 'who flung themselves about all over the stage'.

Before returning home a one-night stand was arranged at a cinema in Thurso, which had been converted for the night to fit the variety bill. It was to be the scene of a bizarre coincidence which Chic's Aunt Tizzie would have relished.

The date was 5 March 1951 and Chic and Maidie patiently stood in the wings, watching the end of an elaborate singing and dancing tribute to Ivor Novello. As the artistes reached the end of their performance the stage was suddenly plunged into darkness. An electrical fuse had blown and in the panic singers and dancers stumbled blindly about, trying to get off the stage while the audience, baffled, began to show signs of growing displeasure. Chic felt that something had to be done—and that he was the one to do it. He bounded on stage and went straight into one of his monologues, as stagehands lit candles round about him.

Maidie listened, as did the audience, to a tale even she had never heard before. 'When I arrived at this vastly beautiful theatre I was told to report to dressing-room No. 53. I thought, they've got more dressing-rooms than seats. So I made my way to No. 53. It was easy enough to find—it was next to 54. And I wasn't there long before I heard foot-steps. I became tense. Still Chic, but tense with it—and I prepared myself. When I say I prepared myself I said, "Who is it?" because I wanted to know and you've got to be so *careful* nowadays when you're out. He said, "It's me," and it wasn't me, it was him. All very puzzling.

'Then I saw the handle of the door turning. I thought, "This fellow knows a thing or two," and in he came. "I won't sit down," he said. I was quite pleased, there wasn't a chair in the room. The fellow came over to me. "The producer wants to see you," he said, in a kind of a monotone. I looked him up and down. "Pardon me for asking," I said, "but is someone working you with their foot?" He said, "How do you mean?" I said, "Oh, don't apologise."

'We left and found the producer's office. I said to him, "Am I here to talk and you to listen, or the wrong way about? What is this embarrassment of riches you have for me? Your winged messenger has brought me straightway to you." He said, "I'm glad you raised the subject. I've a new comic feed lined up for you. My brother." I said, "Him? He couldn't feed lettuce to a rabbit." "You digress," he told me. "No need to state the obvious," I replied, beginning to feel I was getting the better of the argument, if such it was, and beginning to wear down his resistance.

'He opened the door and produced his brother. Well, he is a producer after all, so I shouldn't have been surprised. It was the speed of it—one minute the door was closed, the next it was open, then it was closed again—a dazzling cornucopia of events that I was barely able to take in. Before he shut the door on him again, I noticed an improvement on the last time I had seen him. "Jove," I declared. "He's almost lifelike. I'll bet he makes love nearly every day. I'll bet he nearly makes it on Monday, then nearly makes it on Tuesday, then . . ." "Enough," shouted the producer. "May your shadow cover the earth—and that of your brother," I told him, turning to go.

'"Wait," said the producer. "You misjudge my brother. At least give him a chance to prove himself." "He's had his chance," I said, "and proved himself an incompetent idiot. But even if he were Dame Nellie Melba herself I couldn't use him. You must appreciate that I'm a solo act, at least when I'm on my own. I go everywhere alone, even when there's someone with me. Tell your brother that fame is but a breath on the window of life, so breathe deeply. Although it's a small world, I'm sure he wouldn't like to have to paint it. I know that in your eyes your brother is as simple as a pigeon loft, yet has the majesty of a cathedral, but who wants to appear with either a pigeon loft or a cathedral?"'

Just as Chic got the word 'cathedral' out the lights came back on and blinded everyone momentarily, before a huge round of applause broke out. Chic had held the audience spellbound while the electricians had found and replaced the blown fuse. Now Maidie joined him on stage for 'Silver Threads amongst the Gold' and 'China Doll'.

'Where did you get the new yarn?' Maidie asked later. 'Where do you think?' he replied. 'It came by pigeon post this morning to this cathedral of a theatre. I've got to try new material out somewhere, you know.'

As the company relaxed after the show before leaving for their digs, someone switched on a radio set just as the late news headlines were being read. There was a stunned silence as it was announced that Ivor Novello had died in London earlier in the evening. The singers and dancers were still in their Novello-tribute costumes they had been wearing when the lights had mysteriously failed. 'Oh, my God!' said Chic, rolling his eyes. 'Wait until Aunt Tizzie gets hold of this one!'

*   *   *

Although their income increased steadily the couple were still only just making ends meet. Chic conceded that the Standard 10 had been a wonderful investment, but added that since it had been Maidie's idea, she should definitely continue to do most of the driving. Still she tried to turn Chic into a driver and in the end he did drive, but after a fashion. As with comedy, he seemed to make up his own rules as he went along.

Maidie's other responsibilities included packing and loading the car before they left for engagements. Maidie would often be sitting behind the wheel ready to go, with no sign of Chic. When he did condescend to join her and they had set off, she would be subjected to a non-stop questionnaire. 'Did you pack the hot water bottles?'/ 'I hope you didn't forget the band parts?'/ 'Did you take into account I'll need three changes of shirts?'/ 'What about spending money?' He was consistent, however, in his solicitous inquiry as Maidie staggered into their new digs, accordion in one hand and a suitcase in the other. 'Now are you sure you've got the balance right?' he would ask.

A moment of triumph came for them both when they were invited back to the Roxy in Falkirk. Chic held out initially, saying that the management did not have enough money to tempt them after the fiasco of their opening night there, but gave in eventually when the fee was substantially increased. They scored a great success on this date as joint top of the bill in *The Five Star Show*, sharing with Billy Bowes, Jimmy Wallace, Billy Stutt and Nicky Kidd. They went down so well that they were immediately booked for a return appearance three months later, this time as sole stars of the show.

Early in 1952 they appeared in a bill at the Palace Theatre in Dundee, headed by Dave Willis's son Denny, a good all-round comic and entertainer with a flying start on many of his contemporaries—his father's material—to which he still managed to bring a style all of his own. Billy ('Mrs Wummin') Stutt from Ireland shared top billing on this occasion with Denny, the line-up being rounded off by Campbell Nicol ('Songs of Scotland'), Buddy Crawford and Phyllis Terrell ('Dancing Delightfully') and Allan Young ('Britain's Ace Hammond Organist').

While in the town Chic made a beeline for an old bookshop in Victoria
Road, which specialised in out-of-print and second-hand books. Maidie
was never clear just what it was he was searching for in these forays. 'I
might come across a first edition Zane Grey one of these days,' he
claimed. 'Or a do-it-yourself book on how to earn a living.'

A stray reporter from the *Daily Record* spotted them on this occasion
and gave them a good notice. 'A new trick in the field of comedy is the
act of Chic and Maidie. This husband-and-wife team is on the way to a
very big reputation, although it's hard to explain why. On stage, Chic
doesn't seem to do anything but blether, while wife Maidie supports an
accordion and looks at him. But these blethers are among the funniest
things in the Scottish theatre today.'

They were pleased to be asked back, in the spring of 1952, to do the
Edinburgh Palladium Easter Show. They were particularly fond of this
venue, an unashamed relic of the music-hall era. The big stars and
shows went to the Empire, which did not consider the Palladium as a
rival at all, more of a complementary theatre featuring either up-and-
coming entertainers or those on the way down, in the tradition of the
small, popular, 'cheap and cheerful' venue that had always flourished in
Scotland.

During the afternoon before their first show, Chic took a telephone
call in their flat from Dan Campbell at the theatre. 'I've had an SOS
from Jimmy Hill at the Empire,' he explained. 'He's in dead stook with
his *Folies Bergère* Show. Terry Scott has taken ill and it's impossible for
him to get a replacement at short notice. He wants you and Maidie—if
you're prepared to do it.'

'Keep talking,' said Chic, who could hardly believe his ears. 'The
Empire!' he was thinking.

'OK,' said Dan, 'here's the deal. You have to drop everything and go
there now. Run through whatever you're going to do for Jimmy, then
get your backsides back to me. I'll put you on early, then you taxi back
to the Empire and close their first house, then back to me again to open
my second. Then it's back to the Empire to close their second house.
After that you can go home.'

'Is that all?' asked Chic.

'Pretty well,' replied Dan. 'Jimmy Hill will take care of you financially,
so it's probably more than double money, and of course all
transportation's on him. What do you say?'

After a lightning consultation with Maidie, Dan was informed that the
deal was on, then just ten minutes after putting the telephone down the
Murrays were in a taxi headed for the Empire, scarcely able to believe
their luck. Good as the Palladium booking was, it was small beer
compared with the prestigious Empire, still the jewel in the Stoll/Moss
crown. This was the big time—where reputations could be made, stars

created and careers launched overnight. If they went down well at the Empire, there was no telling what doors could be opened up.

They were greeted on their arrival by a very distraught Jimmy Hill. Chic took his first look at the Empire stage—not since the Usher Hall had he seen anything like it. 'Dear God,' he muttered. 'It's like the Sahara desert compared to the wee Palladium.'

After a very rushed rehearsal they jumped into a waiting taxi to be whisked back to the Palladium. Maidie took the whole thing in her stride like the trouper she was, Chic was like a man inspired—and together they went on to score a tremendous hit with the Empire audiences. The magnificent theatre was almost invariably packed to the doors as the couple opened with 'Wait Till The Sun Shines, Nellie', sung straight. They then followed with 'Melancholy Baby' which Chic introduced as 'Come To Me, My Alcoholic Baby', with a beady eye on his partner. During this number he broke the audience up with his face-pulling behind Maidie, then launched into his monologue to continuous laughter. His timing was impeccable and his hold over the audience never wavered for a second.

'To say Chic rose to the occasion is putting it mildly,' Maidie recalled. 'He was in his element at the Empire and established a tremendous rapport with the audience. By the end of the engagement he had introduced an extra bit of business with the tabs. As they were being closed on us towards the end of the act, he seemed to make them stop every so often just by glaring at them. He'd worked out hand signals with the stagehands in advance, one of which was to plant his finger on his cheek. Even this got a laugh and was adopted from then on. The tabs carry-on had the audience in fits.

'Here he really began to master his comic "looks". I'll never forget one night he didn't follow me on—I'd already started *Nellie* on my own and was wishing the floor would swallow me up, when in he strolled. He got a tremendous hand just for coming in late! He did a little curtsy then and stuck his finger under his chin—another bit of business he was to become associated with.'

With their transfer to the Empire and the sheer hard graft of appearing in two shows at once during the holiday season, the Murrays hit the news pages of the *Scotsman* as well as the local evening papers. The favourable publicity engendered seemed to presage the sparkling reviews that came later.

Thereafter Chic's standard approach to all reviews, which he seldom read for himself, was just the one question—'Is it good?', to which Maidie would almost invariably reply in the affirmative. The *Scotsman* wrote of their Empire appearance, 'As a spectacle the *Folies Bergère* revue would certainly take a lot of beating. In one sphere—that of humour—it has acquired further distinction through the work of Chic and

Maidie. Chic is in a class by himself, with an economy of expression and gesture which can be funnier than any demonstrative technique. Their act last night was deservedly received with a storm of applause.'

The shuttle continued for the full two-week run at both theatres, but despite their dashing about Chic and Maidie felt the benefit of a permanent place of their own in the spacious flat they had bought, secure in the knowledge that they had at last put down some roots and their children were being lovingly taken care of by one or other of their grandparents.

After the excitement of the double-booking it was back to pease-brose and porridge with a vengeance as they went to Paisley's Theatre for Donaghue and Ramsay's *Paisley Pranks*. Next it was a season at the Gaiety, Leith, with their Summer Show. 'I thought we'd been discovered,' Chic moaned. 'We're getting there,' Maidie soothed him. 'Are you sure?' Chic asked. 'Pretty sure,' Maidie replied shakily, confidence leaking all over the place.

*   *   *

The dry spell after their Palladium break ended with word that Tommy Morgan, the resident and hugely successful star comedian of the Pavilion Theatre in Glasgow, wanted to see them. Unlike many other top comedians, Morgan had never been frightened of competition and actively encouraged younger comics to appear on the bill with him. He already had the very funny Jimmy Neil under his wing, but was intent on adding Chic and Maidie to his list of 'discoveries'. They readily accepted his invitation to join him and his company when their present commitments expired, eager to work with and be associated with this giant of Scottish comedy, forever 'Mr Glasgow' to his huge band of followers.

Perhaps in promoting others Morgan considered he was paying off a debt owed to his own discoverer, Tommy Yorke. Born Tommy Paterson, rarely, however, can an individual have been so dissatisfied with his name. He appeared in 1907 with his original partner, Billy Hayes, as 'Salford and Rees'. Tommy was 'Salford', choosing the name because there was a story in showbiz circles at the time that taking the name of a town was lucky. Another name change came with the duo's booking later in the same year at the now-fabled Panopticon in Argyle Street, Glasgow, run by the equally fabled Albert Ernest Pickard, Esquire, who billed the duo by mistake as 'Scapper and Letty'. They decided to adopt this appellation for a while before yet another change, this time to 'Milne and Main'—with Tommy as Milne. Then they split up.

So it was that Tommy Paterson, alias Salford, Scapper and Milne, one night spotted Tommy Morgan, a ba'faced Eastender from Bridgeton— Brigton to the locals—doing an amateur comedy turn at a party. Born in

Tommy Morgan in mufti.

1900, young Morgan had embarked on a series of jobs and was working in a chocolate factory when the First World War broke out. He managed to join up by exaggerating his age and got the notion during his service that he would like to try his hand on the stage. He joined an army concert party as London comedian Alf Vivian's stooge and met artists sent out to entertain the troops in France like Eric Blore (later to gain fame in Hollywood playing butler roles), Leslie Henson and G. H.

Tommy Morgan as Big Beenie—McBride, the Pride of the Clyde.

Elliott ('The Chocolate-Coloured Coon'). In between times he was Sir Douglas Haig's orderly, but he was truly bitten by the showbiz bug.

On his demob in 1919 he was found a job in the Clyde shipyards as a plater's helper, which he hated. Then came the fateful meeting with Tommy Paterson/Salford/Scapper/Milne, who liked what he saw and promptly invited him to appear in a concert party with him as the

Rockets, later Graham and Morgan. 'Graham', I hear you ask? Well, that didn't last long either as Tommy reverted to the 'lucky town' theory in his endless search for the perfect name. He found it in York, adding an 'e' at the end for extra luck. Yorke and Morgan were born.

Their first professional date was in a Kirkintilloch picture hall, which featured two films and three acts, of which Yorke and Morgan were top of the bill. Yorke sang, then did his 'comic's labourer' for Morgan. One of their big breaks came at the Princess Theatre in the Gorbals, run by another formidable worthy, Harry McKelvie, who also owned the neighbouring Palace Music Hall. McKelvie's pantomimes at the Princess were the talk of the country and had been toplined by yet another comic Tommy, Lorne this time, until he had been poached by the rival Pavilion. For years McKelvie and Lorne between them could claim they had the longest-running pantomimes in Britain, and the most lavish. A chorus of no less than a hundred lovelies was recruited each year, which comprised maybe 20 or so professional dancers who occupied the front row, with 80 more behind recruited locally, who made up in enthusiasm for any lack of ability, and whose relatives swelled the theatre for the wily McKelvie. With the loss of Tommy Lorne, McKelvie desperately looked around for replacements—in the 1923/4 season for which Yorke and Morgan were hired, Tommy Morgan said the entrepreneur 'threw new comics on the stage in bundles of six' in desperate attempts to find Lorne's successor.

C. B. Cochran caught Yorke and Morgan's act years later when they were appearing at the Prom Palace in Portobello and declared that Morgan was 'the funniest man he'd seen for twenty years'. By 1931 he was pantomime king of Glasgow at the Metropole in Stockwell Street, then later established a steady routine of winter and spring in panto at the Met, with his own summer and autumn show at the Pavilion.

His catchphrase 'Clairty, Clairty' derived from a saying of his mother's, originally 'Declare to Goodness'. The expression stuck and followed him everywhere—to his delight. 'There goes Clairty,' folk would say on the street. 'Clairty, Clairty,' he would acknowledge with his big silly wide grin, endearing him to young and old alike. *Clairty* even became the name of his cabin cruiser.

He was a sidesplitting Mother Goose in the Metropole's 1939 panto, but there was another, achingly funny portrayal of his still to come in the wartime shape of 'Big Beenie', an oversized blonde perpetually in search of a partner. The character was hilariously developed when she found one among the GIs who flooded Glasgow for a night out from Greenock. The character then became known as 'Big Beenie, the GI War Bride'.

Before they could join Tommy Morgan's show Chic and Maidie had several months to go, from Ayr in April to Glasgow in November. Ayr's

Gaiety had long been one of their favourite venues, Ben Popplewell's natty little bijou palace still having two more years to go before being gutted in a fire—and then lovingly resurrected.

Maidie, as usual, was left to do the packing and loading of the car before starting the journey from Edinburgh. When everything was done Maidie rushed upstairs to find Chic, bumping first into her mother. 'Have you seen Chic?' she said. 'Yes,' her mother replied, 'warming his backside at the fire.' When they were both seated in the car the usual list of questions was asked, with endless variations. 'Did you bring some food for the journey?'/'And a flask of tea?'/ 'Did you remember the keys for the flat in Ayr?'/ 'You didn't leave the gas on, did you?'

Eventually he fell fast asleep as Maidie continued the journey, which entailed driving through Strathaven. Just as she was leaving the town to negotiate a junction on the Ayr road, she observed a lorry approaching from the left, completely dwarfing their Standard 10. It seemed to hover above them and Chic chose this moment to open his eyes, which immediately widened in horror. 'Drive for your fucking life!' he shouted to Maidie.

She proceeded to do no such thing and waited for the lorry to pass by, which it duly did. Inside the normally unflappable Maidie something had snapped. She stopped the car and turned to face Chic as soon as she had cleared the junction. 'Don't you ever talk to me like that again,' she shouted, hot tears of anger filling her eyes. Chic looked at her solicitously, then asked, 'Do you want me to take over at the wheel, pet?' Maidie almost choked. 'Do I what? Heaven forfend! Just stop getting at me while I'm driving. One day you'll take me too far, Chic.' He sat there looking shame-faced for a few minutes, then said, 'Maidie?' 'What is it?' she asked. 'You're a much better driver than I am.'

Chic and Jack Radcliffe went their own ways, annoyance being caused by a remark Jack made to Maidie about the Standard 10 they were so proud of—'I could put the whole shooting match in the boot of my buggy,' Jack had declared.

One of the bright spots of the year was the increasing amount of radio broadcasts they were asked to do by the BBC, the *Workers' Playtime* contretemps notwithstanding. Producer Eddie Fraser was a great fan of theirs and was thrilled by the positive feedback from their shows.

Their very last appearance before joining Tommy Morgan was at the Glasgow Metropole, on a bill headed by the brilliant actress and comedienne, Renee Houston, together with her partner, comedian Donald Stewart. Also featured was a young man named Andy Stewart, at the very start of his career.

But Tommy Morgan was waiting.

PROGRAMME 3ᴰ

The
GAIETY
THEATRE
AYR
•

The Premier
Theatre
of the
West Coast

★

GAIETY

TWICE NIGHTLY
6-30 • 8-40.

MURRAY

9

Enter Billy Marsh

'I went to the butchers to buy a leg of lamb. "Is it Scotch?" I asked.
  "Why?" the butcher asked, "Are you going to talk to it or eat it?"
  "In that case," I replied—with as much dignity as I could muster—"have you got a wild duck?"
  "No," he said, "but I've got one I could aggravate for you." '

In the very first show of his in which Chic and Maidie appeared, Morgan gave the couple an enthusiastic—and prophetic—introduction. 'There's a couple coming on next,' he announced, 'who are the funniest comedy act I've ever seen. Make the most of them now, for I promise you we're not going to keep them long here in Scotland. They're going right to the top as big stars. Welcome—Chic and Maidie Murray!' As Chic later said, 'How could you do any less than your very best for a man like that? He's got a heart bigger than his bank account—and that's saying something!'

Occasionally there was talk of London agencies sniffing around and showing interest, but for a long time this came to nothing. Being part of the Tommy Morgan show at the Pavilion, and on tour with him, consolidated their burgeoning popularity, and Chic and Maidie knew for sure they had arrived as a star act in Scotland that Christmas. It wasn't the extra money or the rapturous applause they got all through that winter season. What brought it home to them was a tiny cartoon in a Scottish daily, the *Bulletin*, which portrayed them making merry with a bunch of Glasgow down-and-outs. The jingle accompanying the cartoon read:

> It's Christmas Day in the workhouse,
> In walked a welfare lady,
> She asked the inmates what they'd like,
> They answered *Chic and Maidie*!

It was a Christmas present that nothing could top, but a sense of anti-climax pervaded the early months of 1953 as Maidie found herself driving hundreds of miles, chasing engagements from Inverness to Ayr and Aberdeen to Glasgow. In addition to the strain of driving for long spells, Maidie found Chic to be an increasingly irascible passenger. If he wasn't complaining about something specific, he was 'nittering' constantly.

The duo began to feel as if they could re-draw the map of Scotland with the number of trips they made to village halls, town halls, drill halls, church halls and the rest between appearances with Tommy Morgan, and for a change they accepted a series of dates in Ireland early in 1954. 'Cinevariety' was especially popular there and at the Theatre Royal, Dublin, they found themselves part of a bill supporting the main attraction, the new Frank Sinatra film *Suddenly*. They were in continuous performance with the picture sandwiched between from 3 p.m. to 11 p.m. daily. Chic's comment was, 'Very glamorous. They might have got us a decent Sinatra movie instead of one of his clinkers!'

Maidie recalls the tiny pit orchestra during this engagement, with backing group of piano, bass and drums on stage. Irked by the racket this trio produced Chic dubbed them 'piano, hoover and drums'. Maidie asked the young drummer for some 'nice soft brushes' in one quiet number—instead they got drum rolls that drowned them out. One night the audience unexpectedly demanded 'China Doll' for an encore. As they hadn't rehearsed it, the conductor asked what key they would like it in. 'F and C,' requested Maidie, to a thunderstruck reaction, until it was realised that Maidie meant the key of F for Chic and C for herself.

When they returned to Scotland they had a few precious days off before rejoining Tommy Morgan. Chic suggested a fishing trip for the whole family. It was not too often that they had the opportunity for excursions like this and together Chic, Maidie, Douglas, Annabelle and Grannie Dickson set off, picnic baskets packed and spirits high. Obligingly the weather was perfect, with the fresh blue skies and sunshine that can bless the east coast of Scotland in the spring. When they were settled down, with the children happily splashing away and Grannie Dickson spreading the sandwiches, Chic and Maidie lay together on a blanket and looked up at the cloudless skies. 'How do you fancy a holiday abroad sometime?' asked Chic. 'It would be lovely, but we don't have the time—or the money,' replied the ever-practical Maidie. 'Then why are we working?' Chic wanted to know. 'What's it for?' Maidie adjusted her specs. 'We're working to make you a star,' was her unexpected reply. 'You've got what it takes, Chic, and you've got the right defiant attitude as well. Me—I'm too much of a feartie cat. I quake before authority—you take delight in standing up to it.'

*　　*　　*

Chic had struck up a friendship with a broker in Edinburgh, Bill Reid, who also acted as the Murrays' legal and financial adviser. His recollection of them at that time is: 'They were at their most uncomplicated. My impression was of one big, happy family. The big break hadn't come yet in terms of their career, but it was just around the corner. They didn't see that much of their kids, but they had a wonderful relationship with them none the less. Annabelle was potty about ballet dancing, and Chic used to listen to her account of the dancing classes she took, while Douglas would be waiting to regale him with his football exploits. All the balls, you might say, were rolling for the two of them.'

One night the couple were having a quiet drink together, with the children tucked up in bed, when Maidie suddenly announced, 'Chic, it's time for something new. Tomorrow let's begin to think of changing the act around a bit.'

Chic was startled. 'What's brought this about? Why change things when they're going so well?'

'Because,' she replied, 'it's time for you gradually to take over more of the act. Occasionally I'll just join you for the finale, or maybe just one song at the beginning. You're the one the crowds want to see now, so let them see more of you. I think it's time for me to take a back seat.'

'I won't hear of it,' Chic snapped. Maidie pressed on regardless. 'We'll start the change from next week,' she continued. 'Chic, I think we could be about to break through. When it comes everything's got to be just right.'

A week later they heard that they had been booked for the Edinburgh Empire in February 1955—their first appearance there since their triumph in 1952. 'It's taken a helluva long time to get around to it. Overnight sensation—after nine years!' was Chic's comment. 'Better late than never,' Maidie replied.

Before their opening day they had a surprise call from Nellie Sutherland. Nellie never called *anyone* and they were tickled to hear her nasal tones over the telephone, but even more tickled with her tip. Apparently the BBC were holding mass auditions for TV appearances— her advice was to get themselves along and 'get tested', as she put it. As Maidie thanked her for the tip, she reflected for a moment on the quiet amount of help she and Chic had received from the redoubtable Nellie over the years. All Nellie would say was, 'Haud yer wheesht, lassie. It wuz mah joab!'

It would be some months before the results of the audition would be known, but Chic and Maidie had other things on their mind as they rehearsed for the Empire show. Their goal was quite simply to create such a hit that this time there would be no going back. Twice already

they had reached milestones in their career, only to face further spells in the show-business wilderness. This time they were both determined it would be third time lucky.

The notices they received indicated that they had achieved their objective. Gordon Irving wrote of their booking in the *Daily Record*: 'It's refreshing to find an act that has slogged it round the wee halls of Scotland getting the real breaks at last.'

Next on their list was a return to the Pavilion in Glasgow with Tommy Morgan. This time the star comic was to be Jack Anthony, but for the opening of the show in April a show-business 'buzz' had begun around Chic and Maidie. Hymie Zahl, a London agent, was first off the mark when he offered to sign them at £3,500 per year. Although their first inclination was to grab it, they cannily decided to wait and see, whereupon the offer was promptly increased to £4,000—still they held out. The 'buzz' told them that other offers would be forthcoming and that Lew and Leslie Grade had been making inquiries. It became common knowledge on the opening night of their show at the Pavilion that Hymie Zahl would be there, still determined to sign them up. What nobody foresaw was that *two* other agents would turn up on the same night—the rumoured Grades' representative, together with Billy Marsh, representing the Bernard Delfont Agency. 'The whole family wanted us,' Chic said later.

After the show there was a scramble to collar the Murrays in their dressing-room. Billy Marsh not only made the highest offer, but he also seemed to have the most concrete plans for their future—an extended tour of major theatres all over the country prior to plum London engagements, a whopping £6,000 a year guaranteed, increasing over a three-year period, with TV and radio fees on top. 'Make it £6,500 and it's a deal,' Chic suggested, 'but let's get it organised now.'

Billy smiled. 'I'll fly down to London first thing tomorrow morning, have the contract drawn up and fly back again tomorrow afternoon. Is that quick enough for you?'

'That'll do,' Chic replied, while Maidie marvelled at his nerve as her knees quaked. 'OK with you, captain?' he asked her, causing Billy a twinge of anxiety in the split second before her reply. 'OK,' she managed to whisper, then they all laughed and shook hands on the deal. 'That's the way!' declared an exultant Billy Marsh.

The next day the announcement was made in the press, when Marsh was quoted as saying, 'Everybody in the business has been after Chic. I think I've made one of the finest signings in my career as an agent.' More than 30 years later Billy had no reason to change his mind. 'I had first seen their double act at the Pavilion much earlier and I remember wondering how Chic would progress. He went down tremendously there, but I wanted to wait. The Pavilion had its own audience, who loved him, so he was comfortable with them, and he kept pushing his style further and further. I wanted to wait until it was distilled to the point he was ready for the circuit, and knew it wouldn't be long.

'You know, what the two of them had was incredible. Chic was a genius, but comedy is a peculiar thing. Often the funniest act can disappoint an audience with a weak ending. I saw that with Chic and Maidie this never happened. When Chic was merely good the act was

Maidie, Chic and agent Billy Marsh signing the Bernard Delfont contract.

lifted by the slam-bang song and dance act finale—but when Chic was *brilliant* the climax *paralysed* them!'

*   *   *

Neither one of them had ever been to London and they decided to do a recce before the end of May and the start of their Delfont contract. Maidie would drive and together they set off one morning from Edinburgh. 'He took turns occasionally to give mc a rest,' Maidie recalled, 'but it was hardly worth it, for if I nodded off for a minute he'd drive up a dead-end street and blame my navigation. Then he'd grab a pedestrian and demand to know the way to London. If they hesitated for even a split second he'd start winding the window up and driving on regardless. I was black affronted—it was easier just driving, believe me. I won't attempt to describe the performance in London when we got there either, though once we got the car into a garage the tension eased a bit. Then we had a tour of the theatres in the West End and stayed for four nights before starting the journey back. Here was our Mecca—and we knew that on our next visit we'd be in one of those theatres.'

Back home again they found that the long-forgotten audition for BBC TV had resulted in an invitation to make their television début in *Garrison Theatre*, to be staged at the City Hall, Perth, in June. Other artistes featured were Duncan Macrae, Margo Henderson and Andy Stewart, and the show was introduced by singer Teddy Johnson.

To Maidie's consternation Chic refused even to talk of rehearsals before they were due at the studio. He later explained to Tom Nicholson of the *Sunday Mail* his approach to the TV début, 'I'm a pretty luckadaisical sort of bloke and I certainly didn't lose any sleep over it. I had a rough idea what I'd talk about, but I didn't get down to thinking about it seriously until I was on my way in the car to face the cameras.' Nicholson astutely observed, 'This could explain why he's so good.'

Other TV critics agreed and the *Dundee Courier* summed it up by writing, 'The outstanding feature of the show was, without doubt, the appearance of Chic Murray, who justified all that was said about him. The success of the show was due to the fact that he gave us something entirely new.'

'Telly,' Chic declared, 'is only different from radio in one respect—you can't wear your glasses.'

Henry Hall watched *Garrison Theatre* with interest and promptly booked the act for his *Face the Music* series. They appeared on a line-up which included Bob Hope, but Chic was in no way overshadowed by that great comedian and again stole the notices.

Now the Delfont organisation moved into overdrive and the couple found themselves with a string of top variety bookings stretching to the end of the year. Two more appearances were fixed for the Empire in Edinburgh and a tour of Moss theatres in England was set to introduce them to variety houses further south. They were already familiar—and hugely popular—with Geordie audiences in Newcastle and Sunderland, but still untested in their other dates of Manchester, Sheffield, Birmingham and Liverpool.

To Chic's relief the tour began in Newcastle and they received their usual rousing reception there. He still managed, though, to suffer from a rare fit of nerves before the Manchester opening. 'What's the matter with you?' asked Maidie, despairingly. Chic had been 'nittering' all the way from Sunderland. 'It's the thought of playing in England,' Chic moaned. 'We've just played Sunderland and Newcastle,' Maidie pointed out. 'Sure,' Chic agreed, 'but that's not England, that's dear old Geordieland, where they're almost as Scottish as we are. The thing is—I can't see them understanding my accent in Manchester.' 'Nonsense,' said Maidie, 'your accent isn't pronounced at all. What's put this into your head?' Chic was beyond comforting. 'You can't hear it the same way the English will, so you can't judge,' he asserted.

When they were assembled for rehearsals in Manchester, an astonished Maidie was approached by the theatre manager. 'I understand your husband doesn't speak English,' he told her. 'Could you explain the cues and running order to him if I write it all down for you?'

Chic was hovering in the background while the manager was addressing Maidie and realised that perhaps he had taken his phobia about his accent too far. He blurted out, 'It's all right. I *do* speak a little English. You can give me the cues and all that.'

This time it was the manager's turn to look astonished. 'But I understood from my assistant . . .'

'That proves my point,' Chic maintained, dead-pan. 'I'm *not* that easily understood.' However, the issue of the accent was never referred to again, by Chic or anyone else. One Manchester review stated: 'The solemn wonderment with which Chic describes the business of minute-by-minute living is as unearthly as a Goon show.'

Following the success of their initial TV appearances, they were asked to sign a BBC TV contract guaranteeing them 18 shows over the next two years. One of these, *Highland Fling*, received good notices, with Chic still managing the lion's share of the praise. One critic wrote, 'Here's a Scot with a quaint knack of making you laugh, although he tells hardly any jokes at all. Mr Murray has a very individual style which might be worked up into a first-rate comedy act.' Chic loved the last line of this review and it was one of the rare ones he kept. 'That's one guy who likes to hedge his bets,' he told Maidie.

The *Scotsman* picked them out again when they returned to Edinburgh in September: 'What can be done with a natural, individual gift for humour, without any straining after effect, is excellently illustrated by Chic Murray, whose manner towards his partner Maidie, is as comical as ever, and whose style of story-telling is unique.'

If 1955 had seemed like a busy year, it was as nothing compared to 1956. The pantomime, *Just Daft*, in which they appeared with Duncan Macrae, Dave Willis and Jack Anthony, ended its run in Glasgow and was promptly transferred to Edinburgh and the Empire, a theatre that would always hold happy memories for them. Many were surprised at their swift re-booking at the Empire in Glasgow only six weeks after *Just Daft* came off. There was doubt that even so popular an act could justify such a quick return, but the engagement was to prove another triumph as they opened yet again to glowing reviews and packed houses.

Out of the blue came an offer from EMI to come down to London and cut a record for their Parlophone label. They had earlier been introduced to Norman Wisdom, another Delfont artist managed by Billy Marsh, and when he heard of the visit he arranged to meet them off the train and take them out to the recording studio. Here they met musical director Philip Green and A & R man George Martin, who would go on to considerable fame as the Beatles' recording manager before founding his own studio.

The duo cut 'Are You Mine?', then Chic recorded several other solo tracks, including 'Satisfied Mind' and 'Lucky Star', all in a country-and-western mould. The decision as to which tracks would find their way on to a single was left to EMI. Afterwards Norman Wisdom invited them to come along to see him on the *Sunday Night at the London Palladium* live TV broadcast. When the show was finished they drank champagne with the comedian in his dressing-room before he saw them on to the night train to Scotland. April saw the release of the record they had made. EMI had initially announced 'Are You Mine?' as the single, then changed it before the release date—interrupted by a printers' strike—to Chic's solos of 'Lucky Star' and 'Satisfied Mind'.

Two weeks later a gap of a whole week appeared in their schedule. 'Nice of Billy to give us a week off. He must be turning soft,' Chic observed. 'Let's not complain.' Maidie announced. 'I can hardly believe the luxury of a week at home. Spring cleaning, getting up to date with the washing,' she smiled, 'all the things I dream about.' The couple were sure they would receive some last-minute booking, but no message came and they returned to Edinburgh on Sunday, feeling almost guilty.

The following day happened to be a local holiday in Edinburgh. Maidie looked up from her pile of washing as Chic announced, 'Right— I'm off to the football. Willie Woodburn's asked me along to see Hearts lick Falkirk at Tynecastle. Back in time for tea.' Twenty minutes after Chic had left the telephone rang—it was a frantic Billy Marsh. 'Why aren't the pair of you in Birmingham?' he wanted to know. 'Why should we be?' Maidie asked. 'We've nothing on this week.' She hesitated, then added nervously, '*Have we?*' Billy Marsh exploded. 'Nothing *on*? Are you *daft*? You're due to open in Birmingham in four hours' time with Ruby Murray. Didn't you get a letter from my office?' Maidie felt her stomach begin to churn. 'No, we didn't. Oh, my God, how are we going to get there? And Chic's at the football.' 'What? Look, get a hold of him while I find a way to get you both down here. I'll phone you back.'

Maidie tried to fight the rising tide of panic she felt, for she had never missed a show in her life—for any reason. Without losing a moment she found the telephone book and dialled Tynecastle football ground, stuttering out the problem to the manager. 'Leave it to me, Maidie,' he assured her. 'We'll find him.'

Just as Chic and Willie were settling down for the kick-off, the loudspeakers blared out their message. 'Will Chic Murray, the TV comedian, please come at once to the manager's office?' Chic looked at Willie innocently, 'Maybe I've left the chip pan on,' he suggested. With the situation explained to him, he turned again to his friend. 'Would you mind, Willie?' he asked. 'Point your car in the direction of Montague Street and let's go.'

Fifteen minutes later he arrived home to find Maidie, dressed and ready packed, the washing taken over by Granny Murray. When the phone rang again it was Billy Marsh. 'Get out to Turnhouse right away,' he instructed. 'I've chartered a private plane from Prestwick to pick you up.'

It was 4.40 p.m. when the tiny three-seater took off from Edinburgh. Maidie sat back and relaxed. For once she was not in the driving seat. Someone else was in charge and subject to Chic's nitterings, for he started soon enough. 'I don't want to tell you your job, but it is Birmingham you're heading for, isn't it?' 'Yes,' the pilot warily agreed. 'Well, why are you heading for Glasgow, then? You're going in the wrong direction.' The pilot none-too-politely explained to Chic that he was following a standard route and he would prefer the flying to be left to him. 'I did some time with Fairey Aviation, you know,' Chic insisted. 'You could have done some time with the fairies themselves for all I'm concerned,' replied the exasperated pilot with an air of finality. 'Leave the flying to me, or get out and walk.'

Chic decided to make the best of it and settled back to enjoy the ride, but found this difficult for two reasons. First, he remained convinced that the plane was flying in the wrong direction. Secondly, it was bitterly cold. He summed up the experience later by saying, 'The pilot must have changed direction at some point, because we *did* land at Birmingham after all. Since my original intention was to attend a contest of footballing skill I wasn't exactly dressed for flying. I don't think sports jacket, flannels and an open-necked shirt will ever take the place of fleecy-lined flying suits in an unheated aircraft.'

Within seconds of landing they were whisked into a waiting car and set off for the theatre, then five minutes after entering the stage-door they were on stage. The packed audience seemed to be aware of their journey and gave them a great reception. Billy Marsh telephoned them at the interval. 'I've got to apologise to the pair of you,' he said. 'I've been in the States for the last couple of weeks with Norman Wisdom and I left word that you should be told about Birmingham. I'm at the office now and I've just found the notification—unposted. Sorry, folks!'

Chic accepted the apology on his behalf and Maidie's, then asked Billy how the US trip had gone. 'Oh, it was fine, more of a recce job than anything else,' Billy told them. 'I want to break Norman in the States, but it's no good just flinging him in. It's got to be planned meticulously. We watched the big TV shows, made a visit or two. Why, Chic?'

'For the future,' Chic replied. 'Eventually I'd like to think we would make a crack at it ourselves.'

'First things first,' Billy counselled, 'let's get London under our belt.'

'When will that be, Billy?'

'When I say so.'

While they continued to tour the halls, they interspersed their appearances with TV spots, which continued to create excellent word-of-mouth publicity for the couple. They appeared in *Home James*, Vera

Lynn's *Tonight at Nine*, *Young and Foolish*, *Rats to You* and *Camera One*, together with a repeat booking on the Henry Hall show. As for London—that decision would be for Billy alone to make.

Chic had taken up the old hobby of model railways he had enjoyed as a boy in Greenock. His story was that he was building up the collection for young Douglas, but his own enjoyment of it was obvious. The whole family was organised around it, as he explained to Archie McCulloch, wearing his journalist's hat at this time. 'It's a great hobby and I'm always adding to it. Maidie never has to worry when she feels inclined to buy me a present—it's always something for the railroad.'

Often reticent in the past about talking to the Press, Chic chose more and more to answer questions designed to probe the source of his humour. He talked frankly to Philip Diack, who had been responsible for some rave reviews in the past. 'I think that storytelling—the telling of real yarns, fantastically tall stories—is a lost art. I think to do it you have to be a terrific liar, and there's a terrible shortage of even competent liars. I mean, the man is rare who can tell a tall tale and get away with it. You may know full well that he's a liar, but you enjoy it just the same. The great thing is to make a bond between you and the audience. It isn't *what* you say, but *how* you say it.' Revealingly he went on, 'What I enjoy most is a real night of good talk with friends. *Real* people, I mean.' He took a deep breath before spelling out his next few words, weighing every syllable. 'Ordinary persons are ten a penny, but characters are very rare. You might say that characters, *real* people, are my main hobby. Even the model trains come second to them.'

Chic would continue to telephone Billy Marsh regularly as the dates rolled in with still no sign of a London venue. 'You're not ready,' he would be told.

'When will we be?' asked Chic.

'When I tell you,' came the regular reply.

'When he tells us,' Billy heard Chic relay to the waiting Maidie.

'Chic, trust me. When the time and the venue is right you'll be there,' Billy promised, 'and you'll see that I've been right.'

At Maidie's insistence Chic agreed to have two suits specially made for him in mohair—one blue and one brown. 'We must improve your stage image, can't have you looking tatty,' she chided him. On the first night at Leeds audiences were treated to the first glimpse of the new-look Chic—wearing his usual tartan bunnet, his brand new blue mohair jacket and his brown mohair trousers. 'I feel more comfortable like this,' he told his partner.

Shrewsbury, Swansea and Portsmouth came and went, then they started going round the English circuit for a second time—Newcastle and Sunderland again, back up to Aberdeen, over to Dublin for a quick appearance . . . the list stretched ahead. The memory of their trip to

London and the bright lights of the West End seemed like a dream. Then at long last the call came from Billy. 'OK, Chic, you're ready and it's all set. September. You go straight into the West End at the Prince of Wales.'

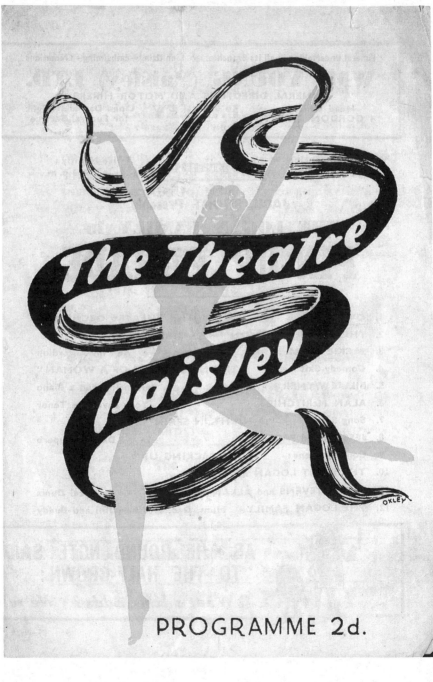

10

London Début—and Disappointment

'I was standing in Argyle Street when a man came up and asked me the quickest way to the Royal Infirmary. I said, "Just lie down between these tram lines. You'll be there soon enough."'

The couple remembered the Prince of Wales Theatre from their London trip. *Folies Bergère* had been showing then and was due to finish its two-year run in September. The management had decided to revert to a variety policy with a fortnightly change of programme and it was for this first bill Chic and Maidie were booked, with vocalist Mel Torme headlining and comedians Jimmy Wheeler and David Nixon also in support.

After attending a few other West End shows to get the feel of London audiences, Chic decided there was no need of any new yarns specially for London and that the limit of his adaptation would be, 'I was walking down *Piccadilly*, one foot in front of the other—oh, that's the best way! . . .' London would have to accept him on his own terms. 'Oh, I *may* fling in the odd Enigma Variation,' he conceded to Maidie, who was none the wiser.

Maidie kept a careful watch on Chic to see how he was preparing himself for their biggest challenge yet and felt confident he would be on his best form on the night. The only unpredictable element was the reaction of the first-night London audience, although Chic had tried to gauge this from his tour of other shows. The other aspect was the London critics, not known for their generosity to Scottish comedians—were they ready to clasp one to their bosoms now?

While they were in London Billy had booked them into Olivelli's, a smart and comfortable hotel which was a favourite with show-business people, conveniently situated just off Tottenham Court Road and only a few minutes from the Prince of Wales Theatre. The night before their opening they both felt like tigers in a cage and decided a dauner round the West End would be in order to settle their nerves, followed by a bite to eat.

As they passed the Prince of Wales Theatre they could see workmen taking down the *Folies Bergère* sign. They turned into Wardour Street and crossed Shaftesbury Avenue on the way to Oxford Street, where they passed the Academy Cinema ('My kind of hall.' 'But they show only subtitled films, Chic.' 'That's right—you know how I like a good read.') Now they headed back to the Prince of Wales, down Regent Street and through Piccadilly Circus. Maidie tugged at his arm as the Prince of Wales came into view. The new hoarding was being set up and already 'Mel Torme' had been erected in large letters. The rest of the billing space had not yet been filled in, although workmen were already grappling with the next set of letters.

'Let's go in here,' said Maidie, spotting a restaurant across the road from the Prince of Wales, one floor up. There was plenty of room and they had no problem in getting the window seat they wanted. While they ordered, the workmen began to adjust the next name under Mel Torme. First a huge C was put into place, then an H, then an I, then another C ('Must have plenty of Cs in stock,' Chic observed.) until CHIC stood there for all the world to see. 'This'll be a helluva anti-climax if it turns out to be Chic Lamour, the famous French fandango dancer,' Chic pointed out, then, 'Jesus, Maidie, it's far too big! They'll be expecting more than we can deliver!' Eventually, the sign was completed and CHIC MURRAY and MAIDIE stood there in all its glory. Maidie put down her knife and fork. 'I can't eat another bite,' she declared. 'Can't you?' Chic asked. 'OK, I'll finish it for you, then fill up with some custard!'

They both returned to Olivelli's refreshed and in good humour. Maidie fell asleep first, while Chic read his latest Damon Runyon, then it was down with the book and off with the specs; propping himself up on one elbow, he looked at his sleeping partner. They had come a long way together and she had selflessly allowed him to take over the act, content to act as his stooge. How, he wondered, does one ever repay a debt like that?

*   *   *

When Maidie awoke at six she could hear Chic reciting away to himself in the bathroom while he soaked in a hot tub. She put the kettle on in the small kitchen and brewed a strong pot of tea. After Chic towelled himself dry, they sat quietly and talked for a while in the quiet of the morning. 'There's only one way to approach it,' he told Maidie. 'It's just another one-night stand, a penny geggie. Remember Gartcosh and those

Marty Paich, Maidie, Chic, Mel Torme and David Nixon, Prince of Wales Theatre.

other hospitals? Basically the audience will be just the same—only they'll call themselves stockbrokers and brain specialists. People still remain just the same, that's what we've got to remember. If we let ourselves be intimidated by thinking it's a sophisticated bunch of prannies out there, then we've had it. We'll do what we've always done—keep it clean and keep it simple and keep it *moving*. Remember, Maidie, it's more difficult to hit a moving target!'

Somehow they got through the tension-filled day of rehearsals. Chic fell silent as Mel Torme ran through his programme, then the couple were introduced to David Nixon, whose act they had much admired on TV. Jimmy Wheeler was next to say 'hallo'—he was an old friend with whom they had appeared on several occasions. They returned to their dressing-room to find a whole batch of 'Good Luck' telegrams awaiting them. Eddie Fraser's ran, 'It's a long way from the Victory at Paisley but I always knew you'd make it. The very best of luck.' Duncan Macrae, Harry Secombe, Jack Milroy and many others sent their best wishes also, but the one that gave them the biggest laugh was from Jack Anthony. It read, 'A big opening, Timothy Tighthole. Love to Maidie. Good Luck.' Isabella's simple greeting ran, 'Good luck Darlings, Mizpah, Grannie Murray.'

From the beginning of their act there was no doubt that things were going well, but Maidie's stomach was in a knot as she left Chic on his own, facing the sharpened Fleet Street knives, together with the stockbrokers and brain specialists. She stood petrified in the wings as the big man launched into his solo spot. 'Who'd be a comedian?' she thought as she looked out over the sea of faces, sat there as if *defying* any comic to make them laugh. For a singer or instrumentalist it was different—they might like your tunes even if they weren't keen on the interpretation, but for a comedian, he was the whole kit and caboodle. She was put in mind of a Roman amphitheatre with Chic the gladiator, as he began.

'I got up this morning.'—Chic was away—'I *like* to get up in the morning, it gives me the rest of the day to myself.' The laughs started, leading Chic to stress, 'Oh, I *prefer* it!' to gales of laughter that sent Maidie's spirits soaring. 'So I dressed,' Chic went on. 'I *always* dress. I like to be *different*, but I think undressed you're just a bit *too* different! As I walked out of the door I turned left. I usually turn right, but this time I turned left—it's the spirit of *adventure*! I walked down Piccadilly, one foot in front of the other—oh, it's the best way. Then I went to cross the street—it was the only way I could get to the other side, and a fellow says to me, "Is that you?" Well, I could hardly deny it, with me *standing* there!'

Maidie could hear the audience were hooked—he had them firmly by the nose and was gently leading them along into his surreal world of fantasy. 'You know, it's a funny thing—I can look at anyone and say whether I know them or not. It's a gift I have! A wee man started jumping up and down, clapping his hands together like this'—here Chic demonstrated to hysterical laughter from the audience—'and I said, "Excuse me, would you mind telling me what you're doing?" He told me he was trying to catch Genumphs.' Maidie was listening to this for the first time herself and burst out laughing. Chic had it timed to the second. 'I said to him—"What's Genumphs?"' Maidie could feel the tears rolling down her cheeks while the audience was in an uproar. 'He said—"I don't know. I haven't *caught* any yet!"' This time Chic almost brought the roof down while Maidie was close to collapse in the wings. He had done it!

Maidie rejoined him at the end of the story and they went straight into the trusty 'Nobody's Darlin' But Mine'. Billy Marsh's dream formula had come off—Chic had been brilliant and the musical finale clinched their success. As they came off to the thunderous applause and yells of 'Encore! Encore!' Billy ran backstage to join them in the dressing-room. Jumping up and down, he shouted, 'You did it! You did it!' and hugged them both in an uncharacteristically emotional display, his unrestricted delight making it a moment they would always treasure.

As they sat chatting excitedly in their dressing-room, Chic shushed them to listen for a few minutes as the velvet fog of billtopper Mel

Torme could be heard serenading the audience in 'Blue Moon'. After listening enrapt through to the end, Chic turned to them both and whispered, 'Hear that—that's what I call a *real* artist!' It struck Billy again, as it had before, that Chic was one of the most surprising men he had ever met. At the instant of his greatest triumph, another artist he admired could stop him in his tracks. 'Consider this, then,' Billy replied. 'You're sharing *his* bill; can't be bad.' He still remembers the quiet smile of pride and satisfaction this thought gave Chic.

If it had been hard to sleep the night before the show, there was no problem after the first night. Billy Marsh took them out for supper and toasted them both in champagne. 'You've justified every particle of faith I had in you,' he told them. 'If people like me have any talent at all, it's for *spotting* talent—and I like to think that's a talent in itself. You know the definition of a critic, Chic? That's someone who criticises someone who *can* do something, although he *can't* do it himself. At least *I'm* on the positive side, pushing talent I believe in—and folks like you make it all worthwhile.'

Chic looked into his glass. 'Look,' he said, 'let's do some plain talking. You're a wee bugger in my book for keeping us away from the West End—our goal—for over a year. And guess what?' Here he looked up at Billy and smilingly raised his glass, 'You were dead right, you so-and-so!'

Next day the notices began to come in and Maidie excitedly ran through them all. In answer to Chic's unspoken question she replied, 'Yes, Chic, they're good all right. *Very* good!' The dailies were led by Donald Zec in the *Daily Mirror* who wrote, 'The narrator of the night was Chic Murray, a hefty Scotsman with a humour as dry as champagne.' Andy Gray in the *Stage* enthused: 'Tall Chic Murray, with a honey of a partner in Maidie, makes a most impressive London début with his inconsequential patter which has a freshness all its own.'

Back in Glasgow the two local evening papers told the same story, the *Evening Times* with, 'The Chic Murray manner took a trick at the Prince of Wales last night when Chic and Maidie made their West End début. Chic, as imperturbable off stage as on, hadn't altered the style of the act for the occasion, and the first-night applause proved he was right.'

The most unexpected review of all came from the *Sunday Times* as its highly respected theatre critic, Harold Hobson, single-handedly elevated the act to new heights. He justified all that Chic had tried to achieve as he wrote, 'I thought the Scottish comedian, Chic Murray, first-rate. His dissection of the process of getting up in the morning is Proustian in its detail, Beckettish in its innumerable qualifications and wholly his own in its irresistible delight.'

In case Chic had missed this review—and he had—Iain Cuthbertson decided it had to be drawn to his attention. Chic was overwhelmed to receive this letter from his old friend:

My dear Chic,

I want simply to say how glad I am that Harold Hobson in the *Sunday Times* saw fit to give you such an excellent notice. He's a clever man, a big noise in the theatre, and one whom the public place great reliance on for his level-headedness. His appreciation of you will go far, I feel, in creating a wider audience for you—an audience which I have felt for a long time you have every right to.

Being up to the neck in the business myself, it is very far from easy for a comedian to make me laugh deeply. You have always been able to twist me into kinks, and all I'd wanted to see in this matter is you getting the audience and recognition you so amply deserve.

Give my love to Maidie. And keep it going. You have all my sincerest good wishes.   Yours,

                                                                              Iain Cuthbertson

Even the unflappable Chic's head was spinning. As usual he had not. deigned to read most of the reviews himself, but he heard enough of them from Maidie. Words like 'original', 'wonderful', 'riotous', 'first-rate' and 'captivating' peppered the notices. He had finally seen his own brand of comedy through from its professional birth-pangs at Carnoustie to its coming-of-age in London's West End.

Such was their impact at the Prince of Wales that they were asked back a month later on a bill with American comic Jerry Colonna who had recently scored a hit with his version of 'Ebb Tide'. They had taken London by storm and there would be no let-up for a long time to come.

Only a few weeks after their London début Billy Marsh telephoned them with some extraordinary news. Stressing its confidential nature, he asked them if they would accept an invitation to appear at the next annual Royal Command Performance on 5 November at the London Palladium—*if* they were invited? 'We were both flabbergasted,' Chic recalled. 'Billy swore us to secrecy, but it wasn't necessary. I was too petrified to talk to anyone—about *anything*—until it became official. It was just totally unbelievable. Maidie was dying to tell Mum, Grannie Dickson and the kids but we just couldn't. I had the feeling right up until the actual invitation arrived that it was all a mistake, that somehow they'd got us mixed up with the Oberkirchen Children's Choir or something, but no—there it was. And to think they could have got Mel Torme instead of us!'

When at last the official announcement was made, the news was telephoned to the family back home. 'Break a leg, Dad,' was Annabelle's response, which had Chic thinking, 'I'm going to have to watch that one—where's she getting all this showbiz lingo?' To one reporter he commented that it was nice the 'do' was being held on his 'thirty-fourth' birthday! This was the beginning of what Murray-watchers would soon recognise as the great age-drain, although lopping just a couple of years off would be nothing once Chic really got into his stride—and if the occasional columnist perpetuated the error, who was he to correct it?

Norman Wisdom joined many others in personally telephoning his congratulations while greetings telegrams arrived by the sheaf and a steady stream of reporters and photographers dropped in. Just 15 months after signing with Billy Marsh and the Delfont Agency they had become one of the hottest acts in the country.

Chic noticed as the rehearsals for the Royal Show approached that Maidie seemed unusually preoccupied. In a quiet moment he asked her if there was something the matter and was met with an unexpected reaction, for Maidie burst into tears. Chic put his arms around her gently. 'Come on pal, spill the beans, what's up?' he asked in a kindly tone.

'It's nothing,' Maidie declared, blowing her nose.

'Come on,' said Chic, 'I know better than that.'

'Maybe it's just the anticlimax after the Prince of Wales or nerves before the Royal Show,' Maidie suggested.

'That's understandable,' said Chic.

'Or maybe it's the fact that you were paying so much attention to someone else in the show at the Prince of Wales.'

Chic looked at her cannily, 'You're not talking about Mel Torme, are you?' he asked.

Maidie had her second wind by now and the sobbing had stopped. 'No, I'm not,' she replied. 'I'm talking about that wee blonde in the chorus—Chic, for God's sake—in front of everyone! I'm not the only one who noticed, either.'

Chic decided a weak defence was better than none at all and came out with, 'Maidie, we were only *talking*!'

'*And* making goo-goo eyes at each other!' Maidie retorted. 'We all know you're a big star now, but did you have to make it so patently obvious? Listen, Chic—I know you're probably only trying to make up for lost time, because I don't think you did much playing around before we were married—but don't hurt me by parading it.'

Chic lowered his head. 'I'm sorry,' he said. 'I think I was just flattered that she was paying attention to me—I'd no idea it was that obvious. It was the first time, Maidie, and it won't happen again. I promise.'

'Let's stay the same as we were before,' Maidie pleaded.

Chic smiled. 'OK, agreed; back to doing our W. C. Fields and Mae West it is, my little chickadee!'

Maidie's effervescence returned—the worst was over, for she had dreaded Chic's reaction to being tackled. Even so, she was painfully aware that Chic and the blonde had done more than just talk and eye each other up. A few days later Maidie took Chic by surprise by turning up with her hair dyed blonde.

'You didn't do that just to please me, did you?' he asked.

'Well, I didn't do it to *displease* you,' came the reply. 'Besides, everyone's having it done.'

On the morning of 5 November the continuing Suez crisis dominated the newspaper headlines. As the performers arrived at the London Palladium to begin rehearsals for the Royal Show that night, the crisis was on their minds, but it took second place to the day's events and for the moment Suez was forgotten as Tommy Trinder called the company together for the first run-through. Alma Cogan kicked off the proceedings, followed by Syd Millward and his Nitwits and then Sabrina. Next came Chic and Maidie, who were followed by French cabaret star Patachou and Harry Secombe, his finale supported by a 60-strong choir of Welsh miners. Tommy Trinder announced the next act, planned as a top hat, white tie and tails song-and-dance routine featuring Sir Laurence Olivier, Vivien Leigh and John Mills, was unable to make the rehearsal, so the Crazy Gang were introduced as 'A Midsummer Night's Dream'. Bud Flannagan quipped, 'This is a tribute to Sir Laurence, Vivien Leigh and John Mills—if *they* can do a variety act, *we'll* have a bash at this!'

Liberace closed the first-half run-through before a break was called. With a cup of tea in one hand he came over to the couple and introduced himself. 'Call me Lee,' he said. 'Everyone else does. I just had to say how wunnerful I thought your routine was—you'd be a sensation in the States. Do you have any plans to appear there?'

'Eventually we'd like to try,' Chic replied, 'But you've already got Burns and Allen—how would you see us fitting in?'

The canny Liberace already had his answer ready. 'Another parallel is Jeannie Carson—Scots girl new to the Big City. There's lots of scope there to develop, folks, but it's a tough market—the toughest, I should know!'

'Aye, but you've cracked it,' Chic said.

'Sure I have,' Lee agreed, 'But if I'm an overnight success as people say, it must be the longest night on record!'

'Join the club,' thought Chic.

Soon they were recalled to start the rehearsals for the show's second half. Standing there on the stage of the London Palladium was like an injection of adrenalin to them both as they watched what amounted to a private showing of the Royal bill, before Tommy Trinder came on to announce the spectacular all-star finale featuring the Eric Delaney band, Dickie Valentine, David Whitfield, Beryl Reid and Gracie Fields. Just as Trinder began to speak another familiar figure emerged from the wings and walked briskly to centre stage. A hush fell on the company as they recognised Val Parnell, a household name since the success of his

Sunday Night at the London Palladium shows. Something was clearly wrong.

'Ladies and gentlemen,' he announced. 'I am sorry to tell you I have just received a message from Buckingham Palace that I know will be a dreadful disappointment to all of you who have worked so hard to make this show a success. The Royal Family have decided they cannot attend tonight because of the international situation, leaving me with no alternative but to cancel the show.'

A shocked silence greeted Parnell's message, the most voluble reaction coming from Liberace, who burst into floods of tears before being escorted off the stage by his brother George. Chic and Maidie could only stare at each other in total disbelief. 'Let's get changed,' said Chic eventually, giving Maidie's hand a squeeze. Columnist Archie McCulloch came round to commiserate.

'All dressed up and nowhere to go was never in it,' Chic told him. 'I'm sure everyone is totally shattered—but maybe Maidie and I will get another chance. And after all, what's a variety show compared to the gravity of the Suez situation?' He looked down at the parchment they had been given on their arrival inscribed, 'To Chic and Maidie, on being one of the representative artistes selected to appear at the Royal Variety Command Performance, November 1956'. 'It's ironical,' he said, 'getting this for a show we're not going to do. However, we were selected and that's the honour, after all.'

Commiserations generally were the order of the day until word came round that Winifred Atwell and her husband, Lew Levisohn, had invited everyone out to their Thameside home for a party, although there was still no disguising the intense disappointment everyone felt. Gradually the Palladium emptied—the occasion was over, the moment had passed. Seldom can the great variety theatre have witnessed a more melancholy sight than the performers drifting disconsolately away. By all rights Winnie Atwell's party should have had all the scintillating atmosphere of a wake, but contrarily it was to prove a riotous success. The drinks flowed freely and gradually the performers' sense of fun took over. Liberace, who had earlier described the cancellation as 'the biggest blow of my life', was dressed in a black wool double-knit sweater with a thread of lurex running through it. 'Isn't it stunning?' he asked. He had recovered well from the shock of the cancellation and comforted everyone with 'Don't worry—we'll be asked back again!' Chic introduced Alma Cogan's mother to him as Joan Crawford, which seemed to suitably impress Lee even if it left Alma and her mother somewhat disconcerted. 'Isn't there anyone in the company who can play the piano?' Chic yelled at the top of his voice as he stood sandwiched between Liberace and Winifred, who asked him if there was something special he wanted. 'I'll have a cheese sandwich and a glass of champagne,' he replied, before

Jimmy Nervo, Gracie Fields, Chic and Dickie Valentine, after the news of the Royal cancellation.

adding, 'Oh, you mean you want to play the piano? I thought you'd be too busy keeping your guests going with food and booze. OK then, give me a "C".' With Winnie and Lee taking turns on piano, and Maidie by his side, Chic went through his repertoire of country numbers, including 'Lucky Star', announcing it as 'The one that got away, but it'll be a sleeper—No. 1 by 1960 at the rate it's going!'

Singer Dorothy Squires turned up at the party, together with her then husband and current 'Saint', Roger Moore—later to be the third James Bond. 'Did you like my "Tree in the Meadow"?' she asked Chic, who replied, 'I don't think we got that picture in Scotland.' Archie McCulloch bumped into the couple again and introduced his wife, the singer Kathy Kay. Chic nodded in the direction of Lee and Winnie, 'What do you think?' he asked. 'I reckon these two should get together—they could make a bob or two!'

Next day the press was full of the show's cancellation. As well as the Suez crisis and the unrest in Hungary, the authorities had also learned of a Communist plan to demonstrate along the Queen's route to the London Palladium against Sir Anthony Eden and the Government's policy on Egypt. Although it was no comfort, the scrapping of the show was not without precedent, all engagements last having been cancelled on the death of Queen Mary. Despite a Palladium statement that they hoped to reinstate the show at a later date, this was clearly impractical. The same cast could never be assembled, as and when 'the international situation dies down', as the spokesman put it. If the show had gone ahead, Chic and Maidie would have been the first Scottish act to have appeared in a Royal Command show for ten years. Jack Radcliffe had been the artiste last honoured just after the end of the Second World War and before then it was necessary to go back to Robert Wilson and Renee Houston's appearances in the 1930s.

Unlike many acts in show-business whose rise to fame seems to be resented by their contemporaries, Chic and Maidie's ascent had been a popular one. After the Royal Command disappointment sentiment was strongly on their side as they prepared to open at the Empire in Glasgow for the Christmas show, *We're Joking*. They were overwhelmed by the warmth of the good wishes that poured in on the opening night from a host of celebrities but it was left to Jack Anthony to underscore what was in everyone's hearts as he wrote, 'May this be a *definite* Royal success.'

PROGRAMME 2ᵈ

1949

II

New York! New York!

From the desk of:
Col. P. Hool

Dear Chic,

Perhaps you have heard of me and my nationwide campaign in the cause of temperance.

Each year for the past eighteen, I have made a tour of Scotland and the north of England including Manchester, Liverpool and Glasgow and have delivered a series of lectures on the evils of drink. On the tour I have been accompanied by a young friend and assistant, David Powell.

David, a young man of excellent background, is a pathetic specimen of a life ruined by excessive drinking of whisky, gin, vodka, wine etc. He would appear with me at lectures and sit on the platform wheezing and staring at the audience through bleary bloodshot eyes, sweating profusely, picking his nose, constantly passing wind and making obscene gestures, while I would point him out as an example of what drinking etc. could do to a person.

Last summer unfortunately David died. A mutual friend [wee Bobby Shearer's dug] gave me your name and I was wondering if you would care to take David's place on my next temperance tour.

Yours faithfully
P. Hool

Bernard Delfont continued to ensure that bookings came pouring in. In 1957 their schedule was almost brought to an abrupt halt, however, as the couple were making their way to Birmingham for their second date at the Hippodrome, where they were due to appear with Frankie Vaughan. Maidie was driving along with Chic snoozing away beside her when a green Morris Minor careered round a corner on the wrong side of the road. All Maidie could do was swerve hard to avoid it, but a collision was virtually inevitable and the Morris crashed into the driver's side of their Standard 10, bringing the two cars to a juddering halt.

Chic was wide awake at the moment of impact and his eyes widened in horror as he saw his wife slumped motionless over the steering column, blood oozing from a gash on the side of her head. As he reached over to her he groaned involuntarily at the pain from his own bruised ribs. The driver of the Morris Minor had meanwhile leapt from the car and rushed to help. He pulled the driver's door open and began to extricate Maidie gently, as Chic rushed to join him. Chic pulled a blanket from the car and laid it at the side of the road as the other driver carried her round. Tenderly lifting her head, Chic flinched as he saw the extent of her injury. Her face was deathly white, but she was breathing. 'Get an ambulance, man,' Chic shouted. 'Be quick!'

At the sound of his voice Maidie started to come round, although everything looked strangely blurred. From a nearby house where he had rung for an ambulance the Morris driver emerged with some brandy, which caused her to splutter and choke. An ambulance arrived after a short but agonising wait and whisked them off to a nearby hospital. Fourteen stitches were required to close Maidie's wound, while Chic had a corset-like bandage tied round his middle to ease the pain of his bruised ribs.

'Your wife's got concussion, Mr Murray, and she's weak from loss of blood,' the doctor told him. 'There is no question of performing in Birmingham tonight. Perhaps later in the week . . .'

Maidie sat up at this. 'Just get me to the theatre,' she told Chic.

'But what's the point?' he asked.

'Just get me there. All I've got is a sore head and I'm feeling better already. Where are we anyway?'

'Ashby-de-la-Zouche,' replied Chic. Maidie thought about that and smiled. 'There has to be a joke in there somewhere, but you'll have to dig it out. I'm too tired and you're the comic, after all.'

While they had been in the hospital a garage had towed their forlorn, faithful Standard 10 away to what was to prove its final resting place. A taxi was organised to take them the last few miles to the theatre, where Maidie insisted on going on, her only worry being that they had no time for a band call. The memory of their last Birmingham Hippodrome engagement and the freezing light-aircraft journey from Edinburgh was fresh in their minds as Maidie plaintively pointed out, 'The Hippodrome will think we *never* bother with a band call!'

Several days later Maidie felt reasonably recovered. Her head still ached a bit, but the threatened concussion had not materialised and she was sitting up in bed having breakfast when Chic burst in excitedly. 'I've sorted out the new car,' he declared. 'We can pick it up today and the mechanic says he'll show you how to work it. There's a new system in it apparently.' Maidie felt as if she was having a relapse. 'New system?' she echoed, inwardly groaning at the thought of having to make her way to the garage and grapple with some mechanical *tour de force*.

In the event the 'new system' turned out to be a column gear change, which Maidie took in her stride. It was just as well, for at the end of their Birmingham week she was required to drive to their next venue at Brighton. From then on Chic would say, 'I'd take over, but you know I can't do the column change.' 'Why don't I just stop the car and show him?' she thought one day, then banished the idea from her mind. Nothing was worth a repeat of what she had put up with when demonstrating the floor change, which he had never yet completely mastered.

After a short breather in Scotland between engagements, the couple flew to London for TV rehearsals. On the second night of their stay Billy Marsh telephoned them. It seemed that Harry Secombe had developed acute laryngitis while appearing at the Glasgow Empire in a show called *Rocking the Town*. Could they fly up there in the morning and take over for two nights? They were due at Butlin's holiday camp at Filey in Yorkshire the following Sunday and had planned to go there direct from London, but off they went to Glasgow to the dear old Empire. Harry had packed the place out, but Chic and Maidie lost not a single customer, for the Empire in Sauchiehall Street had now become their Glasgow home. Sadly, this theatre would be one of the first to go for property development when the big theatrical decline set in. A stone's throw away stood the smaller but enormously popular Pavilion, from whose stage the couple had made their vital breakthrough under Tommy Morgan's auspices. This typical Scottish music-hall would survive the decline, though rather precariously at times.

After their last show at the Empire on Saturday evening it was home on the late train for a quick family reunion before bed and an early rise on Sunday, ready for the trip to Filey by car. Here the two houses they had expected had been extended to a non-stop five shows to cope with the demand. In between, another call came through from Billy Marsh. 'He thinks we're not working hard enough,' Chic groaned. 'What a guy!' Harry Secombe had been due to transfer to Edinburgh in *Rocking the Town* on Monday, but was still unwell. Could they do the necessary?

Edinburgh was followed by another visit to London for the rescheduled TV appearance, then it was up to Aberdeen to join Petula Clark at the start of Harold Fielding's *Music for the Millions* tour. For the first few nights they had little contact with the young singer, who seemed a bit distant and above it all, until one night she visited them in their dressing-room. 'Chic, I thought you were so funny tonight,' she said. 'And Maidie—how on earth do you cope with him? Do you know what he's coming up with next?'

'Not all the time, Pet,' Maidie confessed, 'but I think that's what keeps the act fresh.' Chic explained that they both loved her record of 'The Little Clogbasher', which brought a smile to Petula's face. Later she confided that she was missing the company of Joe 'Mr Piano' Henderson, with whom she was romantically involved at the time, this being before France and her 'Ya Ya Twist' days. Already a screen veteran, she talked at length about her early appearances and what she regarded as the high spot to date, *The Card*, with Alec Guinness. 'You should meet him,' she told them. 'He's such an incredibly talented actor—and a very funny man, too, in a dry, courteous way.'

Chic's eyes grew larger as he stared at Petula in mock-horror while she told him this. 'I hope he hasn't any plans to enter variety, Petula,' he said.

Petula giggled. 'I don't think so, Chic,' she replied.

Chic sighed with relief, then added—towering over both Petula and Maidie—'Oh, thank goodness, but are you *absolutely sure*, Pet? I mean, look at *you* . . .' and saying this, he dimpled his cheek with a finger and stared at her quizzically, jutting his head forward. Petula burst into helpless laughter, then they talked for hours, swapping show-business stories and reminiscences.

Later in the week the couple learned that they had a Cyprus tour of army bases fixed for October. Chic got in some early language practice as he endlessly enunciated 'Fa-ma-gust-a' and 'Nic-o-si-a', intrigued by the idea of setting foot on foreign soil for the first time. 'I hope the natives are friendly,' he said to Maidie.

'Well, they can't all be, that's why the troops are there in the first place,' replied the ever-practical Maidie.

When comedian Jimmy Edwards heard they were going he offered them some advice. 'Don't go on the army aeroplane they'll offer you,' he told them, 'unless you fancy being rattled out of the sky.'

'What are you suggesting, we go there in a banana boat?' asked Chic.

Edwards's moustache bristled. 'No, you *clot*. Don't be such a miserable bugger—fly and pay your own fares. Believe me, it's worth it.' Turning to Maidie he said, 'If he doesn't, divorce him and marry me!'

Maidie knew only too well what the outcome would be, and in due course they boarded the army Blackwood DC6 for the flight to Nicosia. An hour later it was still sitting on the ground full of cold, miserable passengers, including Glasgow comedians Berta Ricardo and Billy 'Uke' Scott. When it finally did take off, amidst such shaking and rattling, air-sickness bags were passed round among the unfortunate passengers, who were beginning to lay odds against arriving in one piece. They did, but Jimmy Edwards's warning rang in their ears all the way.

In Nicosia, and later on a visit to Famagusta, Chic was in his element under the hot Cyprus sun, more than once getting carried away with himself and coming home slightly singed as a result. For Maidie it was the closest thing to a holiday since their marriage and she made the most

of it, although even on shopping trips to the towns she had to be accompanied by an armed soldier. The shows they gave were most rewarding, with the troops roaring their appreciation.

At the end of the first week Maidie was relaxing in their hotel room when Chic limped in. He had been swimming and sunbathing and looked very sorry for himself. 'Maidie, my big toe's hurting something terrible,' he complained. 'I think I tripped over a mussel-shell coming out of the water and I think I've broken it.' A doctor was sent for and confirmed that the toe was indeed broken, before ceremoniously wrapping it in the tightest of bandages.

When the doctor had gone Chic turned to Maidie. 'I've got to walk and I don't want anyone to know about this.' Maidie looked at the bandage on Chic's foot. 'What option have you got? You'll never get your shoes on.' Chic looked desperate for a moment, then brightened up. 'I've got it,' he declared. 'Down you go to the QM stores and get the biggest pair of army boots you can lay your hands on. Tell them anything—tell them it's for a sketch. That'll do it!'

The boots were duly fetched and Chic managed to get his bandaged foot inside. His already large feet now looked even bigger with the oversized boots and their enormous toe-caps. 'What are you going to say when people ask why you're wearing them?' Maidie wanted to know. 'I'll think of something,' Chic replied. 'Anyway, we *are* on a Forces tour. It behoves us all to dress accordingly!' And so saying he took a few tentative steps. 'Ouch,' he cried, then, 'on second thoughts, *ouch*!'

'Chic,' said Maidie, 'if you're going to be a soldier . . .'

'Yes?'

'. . . be a *brave* one!'

On the last night of their tour they were in the middle of their act on an open-air stage with a backdrop of real palm trees when the audience began leaving their seats in droves. Chic looked at Maidie. 'I've heard of unprofessionalism among *performers*,' he declared, 'but this is the first time I've seen an *audience* act unprofessionally!' At this a tour organiser came dashing on to the stage. 'We've received a bomb warning,' he explained. 'Why are we the last to know?' Chic asked. 'I thought they were leaving because of something I said! Hey—if a bomb goes off now, I can see the headlines—"Murrays Go Out with a Bang!"' Maidie was busy unbuckling her accordion while this conversation was taking place. Chic's response was, 'Look out! Maybe the bomb's inside it!' So saying, he hobbled off in his tackety boots.

The whole thing turned out to be a false alarm, but it kept Chic and the company going for the next few days before they left the island. 'I know we didn't *finish* the act,' he confided to Berta Ricardo, 'but do you really think the army will insist on a *refund*?'

The broken toe and the bomb scare apart, their five-week tour of Cyprus was successful on every level. The troops loved them, the sun never failed to shine and they both left the island tanned and relaxed.

*   *   *

On their return to Scotland they began rehearsals for their first pantomime, *Cinderella*, at the Glasgow Empire, a lavish Tom Arnold presentation that would prove yet another great success. They both popped in and out of the scenes in various guises, before driving on stage for the finale in a bubble car with the registration number CHIC I.

On the first night Chic's initial appearance was to be as a fairy complete with wings, tights and a magic wand. The idea was that he should emerge through a trapdoor in the floor, but only his head and shoulders emerged before the mechanism stuck. The audience roared as Chic looked around helplessly, before raising himself up by his wrists. The audience loved it. 'Why is it,' Chic asked later, 'that we often get the biggest laughs when things go wrong? So much for all our wit and wisdom!' Jack House reviewed the show enthusiastically, remarking however that Chic was at his best when left to do his own thing.

A month into the run of *Cinderella*, during the second week of January, the winter weather that had been late in arriving began to get into its stride. A heavy snowfall was followed by a bitterly cold spell, rendering road conditions increasingly dangerous. A grim-faced Maidie returned from a phone call made to the theatre with the news that Isabella had fallen in the snow outside her front door and cracked several ribs. Chic went ashen at the news, but finished the last show of the evening before telephoning the hospital himself. When he came back, he had a drink in his hand which the show's sympathetic producer had provided.

'They say she's comfortable, but they're worried in case complications set in. She's a heavy woman and they're concerned about pressure from the ribs on her lungs,' he reported.

'Can we see her tonight?' Maidie asked.

'They say no, they want her to rest, but we can see her in the morning. I think we should drive to Bank Street and stay there tonight after the show.' So saying he downed the contents of his glass and sat down heavily, his head in his hands.

On reaching Greenock they skidded their way up to Bank Street, coming to a halt on the steep, icy road outside the front steps of number 21. A light was on in the hall, so they knew Uncle Tom was at home, but the door was firmly locked. As Chic hammered furiously the hall light was switched off, leaving them standing there in inky darkness. 'That crazy bastard!' he yelled, attacking the door anew with the side of his clenched fist and kicking it at the same time. Eventually they heard the lock being slipped and were able to push the door open. As they did, they saw Tom's bedroom door being pulled tight shut.

After a restless night they were at the hospital early next morning. Isabella looked pale and drawn, but managed a wan smile when they entered. 'Oh, my loves,' she greeted them. 'I feel such a fool—I must be getting past it—fancy falling in the snow!' Despite her cheerful demeanour it was clear she was in considerable pain and her breathing sounded forced and unnatural. 'We'll bring the children through at the

Chic in his fairy gear with daughter Annabelle.

weekend to see you,' Chic promised as they rose to go, kissing her fondly on the cheek. 'And Maidie and I will be in to see you every single day.'

On their way out the doctor told them it was too early to say if there would be any complications, but assured the still distraught Chic that his mother would receive the best possible care.

The weekend visit with Douglas and Annabelle seemed to cheer Isabella, but she fielded every question as to when she would be allowed out of hospital. 'Soon, soon. I'm on the mend,' was all she would say.

Maidie visited her alone on their matinée day and Isabella stroked the fur coat she was wearing. 'Did my Chic buy you that?' she asked fondly. (Maidie just smiled, she had bought it herself.) Then, 'How are things between the two of you?'

'Never better,' Maidie replied. Isabella looked at her searchingly. 'Remember your promise to me, Maidie. If anything happens to me, you're all he's got.'

'Nothing's going to happen to you, Gran,' Maidie assured her. 'And as for that big galoot,' she laughed, 'he could buy and sell us all!'

This time the doctor's report was less reassuring; there was concern about fluid gathering in Isabella's lungs.

That night another call came through to the Empire. Isabella's condition had deteriorated alarmingly in the last few hours and pneumonia had set in. The couple dropped everything and drove through to Greenock to be with her, arriving just as she was being transferred to an emergency ward. At five o'clock in the morning Isabella died.

Chic stared in front of him silently after being told the news, then turned to weep quietly on Maidie's shoulder.

Hundreds of people attended the funeral, most of them complete strangers to Chic. Many floral tributes were sent from friends and colleagues unable to attend. Although he had an inkling of the admiration for his mother in the town, he had no real idea of the extent of it. Isabella had been an active member of the Scottish National Party, President of the British Women's Temperance Association and an Officer in the St Andrew's Ambulance Association, from whom she had gained three diplomas. She was also involved with the People's Dispensary for Sick Animals, the Business Women's Club, the Philosophical Society and the local Fourth Ward committee.

'I didn't know all that,' Chic admitted. 'I've always been so damned preoccupied with myself that I never took the opportunity to find out.'

*   *   *

Intense speculation began early in 1958 when the first Scottish Royal Variety Performance was announced to take place in July. Although it was hoped to include some top international names, it soon became common knowledge that many had declined the invitation, pleading 'other commitments', among them Perry Como and Bing Crosby.

When asked who *had* accepted, the organisers released a first list, pointing out that a second would be forthcoming to cover the number of turn-downs. The newspapers had a field day in advance of the first list being published, the consensus being that Chic and Maidie simply had

Duncan Macrae, Jack Anthony, Robert Wilson, Chic and Alex Don.

to be included, if only to make up in some measure for their cancelled English Royal Command Performance. Despite this pressure the organising committee was apparently unmoved and the first list appeared without their names on it.

Among the artistes who were included, Frankie Vaughan took the unprecedented step of announcing, 'I know every artist longs to be selected to appear before the Queen, but if I had a wish at the moment, it would be for Chic Murray and Maidie to be selected. They were chosen for the Command Performance which had to be cancelled because of Suez and they have still to perform before the Queen. I do hope that when the final list for the Glasgow performance is announced their names will be on it.'

'What a pal,' Chic said. 'Maidie, order me ten copies of "Give Me the Moonlight". On second thoughts, make it a round dozen. No, hold it. We'll save up for his next LP instead.'

A few days later all their hopes were dashed as the second list was issued. To be included were Jack Anthony, Jack Milroy, Duncan Macrae, Larry Marshall, Andy Stewart, Aly Wilson, Johnny Victory, Lex McLean and Mary Dalziel (Jimmy Logan's Mum)—no sign of Chic or Maidie. A reporter who ventured to ask Chic his feelings on the subject found him untypically tight-lipped. He and Maidie had received a communication from the organising committee of the show, the Scottish Variety Artistes Benevolent Fund, but the letter was only to ask if they would be interested in buying any tickets. All Chic would state to the press was,

'I'm strictly non-committal about the whole thing. I want to stay out of any controversy. Just let them get on with their fun and games.'

Columnist Gordon Hyslop summed up the feelings of many when he wrote in the *Sunday Express*: 'I say the Murrays should have been asked. Chic is a bigger name than many of the comics picked. His name is known all over Britain. There's talk that America wants to see him. He's just signed a contract to top the bill on TV in *Sunday Night at the Prince of Wales*. If he's good enough to be seen nationwide on our small screen, surely he warrants an invitation to our Royal Variety Show.'

The incident provided a heartbreaking coda to their London Royal Show cancellation, for instead of making up for the disappointment in some measure, it looked as if the organising committee had decided to rub salt in the wound.

In 1959 Chic and Maidie decided to move from their flat in Montague Street to a terraced house in Bruntsfield. Their busy schedule of theatre shows and TV appearances continued unabated as they tried to settle down in their new house, usually for only a day or two at a time. Unfortunately their move coincided with another confrontation—one that Maidie had been trying to avoid since the Prince of Wales incident. She could see that Chic was moonstruck. As soon as he had clapped eyes on the young dancer who formed one half of a ballet duo, he was smitten. Maidie steeled herself for the worst.

When they returned home from a matinée one afternoon and Chic announced he had some business in town to take care of, Maidie further recognised the signs. After he left, she took a taxi back to the theatre. Their car was sitting outside, then a few moments later Chic left with his new conquest in tow. As she watched them drive off, Maidie was in a turmoil. 'I was hiding in the corner, like something out of *Back Street*,' she recalled. 'The first house was only two hours away—long enough for their assignation, I dare say, but too long for me to spend trying to keep in my anger and frustration. By the time I was able to tackle him, when both shows were over, I was ready.'

Chic quickly clammed up when Maidie broached the subject in their dressing-room. 'Do we need to have this conversation?' he asked.

'*Need* to have it? We should have had it a long time ago! Was the Prince of Wales really your first little dabble? If it was, it wasn't the last. Now this —'

'Have a heart!' Chic protested, without even an attempt at a denial. 'I'm only human, for God's sake.'

Something snapped inside Maidie. '*You're* human? What about me? What am I—*inhuman*? How do you think your sleeping around makes me feel?' she stormed. 'Goo-goo eyes was bad enough—now you're meeting another tramp behind my back. What have you got to say for yourself?'

Chic looked glumly at his feet. 'Not much,' he replied, 'except—none of it means a damned thing, Maidie. I'm really sorry. This time I swear it won't happen again.'

Maidie slumped into her seat. 'You know, Chic, I'm awfully tired,' she sighed. 'Tired of touring, tired of endless band-calls, tired of packing suitcases and unpacking suitcases. Sometimes I'd throw the whole lot up tomorrow if I could. Does my life need to consist of seeing my kids on high days and holidays? And now this playing around—it's just too much.'

He tenderly squeezed her shoulder. 'No more birds and no more battles—how does that sound?' he asked.

'It sounds fine,' Maidie replied. She looked at him long and hard— this man she loved so very much, this Greenock refugee she had rescued from the land of sugar, ships and showers. What was the use?

*   *   *

With their act well and truly established in Britain, Chic found his thoughts turning more and more to the States. Billy Marsh recommended that he speak to Neil Kirk in New York, a Scot who had for years organised the highly successful White Heather tours of North America. An ex-comic from Dundee who had emigrated in the late 1930s, Kirk had carved a comfortable niche for himself with his tours and brought a breath of the old country to expatriate Scots throughout the USA and Canada. Although this was not what Chic had in mind, talking to Neil would be a start.

Maidie elected to stay at home during Chic's reconnaissance, deciding that the break was the perfect tonic both of them needed. It was the first time she had spent more than just a few consecutive days at home since the 1930s.

Although he had underplayed to Maidie the excitement he felt, every nerve in Chic's body was ready for the new experience he was confident America would bring. The US customs brought him down to earth a bit at Idlewild Airport as he had to wait over two hours for clearance. His visa was for only four weeks and he found himself asked to declare his visit was of a 'non-political nature' and he 'was not now and never had been a member of the Communist Party'. Chic glumly went along with the rigmarole, which took him back to the McCarthy hearings he had followed so avidly.

Chic did not underestimate the formidable challenge he faced, his greatest asset being the fact that no one had any preconceived ideas about him. For Chic it had been a major surprise that he had even been accepted south of the Border back home, so what was America but one more frontier? And since he hadn't lost any sleep over England, why should he get his knickers in a twist over the States?

Chic felt himself to be an expert on all things American, thanks to his exposure—especially in his misspent youth—to all the grade 'A' and 'B' products that Hollywood had to offer—or dump—in the cinemas of Scotland. Among the many picture halls patronised by Chic and his pals was the Central, known locally as 'The Ranch' on account of the number of Westerns shown. One thing led to another and a taste for cowboy films led to the novels of Zane Grey.

When he had cleared customs and collected his solitary bag, Neil stepped forward and introduced himself. He was tall, almost up to Chic's height, but wiry and several stones lighter than Chic, who now weighed almost 14 stone. 'How did you know it was me?' Chic asked. 'Something to do with the tartan bonnet you're wearing,' Kirk replied wryly, still with clear traces of his Scottish ancestry.

In the cab from Idlewild to Manhattan Neil filled Chic in on the agency. 'Although our main work is in setting up the Scottish tours,' he explained, 'we have access to people who might be right as managers for you. Getting the right guy is the most important thing, then you've got the springboard for your next visit.' Chic sat hypnotised as the New York skyline came into view. It was early evening and already he could see skyscraper lights flickering away, like a scene from one of the many movies he had seen. 'Is that —' he began.

'Yep. The Empire State building, Chic. Unmistakable, isn't it? That other beauty's the Chrysler building. Once you're checked in I'll take you out for a meal and let you have an early night. I know it's only 8 p.m. here but you're working on 1 a.m. back home. Tomorrow morning I'll call and show you the sights, then you can relax on Sunday and be all freshened up for the rounds on Monday. How does that sound?' Chic brightened up immediately. 'Sounds great,' he replied. 'Neil, I'll be like putty in your hands—well, Scottish clay anyway.'

Soon the cab was in Manhattan and Chic was deposited at the Hotel Belvedere on West 48th Street. He looked up at the sight of the first skyscraper actually to tower above him. 'Back in an hour,' Neil assured him. Chic was quickly settled in his 27th floor room, with a bath running and the contents of his case all over the bed. He examined everything quite critically until he realised that as usual Maidie had omitted nothing. He had all he needed to survive—everything that is, except her, for already he missed her.

Neil took him to a restaurant called the Press Box where the quantities were such that even Chic was hard put to clear the plates. After the meal the two men talked for hours. 'You know,' Neil told him later, 'there's something about your humour that's hard to pigeonhole. I just hope you're not *too* damned original. It doesn't mean you won't be able to make a breakthrough here, it may just make it that much tougher.'

Chic nodded. 'I've always had the same reaction,' he assured him.

'When I started out, hanging on to Maidie's coat tails, no one wanted me—they couldn't see the point of what I was trying to do. Finally they got the message and seemed to like it. Have you heard much of my stuff, Neil?'

'Only a disc that Maidie sent me. I think it was your first broadcast together—Betty Grable trying to get a night's sleep. I thought it the sweetest, silliest story I'd ever heard and I've been a fan ever since.'

Back in his room Chic fell asleep almost immediately, intoxicated by the atmosphere of New York, the wonderful meal and the warm friendly reception afforded him by Neil Kirk.

He awoke with a start to find it was already eight o'clock. Thinking it was no wonder he was so hungry, he had a quick splash and ventured downstairs in search of breakfast, to find the coffee shop closed. He walked through the revolving doors into the street outside, struck by how dark it was.

After walking for several blocks, he found a coffee shop that was open and sat down, asking to see the menu. As he studied it, the gum-chewing waitress poured him a glass of iced water. 'What can I get you?' she asked.

Chic was bemused. Everything seemed to be 'Special'. 'How are the scrambled eggs?' he asked.

'Good,' the waitress replied. 'Scrambled eggs are always good. You want the Special?'

'No,' said Chic. 'I'll have two *fried* eggs with bacon and sausage.'

Expressionless, the waitress asked, 'How do you like your eggs?'

Baffled, Chic repeated, 'fried', thinking she must be hard of hearing.

'Yeah I know, but sunny side up or easy over?'

'Oh, sunny side up first, *then* easy over, and the bacon wants to be well done—crispy—but not the sausages.'

'How about I just show you the kitchen, buster?' asked the waitress, although she was beginning to see the funny side of this strange customer.

'If my wife were here, I'd accept the invitation on her behalf,' Chic replied.

'Toast?' she asked, getting her second wind—not long until the end of the shift now, she was thinking, we may just get this order through in time.

'Yes, please.'

'White bread, cracked wheat, rye or a bagel?'

Chic by this time had had enough of this foolish banter. 'I'll leave that to you,' he replied, smiling ever so sweetly.

The waitress returned his smile. 'Oh, I think *cracked* wheat would be good for *you*. Coffee?'

'Thanks.'

'Coming up.'

Chic was beginning to think he deserved an Olympic medal, and would some breakfast eventually emerge from all this?

First the waitress poured the coffee, then he heard her yell through the service hatch. 'Two easy over with bacon and sausage. Heavy on the bacon, light on the sausage!' Then it was back to Chic. 'You want orange juice?'

'I expect it's compulsory.'

'You got it, bud.'

Chic reflected that half his visit seemed to have gone in ordering breakfast, but his eyes widened when the steaming plateful arrived about two minutes later. Hash potatoes nestled alongside the eggs and bacon and sausage. Why was Maidie unaware of the wonders of hash browns? From now on, he vowed, they would be on the Murray household menu.

After breakfast was over—it turned out to be the 95 cent special—Chic squinted outside. It was still as dark as ever, then the clock on the wall told him why. He was still working on Greenwich Mean Time—in New York it was only four o'clock in the morning!

Chic was longing to see the famous streets he knew about. He stopped a passing policeman to ask the way to 42nd Street, synonymous in Chic's mind with show business and glamour. Unfortunately, it appeared he had been walking in the wrong direction since leaving the hotel. 'You walking, bud, or takin' a cab?' the policeman asked.

'How much would a cab cost?'

'About 75 cents.'

'I'm walking. Which direction? Twelve blocks? Eh—how does that work?' Chic was treated to a potted guide on the city's layout and sent on his way. He was puzzled by the policeman's cautionary, 'Are you sure you wanna go there now? OK, but watch out for yourself, and keep an eye on your wallet.'

Soon he was on the famous street and looking in vain for some familiar sight he might recognise from the movies. Try as he might, he could find none. Most of the theatres that had once lined the street had been converted into movie houses, which seemed uniformly run-down and seedy. The morning light seemed to cruelly expose any pretence of glamour the street might still have retained at night, as the tawdry façades and billboards luridly advertised their current attractions. Despite the early hour Chic was approached within a minute of entering the street. 'You got a match, sport?'

Chic took in the short leather skirt and painted features. He was inclined to give the standard Greenock response, 'Aye—your face and my arse,' but restrained himself and increased his pace somewhat. The 'girl' was wearing the highest pair of high heels he had ever seen, and he was just thinking how much they would suit Maidie, when he got an earful of abuse. 'Whazzamatta? Doncha know how to do it? You got a noive—wasting a goil's time.'

Chic felt a bit like an Edinburgh headmistress inadvertently taking a walk on the wild side. It was with considerable relief that he came out on Times Square and Broadway. This was a famous sight that proved not to be a let-down, although something of 42nd Street's atmosphere still managed to linger. He wandered on, passing a Broadway movie theatre showing Billy Wilder's *Some Like It Hot*, then a block or two further east stumbled on the Radio City Music Hall, where *Ask Any Girl* was the current attraction, together with a stage show and the Rockettes.

Resetting his watch to local time, he slept for a few hours before being wakened by the promised call from Neil Kirk. 'Is there any particular New York area you'd like to see?' Neil asked when they met, unaware of what he was letting himself in for.

'The Bowery,' Chic replied nonchalantly.

'Skid Row? Nobody goes there.'

Chic squeezed Neil's arm. 'Humour me, Neil. There are good reasons.' Neil laughed. 'What can the good reasons be?' Chic looked straight at him with a deadly serious expression. 'The Bowery Boys were cousins of mine,' he explained. 'Now just get your butt in gear and take me there.' Obediently Neil drove down Eighth Avenue, then stopped, waving his hand at the scene opposite them. 'This is it,' he declared.

'OK,' said Chic. 'You sit tight for a while. I won't be long—I just want to stretch the old legs for a bit.'

'Be careful,' Neil called out, as Chic left and walked across the avenue, heading straight for the bunch of derelicts who had congregated on the pavement under the rotting awning of a closed-down bar. A bottle wrapped in a brown paper bag was being passed around as he arrived.

'Any chance of a belt from that bottle?' he asked. After staring at him in disbelief for a moment, a particularly surly-looking member of the group growled, 'Fuck off, Jack.' Chic looked down at the speaker with a hurt expression on his face. 'I was told the Scots could expect a warm welcome in New York,' he said quietly. 'Seems that was a mistake.'

'He's from the old country,' the surly one announced, brightening up. 'And a Scot—our favourite guys. Sit down, Scottie. We don't see nearly enough of you.' Neil watched in disbelief as Chic hunkered down on the pavement and the bottle was passed to him. Christ, he thought, there was a first time for everything and this was it. Something about Chic was beginning to get to Neil—this guy *is* unique, he thought, with a style all his own. There just had to be a way of getting him over to the great American public. Neil was surprised again 20 minutes later when Chic got up to leave and was given a hearty handshake from his new-found friends. To each of them he handed a green bill, then waving them a cheery farewell, re-crossed the street.

Chic 'addressing the ball'.

'Drive on, MacDuff,' he told Neil. 'I hate to disillusion them about the Scots, but I like to step out of character now and again and that was the one time I had to stand my round. Mind you, that's the budget buggered good and proper.'

'Right, now it's Chinatown and Little Italy, then the Battery and Staten Island,' Neil informed him. 'Tell me, Chic—*apart* from being related to the Bowery Boys, why were you so keen to visit the Bowery?'

'For two reasons,' Chic replied. 'First, the Bowery Boys made the ace number one series as far as Scotland was concerned. I believe they even made the pictures latterly almost for Scotland alone, when they'd run out of steam everywhere else. We still played them as "A" films and eventually they even made one in colour! Secondly, Neil, you're probably not aware of it but I'm a vagrant myself—at least according to many British institutions—so I have a fellow-feeling for these guys. Thirdly —'

'You said two reasons, Chic.'

'All right, call me a liar for one reason. Thirdly—they are guys who are down on their luck, wasted men . . .' (Neil looked at Chic and saw a far-away look in his face. He was staring straight ahead, but not down Eighth Avenue; could it be a street in Greenock? Clearly the situation had struck a nerve) '. . . who deserve a break, a helping hand. Everybody needs one at some stage in their life and if they don't get it—well, there but for the grace of God and all that! Instead of sitting in your undoubtedly plush Broadway office'— Neil grinned—'you could have your arse on the pavement in Skid Row. My poor old Dad and my uncle Tom never recovered from their army service. As for me, Maidie helped me through . . .'

'Tell me about it,' Neil urged. 'Have you got a week to spare?' asked Chic. 'Yes,' Neil replied. 'Well, I'm surprised at you—a big Broadway agent! You should have better things to occupy your time! OK, you asked for it, here goes . . .'

At the end of the trip Neil knew as much as anyone about Chic and Maidie's rise to the top of the show business tree in Britain, and felt privileged to be hearing it first hand.

'OK, Chic—let's do a Broadway show. What do you fancy?'

'What's the choice?' Chic asked.

'Well, for musicals, there's Ethel Merman in *Gypsy* or Rodgers and Hammerstein's *Flower Drum Song*. If you fancy a straight play, there's *Sweet Bird of Youth* with Paul Newman and Geraldine Page at the Beck Theater, or *The Miracle Worker* next door.'

Chic wanted to see them all, then asked to see a newspaper with the listing. After studying it for a moment he chose *Sweet Bird of Youth*, explaining, 'Well, it's got seats at $6.99—all the rest are over $8—then it's got Paul Newman, but most of all because of the title, you could sell me that play on the title alone. *Gypsy* would come second, but I wish Maidie were here to see it too.'

'To hell with poverty,' Neil declared. 'I'll get tickets for them both, then you can tell Maidie all about it when you get home.'

Although the visit lasted for only two weeks, Chic felt as if he had learned a lot and soaked in the Manhattan atmosphere. Switching on TV he saw *Huckleberry Hound* and *Sea Hunt* for the first time, and listened to Walter Cronkite with the background on the daily news. There was so much to tell Maidie, for he was becoming convinced that the two of them could make it in the States. Neil promised to find a suitable manager in time for Chic's return visit, then as they waited for his plane, he asked if he had a special memory he would retain from his first New York trip.

'That's easy,' Chic replied, 'although there are so many, like the

Empire State, where I came across a bit of King Kong's fur still hanging about—or maybe it was a dead cat, or the Staten Island Ferry, or the Bowery guys. But the bit that will always stick in my mind is the afternoon you took me for a cocktail in Manhattan.'

Neil was surprised, but recalled that Chic had fallen quiet as they entered the lounge. 'It was like a spell out of time,' Chic explained. 'There was no natural light and what lighting there was, was low— although it was a bright sunny day outside, inside it could have been midnight or the middle of the day, any time. The sounds were muffled—you could hear traffic noises but it was like a distant soundtrack. Everyone in the lounge was talking in whispers, either that or what they were saying was being soaked up like a sponge. It was eerie and it took an effort to leave and rejoin reality. In fact, if you hadn't pulled me out I believe I'd still be sitting there!' The faraway look on Chic's face gave way to a broad grin. 'On second thoughts, no I wouldn't. At the price of drinks in that joint I'd have been skint!'

G. B. BOWIE PRESENTS

THE FOLLIES OF 1949

6.45 | **TWICE NIGHTLY** | 9 p.m.

BARRFIELDS
PAVILION

LARGS

2D.   1949

Booking Office Open Daily from 10.30 a.m.
to 5 p.m. at Kiosk in front of Pavilion

12

Troubles and Tiffs

'I sometimes feel about as awkward as a left-handed violinist in a crowded string section, but let's face it, only a mediocre person is always at his best. At least I got one thing settled today. I spoke to the Duke of Edingburgh, who spoke to the Queen and she's passed a law that if anyone beats Glasgow Rangers it's only a draw.'

A few months later Maidie was busy attacking the family wash when Chic strolled in. 'I've fixed us up with a complete break,' he declared. 'It's at the seaside—just like you wanted. Well, doon the water anyway, same thing. We can take the kids and make a real summer holiday out of it. Oh, we've a wee job to do as well, but nothing that'll get in the way of our having a great time.'

Maidie could have hugged him. 'Chic, that's marvellous,' she replied. 'Our first real holiday together—'

'Don't forget the honeymoon weekend—and Cyprus'.

'Our first real holiday together,' Maidie repeated, unabashed. 'Did you say we had a wee job to do?'

Chic rubbed his hands together. 'A real family break, that's what it'll be. *And* it'll pay for itself.'

Maidie paused for just a moment before doing a double take. '*Pay* for itself?'

'Yes, it'll be just the job. A full summer season at the Winter Gardens in Rothesay—but we're the bosses, Maidie. What we say goes. It's our show and we can do what we like. We hire the rest of the bill and get a percentage of the take. All that free sun . . .'

For Maidie the gilt was suddenly off the gingerbread. 'A summer season at Rothesay,' she repeated, as if stunned. 'Two shows nightly and matinées on top. Chic, I'm surprised you've nothing lined up for the Sundays.'

'I'm glad you brought that up. You know how fond you are of a sail

Annabelle, Maidie and Douglas at home.

Maidie. Well, Scottish Television want to pick us up every Sunday morning, ferry us across to Wemyss Bay and then whisk us off to their studios in Glasgow. It's all for a new show they're putting on.'

Maidie slumped into the nearest chair, a handful of shirts clasped in her arms. 'Chic, I don't know.'

'Oh, come on Maidie,' he coaxed. 'The kids will be with us. Here I am arranging all this and you're not pleased.'

Maidie stuck to her guns. 'Chic, I had a summer *holiday* in mind.'

'And that's just what it will be! Oh—I saved the best news till last. We're going to stay just outside Rothesay on a real working farm.'

Maidie tried hard to suppress a smile at the very thought of it, but gave in. 'OK then, Chic,' she conceded. 'You're on, but on one condition—I don't have to milk the cows or feed the chickens!'

Chic grinned. 'Of course not. You might be called on to plough the odd field, though.'

The family did have a tremendous time at Rothesay, the farm lodgings proving to be an inspired idea. The children loved it and were never at a loss for something to do, between visiting Rothesay, being near the seaside and the delights of the working farm. The old tram tracks that had run from Rothesay to Ettrick Bay stopped outside the farm at Mid Colmas, providing a poignant reminder of bygone times, for Chic shared with Maidie a nostalgia and affection for the old trams, missing them terribly after their removal from the streets of Edinburgh and Greenock. For the moment they still operated in Glasgow, but here also their days were numbered.

The couple never went straight home after their last show at the Winter Gardens, for Chic had discovered a splendid Italian restaurant, Tony's Place, where he nightly consumed vast quantities of spaghetti bolognaise before driving back for a nightcap and bed. Chic was surprised at his reaction to the early start involved with the Sunday trip to Glasgow and recalled, 'Traditionally I never was an early bird, but here I had to be. Half past three we got up—can you picture it? Maidie was always wide awake, but it was still like the blind leading the blind. Believe it or not though, the whole thing turned out to be a tonic. Scottish Television hired a motor boat to get us across to Wemyss Bay and the Firth of Clyde had never looked bonnier as it did on these mornings—we both felt it; it was dreamtime. There was this uncanny peace about that you only get around dawn, like a new beginning, and at the same time it was decidedly supernatural.'

In between the Winter Gardens and the weekly Glasgow expeditions, Chic managed to fit in the first of a series of voice-overs for television commercials, another new field that had opened up, and for the first time the Murrays were in competition with themselves 'on the box' as the first instalments of the STV series *Holiday Showtime* were screened each Wednesday evening. Far from hurting their takings on the night, the TV appearances created an extra buzz that quickly boosted the box office. The sacrifice of their one precious day off was certainly not in vain, therefore, although newspaper critics had a field day with the show. Fortunately, this did not prevent it shooting to the top of the Scottish television ratings charts, where it outdid all the network shows.

To Maidie's intense relief Chic's roving eye was scarcely in evidence at all during the run, though it was possibly because he was becoming increasingly short-sighted. Many of the girls in the show had their eye on the still-dashing Chic none the less, and on one particular evening Maidie noticed that he seemed to be directing his patter toward a plump blonde who was seated in the middle of the front row. Maidie stood with him as the audience burst into applause half-way through their act. As they took a bow she whispered to him. 'You surely don't think she's good-looking, do you? Get your specs on, Chic—the woman's cock-eyed. One eye's going for a message and the other's coming back with the change!' Although Chic gave his partner a thorough glaring as this information sank in, he couldn't help feeling that the blonde didn't look half as attractive as she had before.

When the season was over and they returned to Edinburgh it was to a period of renewed tension, with Chic's idiosyncrasies again to the fore. Maidie had to be careful that she did or said nothing that would spark his anger. A simple meal of bacon and eggs for breakfast—his favourite—could be an ordeal if everything wasn't just perfect. When everything was just right, however, he was lavish in his praise of

Maidie's cooking. Another breakfast favourite was a plate of kippers and as they were served he would sing away merrily, 'Oh, them golden kippers!'

One morning after a late breakfast Chic had a bath that stretched to lunchtime. 'I felt like a good soak,' he later explained. Maidie had the lunch made and sent Douglas up to tell Chic it was on the table. 'He says he wants it in the bathroom,' Douglas said on his return. Maidie just stood there in the kitchen, not knowing whether to laugh or cry. Douglas shrugged his shoulders, looking for all the world like a younger version of his Dad as he said, 'Just give it to him, Mum. Why bother if that's what he wants?' From this start Chic would regularly take a tray up to the bathroom when he wanted to dine alone, so that it ceased to be an event to be talked about and became just one of Chic's funny ways. He would disdainfully claim, 'There was nothing funny about it! I was always relaxed in the bathroom and you should be relaxed when you eat. It aids digestion.'

Normally Chic kept clear of all the household chores, with a single exception in which he took great pride—for he seemed at his happiest when building and lighting a simple coal fire, although even this involved tension for those around him. Their return to Edinburgh coincided with a coal shortage and one day Chic took the initiative, driving to a coal yard and proceeding to load up the boot of his car. He decided against unloading the coal when he got back home—no, it was his coal and it might as well remain in the boot until required. Henceforth he would use the car boot as a coal cellar, bringing it into the house as required, a shovelful at a time.

When building the fire he would make the base of twists and sticks before picking up the pieces of coal one at a time. Each would be examined and polished before the holy moment arrived and the fire was lit. He would then sit, transported, an expression of childlike contentment on his face. 'You'd have thought he was witnessing the very dawn of creation,' said Maidie, 'but I knew it took him back to the hearth in his parents' home in Bank Street.'

Another of his rituals was the simple luxury of having his feet washed and dried by Maidie. He would ask her to bring him a pan of hot water, then would sit with his trouser legs rolled up, in seventh heaven. 'Don't forget the joins!' he would specify as Maudie towelled his feet dry. Baffled, she had first asked him in the early days which area the 'joins' constituted. Chic replied impatiently that this was where the dry bits met the wet bits—surely everyone knew that?

One night while he was having his feet washed and issuing the usual instructions, he suddenly stopped and stared pensively ahead, a blissful smile on his face. 'Maidie,' he said. 'We're going to give up show-business completely. I've had a great idea.' Maidie was too tired to consciously act the stooge, but carried out the function anyway on automatic pilot. 'What'll we do instead, Chic?' she asked. 'What's your idea?'

'It's a sure-fire money-maker. We'll open a chain of wishing-wells!'

After this uncomfortable and tentative spell at home Maidie began to wonder if there was something niggling at Chic, like a health worry he wasn't prepared to talk about. Their next engagement—at Blackpool—confirmed her fears. After the last show of their first night there, they had a supper of fish and chips brought to them in their dressing-room, before driving back to their small private hotel. All the way Chic complained of feeling unwell. 'I'm starting to get pains,' he groaned. 'They're like birth pains.' Maidie permitted herself a smile, 'How would you know?' she almost asked, but bit her tongue.

On arriving at the hotel they found the owners at the door to greet them. They were off to spend the night with some friends, they explained, and would be back at breakfast time the following morning. Chic and Maidie could have the run of the house since they were the only guests. When they left, the couple climbed the stairs to their bedroom, Chic moaning all the way. 'The pains are getting worse,' he complained. 'Try to get some sleep,' suggested Maidie as he paced up and down the bedroom. Chic got into bed and lay with the light on, then after a while got up and continued his pacing up and down.

'Maidie, why don't you do something?' he cried.

'Chic, I don't know how bad it is. Do you want to get a doctor?'

'Don't be so bloody silly. Haven't you got any aspirins or something that would ease the pain and let me get a night's sleep? Am I not even entitled to *that*?'

Maidie paced the floor with him. 'I do have some aspirins. Maybe between them and a hot bath—' Chic brightened up immediately, 'That's it! A steep!' He groaned again as another spasm hit him. As he got into the bath he said to Maidie, 'This might be the very dab. Worth a try. Why couldn't you have thought of this earlier?' After soaking for over an hour he donned his towelling bath robe. 'Is it any better?' asked Maidie anxiously. 'No, it isn't,' he replied, and Maidie noticed that he was beginning to look decidedly subaqueous around the gills. 'Chic, I'll need to get you to hospital,' she told him, feeling a sudden twinge of panic. This time there was no argument. He was in agony.

After dressing hurriedly they both went downstairs, to find they were locked in. In vain Maidie searched for a key, then ran round the windows of the ground floor, finding all of them either stuck or locked. Meantime Chic's groans were becoming more and more heartfelt. Rapidly becoming panic-stricken, Maidie now dashed upstairs to their bedroom, then shouted for Chic to come and join her. 'This window's open,' she explained. 'Come on, Chic. We'll have to go down the fire escape.'

His breathing was becoming laboured. 'I don't know if I can make it,' he informed her. 'You'll need to try,' she told him. 'We've got to get you to a hospital.'

Somehow or other they made it through the window and on to the rickety fire escape, quickly getting soaked in the heavy drizzle that was falling. The gate leading out of the back garden to the path next to the garage seemed to be stuck as well, so they both had to clamber over the wooden pailings. Suddenly Chic let out a terrifying yell. 'Oh, God,' he said, 'I'm stuck!' Although Maidie was almost beside herself by this time with worry about Chic's pain and fear of his ire—*she*, somehow or other, had to be at the bottom of this whole mess—this was too much. '*Move*, Chic,' she yelled. 'I've done everything else for you, but only you can sort that out.' With the odd yelp he extricated himself, then bravely attempted a laugh as he saw the funny side of it. 'That's torn it,' he declared. 'I'll need *two* operations now!'

By the time they reached the car they were both soaked. 'Do you know how to get to hospital?' Chic wanted to know, as Maidie reversed the car out of the drive. 'I've got a good Scots tongue in my head,' Maidie replied. Soon Chic was being loaded on to a stretcher at Blackpool Infirmary. With gall-stones diagnosed, a painkiller was administered before Chic was put to bed for the night, looking forlorn and distraught.

As Maidie drove back to the deserted house, she tried to relax, but her heart was pounding. Once again her nerves felt as if they had been shredded and mangled. 'If one of us had to have gall-stones,' she thought, 'why couldn't it have been me?'

In the morning Chic looked even more forlorn, not to say downright sorry for himself. 'I'll never get out of here,' he whispered despondently to Maidie. 'I'll bet they're going to keep me in. They say it's gall stones, but I'm not so sure. You'd better tell the theatre to have Frank Sinatra standing by.'

A moment later a young doctor stopped by and cheerfully told Chic he could leave immediately. A complete end was put to his melodramatics with a brisk, 'Just take plenty of liquids, Mr Murray, and you'll be right as rain.'

'They're barbarians,' grumbled Chic as he piled into a taxi. 'What do they know?'

Six months later the pains recurred and Chic was admitted to the Royal Infirmary of Edinburgh, where he was successfully operated on. The break gave him a chance to stop and take a look at himself. At 40 he was no longer a kid and all the expressions he had ever heard about ageing now ricocheted around in his brain. 'More years behind you than you have in front' and 'You're on the slippery slope' seemed to register more strongly than 'Life begins at 40', since the logic of that escaped him.

He had prided himself on his abundantly wavy hair. Now the hair line was receding and he was getting thin on top, something his tartan bunnet served to hide. It had been necessary to get a second pair of spectacles within a year—dear God, he was falling to bits. It was like a horror movie. Was this what they called the midlife crisis?

On their first engagement after his discharge, at the Newcastle Empire, Chic began to disappear each night after the last show, leaving Maidie to make her own way back to the hotel. When she tackled him, he explained that he needed lots of fresh air since his operation and a long walk before turning in to ensure he had a good sleep. Maidie let it go.

When the change of programme came on in the second week, Maidie steered their band-call through with her usual skill while Chic lugubriously hung around. Since the rehearsal was overrunning, she tried to cut it short. On their last song, 'Nobody's Darlin' But Mine', where the melody in the three verses and three choruses was identical, she shaved a few precious minutes. 'We'll take it from the top,' she told the conductor, 'as written. Give me just the intro, the first verse, then jump straight to the sixth and rallentando.'

After the first show that night, Chic grumbled about the band being ragged. When there was no improvement after the second show, Chic strode into the wings after their curtain call and let fly. 'You should have taken them through the whole six fucking verses this morning!' he raged. Maidie went bright red with embarrassment as the rest of the cast came and went. 'Look, Chic,' she said, 'don't shout and swear at me in front of the stagehands. If you want to give me a row, do it when we're alone.' Chic glared at her for a few seconds, then strode into their dressing-room, while Maidie meekly followed behind. As soon as the door was shut he started again.

'All right to speak to my wife now, is it? I suppose you *liked* that ragged accompaniment!'

Maidie slumped into a seat. 'All right Chic,' she said. '*You* take charge of rehearsals from now on. I'm tired of it. I've had enough. From now on it's you.'

'Now you're being *silly*!'

'Am I?' She felt a burst of defiance, the 'feartie-cat' finding her voice. 'Am I being *silly* about your nightly disappearances as well? Who have you got in tow this time, another of your old boilers?'

'None of your damned business!' he exploded, then turned and walked out the door, slamming it shut behind him. Maidie sat for a moment and stared at her reflection in the dressing-room mirror, with its little semi-halo of lights, while Chic strode toward the stage door, furiously wiping the last of the grease-paint from his face with a towel.

He knew that with every escalation of the scenes with Maidie they were becoming inexorably torn apart. So the hair *was* falling out and the eyesight was away to hell. At least something was still in full working order—for the moment at least, he reminded himself wryly.

As usually happened after each confrontation, there came a period where living together was like walking on eggs, followed by a truce, then a period of relative calm and even a semblance of normality. The family knitted together again and all went well—Chic would be like his old self, still fairly impossible, but lovable at the same time.

'I fancy something tasty for supper,' he declared one night while they were enjoying some time off, reading and watching Douglas and Annabelle do their homework. Maidie put down her book. 'I'll make you something, Chic. What do you fancy?'

'No, no, you take it easy, Maidie,' he said. 'It's a fish supper I fancy. Food of the Gods! Off I go, won't be long.'

Maidie stared after him in disbelief. Chic proved time and time again that he was never a man to be sold short. It was like a scene from *Happy Families* and while Maidie felt a sense of incongruity, the change was a welcome one. She fussed around while Chic was gone, for she knew his very precise requirements with fish and chips. There had to be masses of freshly buttered plain bread, mugs of hot tea and 'Daddy's Favourite' sauce on the table. Fifteen minutes after leaving a distraught-looking Chic appeared at the door. 'Come out and see what's happened, Maidie,' he implored.

He had been unable to find a parking space and had double-parked in the street. He had placed the fish suppers on the bonnet, then inadvertently shut the driver's door with the lock button down. Unfortunately the key was in the ignition and the car was still running. Maidie surveyed the damage—surely, she was thinking, I can't possibly be blamed for this? To make matters worse Chic had parked virtually in the middle of the road, with stationary cars on either side and no room for anyone else to get through. Now there was a car positioned at either end waiting impatiently for Chic to make a move.

'Why haven't we got a spare key?' shouted Chic to the heavens. 'Oh, God, no,' Maidie thought, 'I knew it would be me!' Then 'Hold on,' she told him, 'entertain the other cars for a moment,' before she disappeared into the house to hunt for a wire coat-hanger.

In less than a minute she reappeared with it and the car door was opened, while Chic looked on, open-mouthed in admiration. She then got into the driver's seat and yelled at the driver in front to back up so she could move out. Chic neatly removed the fish suppers from the bonnet before Maidie took off.

One of the drivers loudly demanded Chic's address so he could report him to the authorities. 'C/o the Conservative Club, Moscow,' he yelled back defiantly, before following Maidie into the house. Once inside all was sweetness and light, redeemed by the adept use of the coat-hanger.

'Maidie, what you did there was amazing,' Chic declared. 'If we ever get around to a crest for this family, crossed wire coat-hangers will be given serious consideration!' Soon they were all tucking in to their fish and chips. 'Best I've ever tasted, and piping hot,' Chic declared. 'Must have been the heat from the bonnet!'

'What if Mum hadn't been able to get into the car?' asked Douglas innocently. Chic popped the last chip into his mouth as Maidie gulped and awaited the answer. 'Well now, Douglas—as to that . . . you're quite good at history, aren't you? Then you must know that the whole history of the world could have been changed many times by the use of "What if?" . "What if", for example, your Mum and I had never met? You wouldn't be sitting there now enjoying this magnificent feast. Like one of my old pals, you might have been your auntie's bairn by the lodger.'

This tickled young Douglas. 'My auntie's bairn by the lodger!' he roared, leaving his fish and chips unguarded. 'And,' said Chic, as he pounced, 'I wouldn't be nicking half your chips as I am now!'

'Nick some of mine too, Dad,' Annabelle pleaded.

This remission didn't last, as Chic continued to alternate at the drop of a hat from loving concern to callous—and at times sadistic—indifference. At their very next engagement in Glasgow, he again chose to frighten the life out of Maidie. Minutes before the curtain was due to go up, he flatly declared, 'I'm not going on tonight. On you go yourself.'

'Chic, *don't!*' Maidie pleaded. 'You're terrifying me. My stomach's in a knot—don't do it.'

'That reminds me of a joke,' he replied, stony-faced. 'Man goes to the doctor, says, "Doctor, I've got butterflies in my stomach." Doctor says, "What have you been eating?" "Butterflies," he says!'

Maidie could feel herself breaking and jerked her head from side to side as she heard their cue being struck up. 'Chic—*why?*' she asked as he turned and walked away, leaving her to dance outstage alone.

Accordion to the fore, she started off, 'Be sure it's true when you say you love me—,' before she heard Chic's voice from the wings join in, '—it's a sin to tell a lie,' before he entered to a round of applause. Maidie felt a rush of relief, combined with a hot flush of anger.

One thing was becoming uppermost in her mind—there was a limit and she was nearing it.

The EMPRESS Playhouse
GLASGOW

PROGRAMME   Price 2d

13

Chic, Hotelier

'Lonnie Donegan? He's so nervous he even wears water wings in the shower. And he's so narrow-minded that when he gets an idea it comes out folded. At the drop of a hat he goes into a selection of his hits. Never mind, here's some good news for the deaf—he's got a new record coming out!'

'We'll need to regard it as a challenge, Maidie,' Chic declared.

'I just can't see it,' she replied, shaking her head. ' "There's a Blue Ridge" will have to go, that's for sure. We can't look out of date.'

'Well, there's one thing for sure. I'll be damned if we're going to introduce rock'n'roll into our act just for the occasion.'

'Oh, come on Chic, we have to bend a little. Let's enter into the spirit of the occasion.'

The event in question was a lucrative booking they had accepted at Great Yarmouth, where Larry Parnes was presenting a rock'n'roll bill featuring his stable of discoveries. Billy Fury was the show's topper, supported by Joe Brown, Marty Wilde, Karl Denver, the Tornadoes and the Vernon Girls. The shrewd Parnes saw Chic and Maidie as a way of getting the show over to all ages.

Chic grumbled as Maidie suggested a new song here and a change of pace there, but eventually he saw there was room for compromise and even began to relish the prospect of taking on the teenage favourites on their own ground. Since it was a seaside booking, Douglas and Annabelle were taken along for the season, while Chic declared himself singularly unimpressed with his partners on the bill. Before a full-blown 'them and us' situation could arise, the chirpy Joe Brown effortlessly bridged the gap, for he enjoyed Chic's humour and soon had the whole cast laughing along with him—at his own cockneyfied impersonations of Chic. 'I'm not a bloody relic, you know,' Chic declared in mock indignation as Joe explained that the rest of the troupers regarded him as a cult figure, but he was clearly flattered.

Young Douglas was with them for the season. 'It was funny to be alongside the rockers after seeing them on telly and buying an odd record of theirs. Billy Fury was the biggest surprise. I thought he'd be a total pain in the arse after his telly appearances but one night I sat in the back of the stalls and watched his act. It was incredible. If he'd come along now with all the video paraphernalia and promotions he would have been a top international star. After a couple of nights Billy had to leave the show—nobody could credit a young chap like that was suffering from heart trouble—and Joe Brown was pushed into top billing, with Rolf Harris brought in to replace him. Oh, and Mum and Dad went down really well.'

Chic decided to join in the spirit of things with a vengeance, introducing a comedy version of the recent chart hit by Mitchell Torok, 'When Mexico Gave Up the Rumba', which had exactly the desired effect of cutting across all age barriers. The advent of the rock'n'roll craze in Britain had given variety theatres a fresh injection of life, but Chic could see even then their days were numbered. Television had overnight brought variety into people's homes and it was no longer necessary to troop down to a local theatre in all weathers and pay admission. What variety was experiencing with packed houses for these rock shows was not a revival as many thought, but merely a period of remission before the inevitable decline continued.

*   *   *

When the neighbouring house in Bruntsfield Terrace came up for sale, a council of war was called, Chic's idea being to buy it and convert the two properties into a hotel. There would still be plenty of room for the family and with the hotel paying its way they would be living in rent-free accommodation. His eyes were aglow as he enthusiastically outlined the project to Maidie—why, in the future it would provide jobs for Douglas and Annabelle and in the meantime they would hire staff to start them off. Naturally, it would be called the Chic Murray Hotel. 'And I'll never drink anywhere else,' he promised. 'I don't doubt it,' said Maidie, who had noted Chic's increasing fondness for a tipple.

She went along with the plan, reckoning that if one house was a good investment, then two houses must be twice as good. They had just been invited to do an eight-week Australian tour, which made Chic even more enthusiastic. 'All the conversion can take place while we're away,' he explained. 'That's right, leave me to take care of the workmen,' Anne Dickson chipped in. 'No one more capable,' he assured her, for over the years he had developed a great admiration for the lady.

The purchase completed and the conversion plans approved, the couple looked excitedly at the itinerary for the Australian tour. They were to fly first to New York to meet Neil Kirk, who had landed them a date on the Jack Paar TV show, then it was on to Chicago, San Francisco, Los Angeles, Las Vegas and the Fiji Islands before their arrival in Melbourne to begin their dates. They would be out of the country for a total of ten weeks and had a couple of dates in Scotland on their return before opening in Lonnie Donegan's Christmas show with Miki and Griff at the Hippodrome in Birmingham. 'I'm going to miss the kids terribly,' Maidie whispered as they left in a taxi for their flight to London. 'So will I,' admitted Chic, 'but Maidie, this is a grand chance for the two of us to have a complete break on our own.'

'Show me a good time, baby,' Maidie implored, half-joking and wholly in earnest.

'I'll do my damndest,' Chic replied.

He delighted in showing Maidie round the sights of New York, although he never quite got the knack of avenue-skipping. Finding his way from street to street was easy with the numbering system, but the avenues were trickier and often defeated him. First they would go from number to number, then Lexington and Madison would creep in. 'It gets so you don't know where you've been,' Chic complained.

Maidie had no desire to join Chic in another Skid Row expedition, but Chinatown and Little Italy were of great interest, followed by the famous Staten Island ferry trip. Together they climbed the Statue of Liberty, looking out from the spikes on the helmet to the breathtaking view below. 'Look, Maidie. You can almost see Gene Kelly, Frank Sinatra and Jules the Munchkin from here,' he whispered. Altman's famed Fifth Avenue store was the next stop ('A bit like a superannuated Woolworth's,' said Chic) followed by Lord & Taylor's and Bendel's. 'Have a Bendel's bonnet,' he urged. Maidie laughingly declined.

All too soon their free weekend had almost come and gone, but Neil Kirk had a special treat lined up for their Sunday dinner date, booking them a table at Jack Dempsey's restaurant. The famous boxer came up to their table and personally introduced himself with: 'Neil tells me you're hotter than hell back in blighty. Remember, when you make it here—I knew you when!' He insisted they have their photographs taken together for his personal collection, prominently displayed along the walls of the restaurant, then they just had to sample some of his famous cheesecake. The evening ended with the ex-champ signing the menu for the couple before waving them on their way.

On the way back to their hotel, Neil mentioned he had someone in mind who might be ideal to handle them in the US. 'You'll meet him on your way back from Australia,' he told the excited pair. Back at the Belvedere Chic got into conversation with the liftman and discovered he was from Port Glasgow of all places. The three of them chatted away about the 'dirty wee port', then it was off to bed with a farewell of 'See you the next time I'm in the lift!'

Neil had promised to telephone them in the morning regarding their appearance on the Jack Paar show, for which they had been tentatively booked. Unfortunately, the news was not good. A major show-business scandal had just broken and Paar intended to devote the entire programme to the combatants, with his other projected guests now on hold. Since they had to be in Chicago the very next day, that was the end of the Paar show.

For Chic the highlight of the week in the States would be the Dempsey evening; for Maidie it was the discovery of San Francisco, the City by the Bay. They took the ferry over to Sausalito and together explored the wonders of the giant redwood forest nearby. 'What does it remind you of?' Maidie asked, as they stood in the majestic stillness. 'The Firth of Clyde at five o'clock on a Sunday morning,' he replied. 'Me too,' Maidie agreed.

Their shows in Melbourne were to prove a great success and the Chevron Hotel chain for whom they worked pleaded with them to stay longer. 'You could run for a year in Melbourne alone,' they were told, but their answer was, 'Perhaps another time,' for they knew they had to move on. Quite apart from the dates they had lined up back in Britain, Maidie was already desperately homesick. They triumphed again on Australian TV's Channel 7, then it was on to Sydney for their last cabaret performances before the start of their journey home.

After a stop-over in Las Vegas it was back to New York, where Neil greeted them excitedly at the airport. 'I'm sure I've got just the guy for you,' he declared, 'name of Nathaniel Silverstein. Unfortunately he's in Chicago, but his plane gets into Idlewild tomorrow two hours before you take off for blighty—there'll be time enough to talk.'

With their flight to London leaving at 9 p.m. and Silverstein's domestic Chicago flight due at 5.30 p.m., Chic watched as Maidie packed for their return to the airport. She was quiet and withdrawn. 'Let's sit and talk this out,' he coaxed her gently. 'Tell me what's on your mind.'

Maidie came straight to the point. 'I'm quitting the act,' she declared, 'as soon as we finish our commitments back home.'

Chic was ashen. 'Quitting? *Quitting*? How can you talk of this when we're due to meet Silverstein—'

'That's just the whole point,' said Maidie. 'If he takes you on—*when* he takes you on, it's like a new beginning. You know I've edged myself out of the act anyway, Chic—you're the star, you're the comic. And I've had it with all this travelling. I've been doing it since I was four. I think I've earned a rest. I'll be there—but on the end of the phone. As for the rest—you'll need to buzz along on your own. You'll manage. You could get a jeely piece at any door, for all your helplessness! Now come on, Silverstein's waiting.'

He turned out to be a small, conservatively-dressed individual with distinguished grey hair and a cool, imperturbable manner. 'Neil's told me all about you,' he informed Chic, 'and I'm kind of intrigued by the challenge. By the way, I would never take you on if I didn't think I could break you big in the States—it would be a waste of your time and mine. Let's you and me and Maidie talk for a while.'

'Mr Silverstein' Chic interrupted.

'Call me Nate.'

'Nate, the act is *me*. Solo.'

Nate smiled. 'Maidie wants to be included out? So—let's talk.'

For the next hour Chic talked as if his life depended upon it. Maidie felt proud as she listened to the way he put himself over, parrying and anticipating Silverstein's questions and letting some of the Chic Murray flavour bubble to the surface in every answer. 'Dear God,' thought Maidie, 'if it was me—I'd hire him!' Silverstein's face remained impassive for the most part, although Chic would have sworn he saw the start of a smile once or twice. Or was it his imagination? After a full hour, Silverstein turned to Neil Kirk. 'Neil,' he said. 'I'm impressed with your boy. I think we could do something together. I've already got just the germ of an idea, but I need to mull it over for a couple of days, then I'll phone you.'

Turning to Maidie he said, 'It was a privilege meeting you—you're a real lady and you've made a very unselfish decision. There could be something for your husband on his own. He could be a very big star— with a little bit of help, of course.' All he said to Chic was, 'You'll be hearing from Neil. Meantime, don't take any wooden nickels!' Then he was off, leaving Neil to comment, 'I think it sounds hopeful.' Chic was silent until Neil asked him what he thought. 'Me?' asked Chic. 'My mouth's too dry to think! Oh, I'm probably in with a shout. I don't know if he's impressed with me or not, but I'm certainly impressed with him!'

Their goodbyes made, they boarded their flight to London. Silverstein had certainly given nothing away, but there was hope. While Chic dreamed his dreams of fame in America, the thought that kept Maidie going was of holding her children in her arms once more.

A week later a call came through from Neil Kirk. Nate Silverstein, he explained, was not a typical show-business manager. He never got over-excited or carried away with hyperbole, but had called Neil to tell him how enthusiastic he was about working with Chic. In trying to decide how best to present him he had come up with a plan that was audacious and far-seeing. He would open him in cabaret in Greenwich Village initially and let the word spread around town that a new comic had arrived. With guest appearances following on television, the aim was to present Chic in his own one-man show off Broadway within the year. He intended to fly to Britain in a few weeks' time to discuss Chic's availability and the likely timetable for the New York launch.

Chic was stunned and could hardly communicate the news to Maidie and the family at first, but when he did he was met with excited hugs and kisses. He told Maidie he would immediately begin to put down on paper the ideas that had been simmering for the States. 'For once I'm going to discipline myself to do it,' he said. 'I can't let that man down.'

The season ahead with Lonnie Donegan brought its own anxieties, which Chic spelled out as they drove down to start rehearsals. 'I just hope he hasn't got any illusions about acting the big star with *me*.'

Maidie sighed. 'Come on, give him a chance—what's wrong with you? You've never even met him.'

'I know, I know,' Chic nittered away. 'I'll just keep my powder dry and if he starts acting the goat—I'll blast him off the face of the earth!'

For some reason Maidie could hardly keep her face straight at this. 'I'll bet Donegan turns out to be a real sweetie pie,' she offered. 'He's a *pie* merchant all right,' Chic conceded tersely. 'Well, he's on the Pye *label*, that's near enough! And me a Parlophone Recording Artiste—well, for a day anyway. Never the twain should meet! Parlophone's like royalty compared to little Pye, you know. I shouldn't even be *talking* to him!'

Even so, they duly reported to the Hippodrome to begin rehearsals for the *Lonnie Donegan Christmas Show*. Donegan was at the top of his career, having left the Chris Barber skiffle group to go out on his own and landing himself a whole run of smash hits. Naturally, the inevitable happened—Chic and Lonnie hit it off immediately and became firm friends. Maidie found that she could comfort herself when Chic had disappeared in the fairly certain knowledge that he would be in Lonnie's company, swapping endless stories of their musical and other adventures over the years—and slagging each other off.

'Of course *I* invented skiffle in Britain,' Chic told him, perfectly deadpan.

'Oh, yes. How do you work that out, you old codger?' Lonnie asked, 'and where was I?'

'You weren't even a plucked string on your daddy's guitar, laddie,' Chic bellowed, 'there's no doubt about it, I laid the groundwork for you. I expect you'll get around to stealing "I'm Gonna Drink My Coffee from an Old Tin Can" next. Just you try it! I'll do a Vipers on you and put out a cover version!'

'I hear your recording career began and ended with one solitary Parlophone record,' Lonnie riposted, a remark Chic could not let go by.

'*One* Parlophone record is worth a *million* of your Pyes,' he replied. 'That's all you are, Donegan, a flaming pie merchant—imagine getting a gold disc for selling a dozen pies! Myself, I always buy the Vipers versions of your songs—I find they're superior, *listenable* even. "My Old Man's a Dustman" indeed—at least I'll say this, you're honest about it. Must be the first autobiographical hit ever!'

Lonnie affected his best 'slow burn', then shot back with, 'Chic, I know you and Maidie are the hottest thing since Old Mother Riley and Kitty McShane—the only question is, which is which?'

Chic moved in for the kill. 'Away you go back to Chris Barber—not that he'd have you back, not after that farewell record he dedicated to you, "Petite Fleur". Donegan the hooligan—you're well named!'

And so it went on endlessly, with Maidie suggesting the two of them should get together as a double act. 'Don't give him ideas above his station. Don't build up his hopes,' was Chic's reaction.

'I don't need another roadie,' cracked Lonnie.

On Christmas Eve the couple were relaxing in their hotel suite before leaving for the theatre, Chic dozing in the sitting room while Maidie fussed about getting ready. She answered the telephone, then ran over to wake her husband. 'It's Neil Kirk,' she told him. While Chic took the call, Maidie packed their change of clothing for the Christmas Eve party Lonnie had invited them to after the show.

Five minutes later Chic came through to the bedroom and stared at Maidie with a stricken expression on his face. 'It's Nate Silverstein,' he said finally. 'He's been involved in a multiple pile-up on the New Jersey Turnpike. Maidie, he's dead.'

She saw Chic struggle through his performances that evening, like a robot going through the motions. They explained to Lonnie why they could no longer attend his party and left the theatre quietly after the last show. Chic had started a notebook with America in mind, which he showed Maidie before closing it and throwing it on the fire. Maidie could see the scrawl 'American Gag Book' before the flames blackened it over. 'There it goes up in smoke, just like my American conquest,' he said, shaking his head as Maidie looked on helplessly. 'Every artist needs someone who believes in him and that wee guy was the one. I'd have jumped in the Hudson if he'd told me to.'

*   *   *

With the licence eventually granted the hotel opened for business, the large sign outside proclaiming the Chic Murray Hotel. Douglas, now turned 17, started work under the manager they had appointed, together with Black Bottle Bill, a handyman so named since he drank only Guinness or Johnnie Walker Black Label whisky. Chic was as good as his word and did most of his drinking on the premises, but Maidie soon found this was far from being an advantage. Often he would take a pint glass, fill it half-way up with dark rum, then ask Maidie, 'Do you think that's about a measure?'

Another family 'holiday' came about as they fulfilled a booking for the summer season at Gwrych Castle near Abergele. The grounds had been turned into an entertainment centre with all the attractions free once the visitors had paid their shilling entrance fee (sixpence for children). Billed as 'the most amazing shilling's worth ever!' the castle grounds boasted a miniature railway, a vintage fire engine, a mini-zoo and a chamber of horrors. ('That's probably what they want us for,' Chic declared.) The couple were featured in a large marquee in the grounds, the same one in which boxing champion Randolph Turpin had been engaged to do his sparring matches. They did a matinée each afternoon, then two shows in the evening, but with Douglas, Annabelle and Granny Dickson along it really was more like a holiday than work.

Their quarters at the site consisted of an up-to-the-minute luxury caravan. Apart from the occasional reassuring telephone call from Black Bottle Bill to say that the toilets were flooded or the roof was falling in back at the Chic Murray Hotel, their spell at Gwrych Castle was a relaxed family affair.

On their return to the hotel, it seemed that there had indeed been a catalogue of disasters in their absence, culminating in Black Bottle's fall from the roof while trying to fix up a new aerial. Luckily his fall had been broken by Maidie's rosebed, which looked distinctly forlorn and battered. In the post was an offer for the duo to tour South Africa on a bill with Kenneth McKellar and Moira Anderson. 'All that sunshine,' said Chic, rubbing his hands with delight. 'Jo-han-nes-bur-g, here we come. Oh, I'd love to go to Durban in a turban!'

'Here *you* come,' said Maidie. 'I told you in the States I'd finish the run of gigs we had and that would be it.'

'But, Maidie—'

'*No*, Chic. Leave me to run the hotel and off you go on your own. If you want room service, pick up the phone. If you're hungry, eat. If you're thirsty, drink. And if you want to gallivant around, I won't be there to see it.'

'Oh, be *fair*.'

'Fair? Is that what you've been to me? You're behaving yourself just now—at least I *think* you are—but how long will it last? I resigned myself a long time ago to the fact that I'm no Elizabeth Taylor, but you seem convinced you're Richard Burton. I still love you, Chic, despite your best efforts to kill it—'

'I never—'

'Maybe not *deliberately*, Chic, but the effect's just the same. We'll need to regard this tour as a trial separation . . .'

'A what?'

'A *trial* separation. God, Chic, we've been living in each other's pockets for so long—I can't *remember* a time when I haven't been on the move. I feel pummelled to bits. Let's just have the break and see how it goes. While you're away, I'll act as assistant manager and try to get this place off the ground.'

Maidie had been able to hear herself speak, but the words that came out did not seem to be her own. Afterwards, she could hardly believe her resolution; even feartie-cats had their moments of courage, it seemed— or was she just the worm who had turned?

'No more Chic and Maidie?' she heard him say. 'I can see the headlines now: "SMALL DOLL LEAVES TALL DROLL!" "TALL DROLL THROWS HIMSELF INTO LARGE HOLE".'

Maidie smiled. 'There'll be no headlines,' she replied. 'We'll do it quietly—we've one more show at the Gaiety in Ayr. Let's just finish it there without any announcement or fuss.'

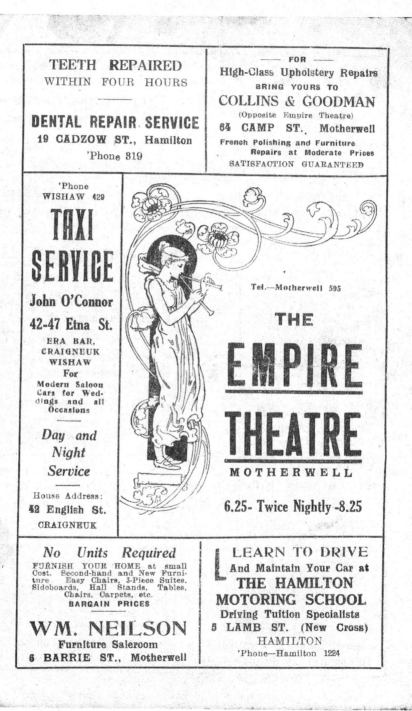

MURRAY

14

Split-Up

'Orson Welles? The man's a nutcase. Imagine doing a remake of King Kong and calling it Citizen Kong. I told Orson I think he's the laziest man I've ever met—fancy marrying a pregnant woman! And he's very illogical. He bought a book on pornography and doesn't even own a phonograph! And did you know that his idea of a balanced diet is a large glass of brandy in each hand?'

The entire South African trip felt to Chic as if it wasn't really happening. Despite the help and camaraderie from Kenneth McKellar and Moira Anderson, Chic missed his wife desperately both on and off the stage, as he related to anyone who would listen, although the reception he got bolstered his confidence.

A mysterious telephone call while in Durban gave him something to think about, although at first he put it down as one of Moira Anderson's famous pranks. As the call progressed, however, it began to sound more and more like the real thing. When would he be back in London? Would he be free to start shooting a film in July? He answered the questions as best he could, then with nothing whatsoever resolved at the end of the conversation, he made his way downstairs to the hotel lounge, where he spotted Kenneth and Moira having coffee.

'Are you at it?' he demanded of Moira. 'Of course, I'm always at it,' Moira breezily replied. 'I know you are, Anderson. But are you behind the movie offer I've just had?' Moira assured him that she had no idea what he was talking about and excitedly pressed him for all the details. 'Well,' said Chic, 'it seems that the producer of *What's New, Pussycat?* is making a new James Bond picture with Orson Welles as the baddie. He wants me to play his henchman.'

As the three friends discussed the offer, a drama was unfolding even then in the already chequered history of *Casino Royale.* Hollywood agent-turned-producer Charles K. Feldman had produced an unexpected smash hit with *What's New, Pussycat?*—a hit with the public at any rate, for the critics had given it a thorough roasting. He had been so pleased with Peter Sellers's contribution that he had presented him with a Rolls-Royce at the end of filming. For his next project Feldman had discovered that the rights to one of Ian Fleming's James Bond stories, *Casino Royale*, had slipped through the fingers of the regular producer of the Bond series, Cubby Broccoli. With these rights secured, Feldman planned his Bond movie as a gigantic send-up of the whole spy genre—to star Peter Sellers, of course. The only problem while the rest of the cast were being organised was—would Sellers come on board or not? David Niven was already set for the picture, as were Ursula Andress, Joanna Pettit and Daliah Lavi. Orson Welles had indeed agreed to play the villainous head of the spy ring SMERSH and Woody Allen and a host of 'guest stars' were set for cameo roles.

It was to be an all-star no-expenses-spared extravaganza, but still in Feldman's mind a nagging doubt remained to keep him off his sleep at night—the uncertainty of Sellers's agreement. With his last two pictures having been resounding smash hits, first as Inspector Clouseau in *A Shot in the Dark*, then in Feldman's own *What's New, Pussycat?*, Sellers had never been hotter and the producer saw him as the pivot around whom the whole project revolved. He was ready to concede to any demands Sellers wished to make—and these were already proving considerable.

As Chic, Kenneth and Moira discussed the offer in Durban, they had no way of knowing any of this, and it was only when Chic stopped off in London on the way back home to Scotland that he finally was convinced that the offer was genuine. In a daze he was informed that the fee would be £4,000 together with all his expenses, and extra money if filming went over schedule. Chic felt as if he hardly needed a plane to make the journey to Scotland—he could have flown all by himself. He could hardly believe that the offer had come along at this particular point— just after the decision to go solo. If he had been stranded at a career crossroads, it seemed he was now being pushed down the road to a film career. OK, he reminded himself, *if* it got made, then *if* he didn't make a complete fool of himself!

Sellers was still holding out at this point, but Feldman was daily living in hope, for in reality, even with a script, director and all the supporting cast lined up, without Sellers there could be no picture. In the next few months, while Sellers dithered and the project was on, then off again, Chic tried to lose himself with other work. To his delight there was no shortage of this and he kept his head well down with radio and TV spots as rumours flew as to whether *Casino Royale* would ever start production. Finally Feldman made his triumphant announcement. Sellers was signed.

Chic found himself called to London regularly for costume fittings and lighting tests, while his other dates took him to Birmingham, Manchester and Glasgow. Soon he was spending more and more time away from home until a growing sense of isolation began to take hold. He almost seemed a stranger in his own hotel, and frequently quarrelled with Maidie over some aspect or other of the hotel's running he found fault with. If Maidie had imagined that coping with Chic in short bursts would be easier, she soon found it was the other way around. Not only was it more difficult; she found she was not prepared to try.

'I was disoriented having to do so much for myself,' he later explained, 'and there were the months of uncertainty over *Casino Royale*. Maidie had her work cut out every day and got up to certainties, whereas my whole existence was in an uproar, travelling here and there and hanging on for phone calls. I'd set aside 12 weeks for the picture and if it didn't come off there was always going to be one helluva gap in my schedule. When Sellers finally signed his little piece of paper it made life easier for everyone—from Charlie Feldman at the top to Charlie Murray at the bottom!'

Before Chic was introduced to the director of the movie, a fellow Scot, Joe McGrath, he was already aware of the controversy surrounding McGrath's appointment, for it was perfectly clear that he was only there at Peter Sellers's behest. Columbia, who were to release the picture, were said to be unhappy that the director in charge of such a huge-budget project had no experience whatever of major movie-making, having been involved only with Sellers's *The Running, Jumping and Standing Still Film*, as well as some television work. As filming got under way at Shepperton studios, Sellers warmly shook Chic's hand and welcomed him to the film set. To his surprise Sellers seemed quite familiar with his work, to the extent of being able to quote the 'Genumph' story. After this happy start Chic had no further conversation with Sellers throughout the entire 16 weeks the picture would shoot.

Tension mounted as the arrival of Orson Welles on the set became imminent, for Sellers was going through one of his bouts of acute insecurity and was paranoid that Welles would try to tip the balance of the film away from him. Chic and the rest of the cast were astonished when they learned that Sellers was refusing to appear on the set while Welles was there, even in a card game sequence the two were supposed to enact. McGrath was given the task of shooting the two players separately and having to splice the results together—not the most felicitous way to make a picture, but he was given no choice.

When the mighty Orson did appear, he ran through his scenes with such ease that for a while the tension lifted and the atmosphere lightened. While he was there, Sellers was nowhere to be found and Chic found himself getting along famously with the legendary, somewhat awesome, but ultimately charming Mr Welles. He seemed to appreciate Chic's sense of humour, so had Chic cracking, 'He can't be all that bad!' Another columnist interviewed Chic and asked him how he was settling down to his first movie. 'Great!' Chic replied. 'So far I've been in two scenes and uttered five lines. But I've no complaints—it's given me time to open an "advice to the lovelorn" bureau on the set with Ursula Andress, Joanna Pettit and Daliah Lavi as my first customers. Poor girls—I'm doing all I can to help them, even to the extent of looking into their cases personally.'

Chic felt an icy shiver when it was announced that Joe McGrath was leaving the picture, for it seemed that Sellers had grown disenchanted with him. The film company covered the story up by maintaining that it had always been the plan to use a succession of directors for different sequences. Since Chic had most of his scenes in the can by this time he was not too concerned but it put something of a strain on his remaining weeks, for he had been asked to stay on—for extra money—to shoot a sequence involving a pipe band. He was also asked for his advice on where such a band might be found and promptly telephoned Maidie. The Edinburgh Police Pipe Band were quickly conjured up and flown to London for this key sequence, which involved Peter O'Toole in a guest role and Chic banging away at a drum.

Columbia nervously phoned Feldman as the costs on the picture went through the roof, but Feldman was reassurance itself. Since the picture would be a smash, he reasoned, what was an extra million or so? As a succession of directors came and went—John Huston, Ken Hughes, Robert Parrish and Val Guest followed Joe McGrath—Chic tried to remain aloof from all the power politics that went on and assiduously kept his place on the sidelines. 'It was all just funny money to me, anyway,' he later declared. 'I wasn't exactly carrying the film, though I wouldn't have minded carrying some of the cast, if someone had asked me—Ursula Andress for one!'

At the end of shooting, there was no Rolls-Royce presented this time to Peter Sellers by the distraught Charles Feldman, for the actor had apparently not even agreed to shoot the last few scenes necessary to make sense of his role. Chic attended the film's première in April 1967, given in aid of a mental health campaign, then flew home the next morning to meet Maidie and discuss the reviews she had assembled. The critics mercilessly tore the film apart, the only good news being that Chic's role had gone unremarked while all around him were savaged, Sellers in particular. Charles Feldman never recovered from the film's reception and its subsequent disastrous showing at the box-office, for *Casino Royale* was his last picture. A year after its release he was dead.

Maidie summed it up by saying, 'At least you got out of it unscathed, Chic. In years to come you can say you appeared in a Bond movie.'

'I know,' Chic agreed. 'Yet the whole thing seems such a waste. All that parading of egos while the money and the film went down the drain—oh well, I'm a few thousand quid better off—and several million wiser!' Just one week later Chic was back in London to do a BBC recording. He winced as he passed Leicester Square where *Casino Royale* was showing. He felt like tiptoeing past in case anyone spotted him— when someone did.

Chic's friendship with Archie McCulloch—who had been inadvertently responsible for his first booking—and Archie's wife, the singer Kathy Kay, had been kept up over the years. Now they had never seen Chic look so down. 'He asked us if we'd seen *Casino Royale*,' Kathy remembered. 'We assured him we hadn't and that seemed to brighten him up a bit. He really wasn't his usual chirpy self at all, though. We were staying at the Coburg Hotel in Bayswater while I was recording a *Billy Cotton Bandshow* for BBC TV, so we asked him to join us for dinner that night.'

Archie recalls how forlorn Chic seemed. 'He brightened up a bit when we asked him back—he really needed friendly company, it seemed. I'm sure he was lonely on his own in the big city. Anyway, our three boys took a real shine to him.'

Chic kept them amused all through dinner. 'We ate Italian and Chic took a fancy to the breadsticks, which I don't think he'd ever seen before. In our room afterwards he climbed on to a chair and conducted an imaginary symphony with them for the boys' benefit. He had them rolling about on the floor as he swung his arms elaborately bringing in the full orchestra, then made little tiny mincing movements for the piccolos.'

Kathy Kay remembers the end of the evening with Chic deflated again as the time to go approached. 'We knew he was hurting inside. He seemed to feel even then that he'd lost Maidie for good.'

Another relationship began to cool as Chic and Billy Marsh gradually lost touch. Chic came to the conclusion that if he could do without a stage partner, he could dispense with management as well. After *Casino Royale*, the feeling was that things could only get better as Chic personally negotiated a summer season in Perth where the conditions seemed ideal. He was to receive a basic salary for each week and a percentage of the takings when these exceeded a minimum sum. It was a similar deal to the Rothesay summer season he and Maidie had enjoyed, with Chic in charge of hiring the supporting acts. Unfortunately the whole thing was to break up in acrimony within a few weeks, with each side claiming the other had failed to live up to its obligations. Chic sued the company and was awarded a cash sum eventually, somewhat lower than he had claimed.

By this time both Douglas and Annabelle were working with Maidie in the hotel, which if anything served to increase Chic's feeling of isolation when he stayed with the family. On one occasion he arrived home to find Maidie in the living room chatting to an old acquaintance from the Borders. 'Oh, hallo, Chic. This is May Forbes from Selkirk,' Maidie greeted him. He stood there awkwardly at the door. Maidie continued, 'I haven't seen her for years, not since I last stayed in her digs in Galashiels.'

'Fancy that,' Chic said, deadpan.

May spoke up, 'I'm a great fan, Chic. Could you sign your autograph for me?'

Chic stared at Maidie for a moment, then announced, 'I can't do that! I don't even *know* this woman.' He then turned and walked upstairs to the hotel.

'That's just his funny way,' Maidie assured her astonished visitor.

When her friend had left, Maidie tracked Chic down to the bar. 'Look—before you start, I *didn't* know the woman,' he protested, before she even had a chance to speak. 'I can't be expected to go around willy-nilly sticking my name on bits of paper. My signature's a personal thing, not to be given lightly.' He downed his drink and ordered another.

'I know the strain you've been under,' she began. 'Maybe that's why you're drinking so much, I don't know. What I do know is this, Chic. I'm not prepared to have the legs knocked from under me any longer. We've split up professionally and I thought that would end your bully-boy tactics. Now I think nothing short of a divorce will do it.'

Chic stared at her in disbelief. 'Maidie, don't be daft,' he said.

'I'm *not* daft,' she replied. 'The kids are grown up now, well able to fend for themselves. I'm running this place as best I can, doing everything to make a go of it and all I get from you is your very worst side. I don't deserve it, Chic, and I don't see why I should have to put up with it any more. Now you can get another whipping boy—this one's had enough.'

Chic was stunned. When eventually he did speak it was in a whisper. 'And they say there's no place like home for the holidays!' he cracked.

Maidie looked at him, feeling he was like a wayward child she was desperately fond of, but one she simply could not control.

Douglas came over to Chic's table. 'Last call, Dad. Can I get you another drink?' Chic nodded, expressionless.

When Douglas had brought the drink he sat quietly with his father for a while. 'Dad,' he finally said, 'I've met this smashing girl and I want to get married.'

'That's good, son,' said Chic brightening a bit. 'Does your mother know?'

'Yes, Dad, but I wanted to talk it over with you both tonight.' Chic fell silent again at this and it was several minutes before Douglas spoke again. 'Dad, what's up?' he asked. 'You look as if you've seen a ghost.'

'I have,' Chic replied.

Chic's answer was to lose himself in work. In rapid succession he did a David Frost TV show, a *Does The Team Think?*, a *Joker's Wild* for Yorkshire TV and a Leslie Crowther TV show. His brief conversation with Maidie before leaving had held out little hope of a reconciliation, although he still chose to regard their spell apart as only a further trial separation. In this he was several paces behind Maidie, for whom South Africa and *Casino Royale* had served that purpose.

He found a bed-sit in Hillhead, Glasgow, strategically close to the BBC in Queen Margaret Drive. There was a bed, a couple of chairs, an electric fire and hotplate and a shared bathroom, toilet and telephone.

After a charity show one night at the King's Theatre in Glasgow he was introduced to a Mr and Mrs Young and their two young children. 'We had to come back and tell you how much we enjoyed your act. It was brilliant,' Anna Young enthused.

'That's what I like to hear,' Chic replied. 'You lot can come back again anytime.' The next time he was to meet the radiant blonde would be under the most tragic of circumstances.

A letter from William Davis, the editor of *Punch*, gave Chic what he regarded as 'a bit of a challenge'. The magazine planned to produce a special issue devoted entirely to Scotland and wanted him to contribute a 1,250-word article. Davis stressed that they were most anxious not to look like a gang of cockneys making jokes at the expense of the Scots, so most of the issue would be written by Scots themselves, and that the idea was to take a sharp, but affectionate look at Scotland and the Scots. Apparently the original cartoon, 'Bang Went Saxpence' had appeared in *Punch*, so they saw this special edition as following up in this great tradition. Chic's theme was to be 'How mean are the Scots?'

When the article was published, Chic had the last word, commenting on his 60-guinea fee from *Punch*, 'They should have asked me to do a follow-up, "How mean are the English?" After that I could have done the Welsh version, based on the lord of the manor and his stingy dresser called, "How mean was my Valet?"'

Willie Woodburn asked Chic along to a Rangers *v* Celtic match at Ibrox soon after this, in the company of Sean Connery. Chic had never met Connery—who turned out to be an admirer—and their conversation before the game centred not on football but on their other common interest—James Bond movies. Chic and Willie were busy cheering for Rangers, and cockahoop when they won handsomely. After the game, as the match's highlights were discussed, Willie was amused to find a note of uncertainty in Chic's conversation regarding Sean's allegiances. Soon it got to the point Chic was going over the top in his attempt to placate what he was convinced was Connery's disappointment with the final score. 'Celtic played a *really* good game, Sean,' he assured him, then later conceded, 'They *deserved* to do better,' and finally it was a totally magnanimous, 'I mean, they could have *won*, Sean!'

Late in 1970 Chic and Spike Milligan got together in Glasgow for a TV recording. Both turned out to be fans of the other, Spike greeting Chic with the words, 'I believe you've worked with a compatriot of mine, Monseigneur Sellers, n'est-ce pas?'

Chic cried, 'Am I ever to be tormented thus?' As soon as filming was finished for the night, the pair got together and disappeared to the studio canteen, where they sat chatting for hours. 'I've read your *Puckoon*, Spike,' Chic told him, 'total crap.'

Spike's eyes misted over and his eyebrows almost met in the middle as he endeavoured to absorb this rare compliment. 'I'll dedicate the next edition to you,' he promised, smiling beatifically. 'I can see it now: "To a little-known wee Scots comic I happened to come across one day in the meadow".'

Chic grinned. 'How dare you refer to my lady wife!'

Spike recalled the meeting with Chic many years later: 'Like W. C. Fields, he had a healthy disdain for the human race and he'd found his own ways to keep it at arm's length. "Did someone make you up?" he asked me. "Yes," I replied, "someone did. But *nobody* made you up, you made yourself up!" . To me he was one of the top comics in the world.' What did they talk about over dinner that night at the Rogano restaurant in Glasgow? Spike fell silent for a moment. 'Well, the bottles kept coming—' Could it be that they both got smashed out of their skulls? 'Oh,' Spike recalled, as if the thought had never before occurred to him and the truth was now revealed in a blinding flash of light. 'Answer: *yes*!!'

*   *   *

From the few conversations Chic now had with Maidie he knew that she intended to go ahead with divorce proceedings. Eventually a date was set in 1972. Chic still had the unreal feeling that the whole thing was happening to someone else, until the papers arrived requesting his presence in court. He looked at the words 'mental and physical cruelty' until they blurred before his eyes, then poured himself a drink. He kept pouring them until he sank into the void that afforded him peace of mind.

He woke up to hear the hall phone ringing. It was Douglas, with the news that his wife was expecting a baby. 'I'm pleased,' Chic told him, but a few hours later he had difficulty sorting out whether he had imagined the call. He woke up on the morning of the divorce after a fitful night. While Maidie would be in court in Edinburgh, he was to be interviewed by Pete Murray at the BBC in Glasgow. 'You should be in court yourself to defend the action,' his lawyer had told him. 'I've no defence,' he had replied, 'so I'm not going.'

He left his flat to have breakfast in a local café before reporting to the BBC. He was like a man in a daze and fretfully kept consulting his watch. Maidie wouldn't have left the house yet, he reasoned. Surely there was still time to stop her. They could start again. He dashed to a phone booth and dialled her number.

'Good morning, Maidie.'

'Oh, it's you. Good morning.' He started at the sound of her voice. It was flat and unemotional, the exact opposite of her nature. 'Maidie, I just wanted to ask you—'

'What, Chic?'

'—not to go ahead with this divorce. It's tearing me apart . . .'

'Chic, you've torn *me* apart for years. I'm sorry, but it's too late.'

'*Maidie!*' He heard the mechanical 'click' as she hung up on him.

Pete Murray was his usual thoroughly professional and sparkling self, but as the broadcast proceeded he could see that something was far wrong. Chic's replies were monosyllabic and lifeless, and it was all Pete could do to jolly along the interview. When it was mercifully over, he asked him if he felt all right. Chic stared glassily at him and replied, 'It's nothing personal, Pete. It's just that while we've been talking my life's gone out of the window. Maidie's in court at this very moment getting divorced from me.'

'God, I'm sorry,' said Pete, thoroughly taken aback. 'Naturally I'd no idea . . .' He sympathetically put an arm on Chic's shoulder.

'Don't feel sorry for me, Pete,' said Chic, drawing away. 'I'm getting what I deserve, but it doesn't make it hurt any less.'

Somehow he made it through the day. In the afternoon, he had a charity matinée to attend, then he knew he could be on his own. In Byres Road he collected a carry-out and made his way back to his flat. He stopped on the street as a thought struck him, then he found a phone booth and rang the number. 'Hallo, Maidie?'

'Hallo, Chic.'

'Is it all over then?'

'Yes, Chic.'

'Maidie, you'd never marry anyone else, would you?'

Maidie stood in her flat in Edinburgh, holding back the tears. 'No, I wouldn't, Chic,' she replied. 'At least—not anyone else like you.'

It was Chic's turn to hang up. Leaving the telephone booth, he walked the few remaining yards to his flat. He had eaten nothing all day and had one Scotch pie in his pocket to sustain him. Opening the first bottle of rum, he took a giant slug, then poured himself another. He took the Scotch pie from his raincoat pocket, then fastidiously removed a ballpen that was stuck in its middle. He looked at it in disgust before twirling it through the open window into the courtyard below and settling down once more to the rum bottle.

Duntermline
Opera House

PROGRAMME

COMMENCING
MONDAY, 22nd DECEMBER, 1947

15

Solo Act

'The chemist asked this lady, "What are your pills for?" She replied, "They're for my ulcer." "Oh", he replied, "there's no need to call me 'sir'. " Then he turned to me: "You're due some pills too. Will I put them in a box?" "Well," I said, "it'll save me rolling them all the way home!" '

Back in Edinburgh at the Chic Murray Hotel one particular customer who frequented the bar seemed to be there for only one reason—to engage Maidic in conversation. In the weeks leading up to the divorce Maidie had felt bruised and vulnerable, and the attentions of the persistent stranger proved an unexpected diversion. 'One kind word and I would have been anybody's,' was how she characterised her feelings at that time. 'Even then I kept asking myself if it had been my fault with Chic. If I'd been different—a stronger person, maybe—but in the end I knew it was hopeless to think along these lines. We are what we are and if in the end I was just too mundane—and meek and mild—for him, what could I do? I was no more able to change than he was. I'd ended up with an inferiority complex a mile wide and when some charmer came along and started paying attention to me, I was a pushover. One kind word did it.'

Anne Dickson helped her daughter out in the hotel occasionally during this time. She and Chic had enjoyed an 'arm's-length' relationship of equal strength and mutual respect, but now the doughty Anne recognised a change in the air and was the first to refer to Maidie's admirer in her own couthy way when she came downstairs from the bar one night to find Maidie cutting sandwiches in the kitchen. 'Your gentleman caller's arrived,' she announced, adding, 'his name's Terry, by the way.'

When the property-split in the wake of the divorce became effective, Chic sold his half of the hotel to Maidie, who intended at that point to keep it going, and then bought himself a brand new Reliant Scimitar ('Same as Princess Anne's got,' he informed all and sundry).

Soon after, Ian Christie at the BBC introduced him to Jenny Wales of the music department. Chic was a familiar figure in her office, popping his head round the door regularly, whether in connection with a programme he was doing or just for a cup of coffee and a chat. Jenny recalled these visits with great fondness: 'We would be upset if we hadn't heard from him for a while. Oh, sometimes he would be a terrible nuisance when he came barging in and demanded your instant attention. I would often be in the middle of sorting out a complicated music requisition and he'd suddenly appear, most of the time in full flood with his latest story. He just expected you to drop everything there and then. You knew instinctively how hurt he'd have been if you gave the impression that you hadn't time for him. I'd heard a few reports about his so-called meanness, by the way, like his reaction to being asked to pay his round—"You pay. After all, there's four of you and only one of me," was typical apparently—but I think that was misunderstood. I felt privileged just to have him spend time with me.'

A few months after the divorce, Chic had been working for the day in Jenny's department, sorting out some records for a request programme and tinkering away on the piano in the corner. 'Chic, I'm away,' he heard Jenny call. 'Do you want to stay for a while?'

'I'll do that. Goodnight, Jenny,' he replied, deep in concentration as he ran through his various ditties. It was the acoustics in the room, Chic decided—they were just too damned good! He felt the weight of passing time as he never had before and there in the darkening room he thought back to his time with the Chicks and Big Neilie, then recalled the thrill of Maidie fronting the group at the naval dance. He had heard the news that Aunt Tizzie had died just a week after the divorce, but he could still hear her words to him as she had looked at the tattoo on the back of his hand: 'Chic, I'll make this prediction now—that's one bird that will never leave you!' Further back still he went as he thought of his Uncle Alex and the practical help he had given him to get over his difficulties at school. Even Uncle Tom had his reprieve—why couldn't he have made an effort to get to know the man, Chic asked himself.

He stopped playing and sat quietly for a few minutes at the piano before reaching for the Safeway bag he had brought with him. It contained four scripts, including one he had recorded the day before. He rummaged among the other papers, which included some very dog-eared notes and a few bills, until he found what he was looking for. The sepia-tinted photograph was of a bright golden-haired youth, still in short trousers, standing on a beach. Inscribed across the bottom was 'William at Whitley Bay, 1892'. 'Hallo, Dad,' Chic said, then a few minutes later he carefully lowered the piano lid and tiptoed out of the room, closing the door quietly behind him. Climbing into his gleaming Reliant Scimitar he drove the few hundred yards to Byres Road, bought a double portion of fish and chips, then drove the remaining 50 yards home. After his supper and a mug of tea he settled himself down and fell asleep in his chair.

When he woke it was 10 p.m. He knew he would never get to sleep again if he went to bed, so he picked up a Zane Grey novel and poured himself a stiff rum. Several hours—and rums—later, he still felt wide awake and decided to retrieve the Safeway bag from the Scimitar and revise some of the scripts. As he entered the car and picked up the bag, his Dad's photograph fell out. Picking it up, he sat himself in the driver's seat and shut the door, then for fully 15 minutes he remained there, just staring at the photograph in the light of a nearby lamppost. The next thing Chic heard was the sound of someone telling him to get out of the car—it turned out to be a young policeman. Tucking his Dad's photograph safely away inside the Safeway bag, Chic obligingly opened the door—and promptly fell at the policeman's feet. After being helped up, he saw that there were two constables.

'Is this your car?' he was asked. 'I don't know,' he replied. 'Who owns the car, sir?' one of the constables pressed him. Chic stared at them morosely before replying, 'I've no idea. I stole it in Edinburgh yesterday.' After being duly cautioned, he was charged with being drunk in charge of a vehicle, then later for failing to provide a blood sample when this was requested. At the station he told the sergeant in charge, 'I've been terribly obstreperous. I have assaulted a vast number of people.' 'No, you haven't,' the sergeant replied. 'You're just a wee bit tired, Mr Murray. Not obstreperous at all.'

Later Chic would claim, 'Obstreperous? I was just pleased I could say a word like that so early in the morning!' At the subsequent trial, where he was represented by the renowned defence lawyer Joe Beltrami, he explained to the court that he used his car as an office and was there to retrieve some papers. He admitted he had taken a drink, but denied having driven the car since the previous evening. He further denied that he had been about to drive the car. 'I don't know of any place in Glasgow you can go at that time of the morning,' he explained. When asked why he had told the policeman who had charged him that the car was stolen, he replied, 'It was meant as a quip—obviously not one of my best.' Chic was found 'not guilty' and discharged. Later he told Jenny, 'I was sorry for myself and that's a stupid, shallow way to be. Now it's on with the motley!'

The Scimitar was not indeed to prove a lucky car, for only a few months later Chic was stopped for speeding along Alexandra Parade in Glasgow and charged with this offence, together with the more serious one of driving under the influence of alcohol. This time Chic knew he was for it, so in a spirit of 'nothing to lose anyway', he chose not to be as contrite as on the previous occasion. When the sheriff said, 'According to the constable who arrested you, you were walking badly on leaving the car,' he tried his best to look humble. 'Sir, I apologise,' Chic replied gravely, adding—'but I *am* a bad walker.'

This time Chic was fined and given three months' disqualification. Driving had lost what little charm it ever had, and the Scimitar was quietly dry-docked. Now it would be the bus, the train, the subway and Shanks's pony—until the advent of Jimmy Hepburn. Before long Chic was a familiar figure on Glasgow's underground.

*   *   *

'I'm getting married again, Chic. I wanted you to hear it from me before you read about it in the papers.' It had been several months since Maidie had last phoned him, on the occasion of her father's death.

'Oh,' was all he could manage at first, until he saw that was a somewhat inadequate response and added, 'I'm very happy for you, Maidie. I hope you've picked better this time.'

'I picked OK the *first* time,' Maidie replied. 'Things just got in the way towards the end, that's all. His name's Terry—will you come to the wedding?'

Chic considered this before replying, 'It's nice of you to ask, but I don't think so—it would hardly be appropriate. Once you've settled down maybe I could call in and see you.'

'Wish me luck, then?'

'I do, Maidie, you deserve it.'

Neither one of them, it seemed, wanted to put the phone down. 'How are you anyway?' Maidie finally asked. 'How's the flat in Glasgow?'

'I'm fine, the flat's fine, the jobs are flooding in . . . and I miss you, Maidie.'

'I miss you too, Chic, but—well, we had our kick at the ball.'

*   *   *

One Sunday Willie Woodburn and some of his football friends decided to drive down to the beach at Gullane, the popular seaside resort near Edinburgh. They were stripping down to their trunks for sunbathing when Willie spotted Chic sitting alone on the beach. He was cross-legged, shirtless and had made a little headguard for himself with a handkerchief. The two men hadn't met since the football match they had attended with Sean Connery. A big smile spread over Chic's face when he recognised Willie. 'When the tide goes out we'll have a game of footer,' said Willie. 'Now let's hear all your news.'

From then on Gullane beach became a regular Sunday afternoon fixture with all of them, weather permitting. When football was played, it was for ten bob a head. With everyone else wearing their 'gutties', Chic invariably stuck to his thick brown crêpe-soled 'brothel-creepers'.

Joe Beltrami, Chic and friends.

'And he was what I would call a "stoic" player,' Woodburn recalls. 'He played the ball only if it came to him. But keen? It was a date he never missed when he was in town.'

Chic also struck up a friendship with Jimmy Hepburn, who booked an occasional act and looked after several up-and-coming performers, dabbling on the outer fringes of show business. He chauffeured Chic as an obligement to a few functions where he was the after-dinner speaker and it soon became understood that he would make himself available on occasions like these. The specific advantages to Chic were that he was mobile again and no longer required to watch his drinking, the only problem being that Jimmy was quite partial to the occasional bevvy himself. 'And it gets the Scimitar out of mothballs,' Chic maintained.

At one Rangers Testimonial Dinner the two of them were seated at the top table and found themselves presented with a 40-ounce bottle of whisky and two half-pint glasses. Within an hour the whisky was downed and Chic had fallen fast asleep. Jimmy started up in alarm as Bobby Shearer got up to announce Chic's act, unaware he had dropped off. He need not have worried, for as soon as his name was announced, Chic suddenly awoke. After looking around for a few seconds to get his bearings, he leapt to his feet and immediately started in on his act—while Jimmy could only look on in astonishment.

'Coming in here tonight,' Chic began, 'I heard someone say, "Charlie," and I turned—not too quickly, but I turned. "Do you remember me?" this fellow asked, sat there like a frog up a pump. He said, "You're Charlie Drawers, aren't you? That's your *own* name, Charlie Drawers." I said, "Yes, it is." He said, "What a funny name that is, Charlie Drawers." I said, "Don't shout it out all over the place!" "Chic Murray now," he mused, "that's a stage name, I suppose. But are you *still* Charlie Drawers?" I said, "I suppose I am." He said, "That's a *funny* name that—Drawers." I said, "What's your name?" He said, "Erskine." I said, "Well, what are *you* talking about?"

'That's my own name, Drawers. It was my father's name—he was Sir Charles Drawers. And it was handed down—the name, not the drawers, of course. And we used to have a shop, it was a draper's shop we had, and he was in partnership with another fellow, a Highland fellow from Islay called Semit—an old-fashioned name. David Semit—Semit & Drawers, the drapers. So it was quite good for business, because people would enter the shop and say, "Mr Semit, can I have a pair of drawers?" and we Drawers—let me tell you—we were a *warm* family. Then there was my brother, my youngest brother, he was Chester.'

As the audience went into convulsions, Chic asked, 'What was that? I missed that. Oh, I see, *Chester Drawers*, aye—' Then he resumed, 'He was a tall boy. But *wooden*. He played violin and I played piano and we used to play duets together. If I finished first I'd put the kettle on for a cup of tea. And I remember on one occasion, my father taking me aside, "Sit down a minute," he said and I knew something was wrong—the way the shotgun was pointing at me! "I think it's about time you went out into the wide world," he said, "and made your way." "Well, if you think so," I said.

'"Well, you've got a good name," he said, "and a good Scots tongue. An excellent name. Always uphold it—always watch what you're doing." "Oh, you can rest assured," I told him. "I'll *never* let the drawers down!"' Jimmy watched and listened in breathless admiration to Chic's command of his audience and the way he never missed a single beat. The 'Summit & Drawers' story was then topped by a virtuoso display of yodelling before he received a standing ovation for his efforts and sat down heavily, falling fast asleep again instantly. Half an hour later he woke up and looked at Jimmy. 'When am I going on?' he demanded to know. 'You've been on,' Jimmy informed him. 'Love of God,' Chic declared. 'Here, Jimmy—did I go down well?'

A few weeks later when Chic was feeling jaded, Jimmy suggested a motor trip to the Highlands. Suitably tanked up with liquid refreshment, they set off, half a bottle of whisky disappearing before they reached Tyndrum, where they stopped for a meal. As they were eating Chic motioned to Jimmy, who was sitting opposite him, 'Look,' he said, pointing to the waitress, 'I've been spotted.' Jimmy noticed that the waitress was indeed looking over in their direction, giggling and whispering to her friend. Chic started to ease himself down in his chair, until he misjudged it and with a crash slid under the table. Now the whole restaurant stared at the sight of Chic on the floor, trying in vain to extricate his legs from Jimmy's chair, in which they were tightly jammed. 'If he had wished to draw attention to himself, he could not have done it in a noisier or more spectacular manner,' Jimmy laughed.

Now they were off to Skye, with the other half of the whisky bottle drained. After a night at Glenelg, where Jimmy knew the manager of a hostelry, they awoke on the Sunday morning to a breakfast of bacon, eggs and toast and another half bottle of whisky. 'We should go to church,' Chic declared, a bit woozily. 'We should keep the sabbath—' Despite Jimmy's protestations that his breath would intoxicate half the congregation, Chic was adamant.

'But me no buts!' he declared. 'Let's go, it's nearly 11 o'clock.'

Jimmy found himself accompanying Chic to the first church service either of them had attended for years. As Chic sat there, head and shoulders over most of the congregation, the minister's eye seemed continually to be on him. 'He recognises me,' said Chic, who in turn seemed quite keen to stare back. When the collection bag was passed around, Chic held the red velvet pouch for a moment under his chin and looked around the congregation, smiling beatifically. Was this the same man who had slid under the table at Tyndrum only 24 hours before, Jimmy wondered, for here Chic was positively *inviting* attention.

After the service the minister approached Chic, as they both knew he would. 'Are you Chic Murray?' he asked. 'I have that honour,' Chic replied grandly, but with a decided twinkle in his eye. 'Well, we're having a march past in ten minutes of the local Brownies, Guides and Scouts,' the minister explained. 'Would you take the salute?' Chic agreed to do this and accompanied the minister to the point in the narrow road outside the church where he should stand. Jimmy stood nearby and watched Chic's tall, burly figure silhouetted against the distant purple hills and clear blue sky. The procession of children could be seen approaching for the salute, while the proud parents looked on.

When the parade seemed almost upon him, Chic raised his arm and saluted. What he hadn't realised was that the children were about to disappear for a moment into the zigzag of the winding shore road. Chic brought his hand down and turned to Jimmy, shrugging helplessly. 'Why are the wee Brownies walking *away* from me?' he wanted to know. 'Hold on, you'll be all right. Give them a minute,' Jimmy advised, then much to Chic's relief the procession reappeared. They were then treated to a truly regal salute.

*   *   *

'He just phoned to say he'll be arriving within the hour for a drink,' Maidie informed her husband of six weeks. 'And he wants to meet his new granddaughter.' For Terry this was only the beginning of discovering just how strong the bond remained between the two.

When Chic did arrive there was a certain feeling of inevitability about it as he breezed in and cheerily introduced himself to Terry before settling down in his favourite old chair. 'Wait till you hear what I've been up to,' he began. 'Oh, by the way, let's get young Deanna wheeled in to meet her Grandad. And while we're at it, is there a bath in the offing, Maidie?'

She could hardly believe her ears. 'A what?' she asked.

'A bath, Maidie—come on, behave yourself. You *know* I like a good soak. Now, Terry, explain this to me if you can—I used to play the field a bit when I was married to Maidie, you know. Now here's the funny bit—since the divorce I've hardly looked at another woman! Is that not peculiar?'

Terry sat there, wondering what he was supposed to say. 'Aye, it's a funny life,' he finally managed, somewhat unconvincingly.

'How about you, Maidie?' Chic continued, while she wished the floor would swallow her up. 'What do *you* make of it?'

She chuckled to hide her embarrassment. 'How would I know?' she asked.

'I've got a theory,' Chic continued relentlessly. 'I did all that stuff only to get at you, Maidie, to get your goat. Now that I haven't got you, there's no point any more.'

Terry looked up. 'That makes you a silly bugger,' he observed astutely.

'The silliest I know,' Chic agreed. 'Now, Terry, there's something else I want to put to you. I've been offered this series of TV commercials and . . .'

This beginning progressed to a spare bed for the night and was to prove only the first of a series of visits, often lasting for several days. 'Are you sure the decree was final?' Terry asked Maidie, adding, 'If it was, he simply hasn't accepted the fact. In his mind you're still here to dance attendance on him!' Despite the somewhat awkward ramifications, the two men enjoyed a companionable relationship, although Terry could never quite shake off the feeling that he had drawn the short straw.

One day Maidie informed Chic that eventually she planned to sell the hotel. 'We'll just keep the basement flat—it's big enough for all of us,' she explained.

'*All* of us?' Chic queried. 'Including me and Black Bottle Bill?'

Maidie smiled, somewhat ruefully, 'No, he'll have to go, but I daresay we'll find a corner for you. There's always the dog basket. Although, I don't know—'

Chic was aghast. 'What do you mean, you don't know?'

'Well, it's just that there's been some talk locally...'

'About what?'

'The three of us—you and me and Terry, something along the lines of a *ménage à trois*.'

Chic covered his ears. 'I'll pretend I never heard that,' he muttered, then asked, 'When did all this start?'

'Oh, since you started your overnight stays,' Maidie replied. 'You've been staying here a fair bit and tongues wag. Two husbands under the one roof and all that.'

'I see,' said Chic, '*Ménage à trois*, is it? They're just silly buggers—we don't *have* these things in Scotland. Shows they're thinking along the right lines, though.' Slowly he got up and walked toward the door. He turned, and Maidie thought she detected a twinkle. 'Surely the neighbours know what they used to say about me?'

'No,' said Maidie puzzled. 'What's that, Chic?'

'That I couldnae *run* a ménage!'

Chic was overjoyed to discover he had become a grandfather for the second time with the arrival of Douglas's son. 'What are you going to call him?' he asked. 'Douglas,' came the reply. 'Excellent choice,' he declared. 'Eh—how did you arrive at that particular name?' He turned next to his daughter. 'When are you going to make an honest man of someone?' he asked Annabelle. 'When he comes along, Dad,' came the reply. 'And I'll know it.' Chic looked at her fondly. 'You will, too,' he agreed.

'It's funny you giving the hotel up,' Chic mused when the hotel sale was almost through. 'You're surely not thinking of coming back into show-business, are you?'

'No, Chic,' Maidie replied, somewhat uneasily—where was this leading?

'It's just that—well, Ian Christie made a suggestion the other day that I dismissed out of hand. He asked if I'd ever thought about re-forming the double-act with you. Naturally, I replied that all that was finished, but if you're going to be at a loose end—'

'I didn't say that,' Maidie quickly pointed out. 'As a matter of fact I'm thinking of opening a hairdressing salon. Be practical, Chic—re-form? It would never work. Who wants that old stuff now?' Even as she spoke, her mind was racing.

'Oh, never mind, then,' Chic replied. 'It was just a thought. Maybe someday—who knows?'

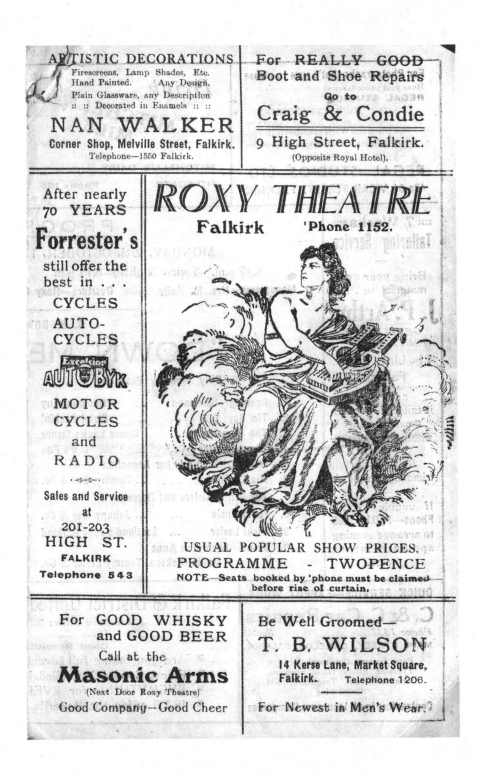

16

Lean Times

*'I went into Boots. I went in the door—it saves walking through the wall—and I said to the assistant, "Excuse me, have you any laces?" "No," she replied. "Oh, my", I said, "that's terrible—Boots without laces!"' *

With the demise of variety Chic did not adapt readily to television, while fellow comedians such as Bruce Forsyth, Norman Vaughan, Des O'Connor and Morecambe & Wise took to it like ducks to water. It was certainly not that television held any terrors for Chic, and he continued to make sporadic appearances on the medium, but without ever really finding his niche. An apparently unlikely outlet for his talents was a series of movies with titles such as *Secrets of a Door to Door Salesman*, *Ups and Downs of a Handyman* and *What's Up, Superdoc?* in which he made fairly fleeting appearances as a comic policeman. These helped to pay the rent, as did the many other assignments he took on, like voice-overs for radio and TV ads and a fairly steady run of work for BBC radio in Scotland. He realised only too well, however, that he had slipped from the front rank.

Out of the blue he was offered a one-hour special on BBC TV in 1975. It had been written specially for him by Joe McGrath—his fellow Scot and the first director of *Casino Royale*—together with Donald Churchill. Bob Hird was to be the producer with Iain McFadzean acting as executive producer. Chic had no idea what to expect when he picked up the shooting script one evening at the BBC and carried it home. Having written his own material from the beginning, he took with a pinch of salt the claim that it had been written purely with him in mind—and even if it had, he had already decided in advance that it couldn't possibly be suitable.

Beginning with a title sequence in which Chic is the only enthusiastic member of an audience in an almost empty theatre, watching a third-rate illusionist act, *The World of Chic Murray* was then ingeniously introduced. There followed a hilarious—and at times darkly surreal—series of sketches featuring footballers coming to life and kicking their ball out of the picture frame, Chic in a drab bed-sit finding a tantalising message left on his Ansaphone by an apparently ardent female admirer, Chic vandalising a phone booth as an art form, Chic as a puppet in a woodland sequence, then—in rapid succession—as a theatrical director, a violin maestro and a disaster film-maker. Another phone booth sequence followed, this time showing a queue of people lining up to 'Dial a Joke', before Chic was featured as a spaceman in flight, returning full circle to the by-now-deserted theatre and the illusionist—all in the time-span of a 50-minute programme.

Three hours after starting it, Chic laid the manuscript down and sat motionless for a while, then slowly shook his head from side to side. 'Jesus Christ,' was all he said. After making a pot of very strong tea, he sat down and picked the manuscript up again. *The World of Chic Murray* was it? He ran through the whole thing again, only more slowly, thinking of all the bits of business he could insert, then at six o'clock in the morning he turned in for a couple of hours' sleep. His dreams were filled with illusionists, their white rabbits and a grubby man in a raincoat sitting in the stalls of a seaside theatre.

The next morning he rang Bob Hird, who had handed him the manuscript the night before.

'What did you think of it?' Bob asked anxiously.

'Well, you know how I feel about other people writing my material—'

'Yes, I know, Chic.'

'—not very happy about that.'

'Oh—so you don't like it?'

'No, Bob, I don't *like* it. I fucking well *love* it!'

'That's fantastic,' Bob enthused. 'So do we—the whole team's wild about it. I didn't want to say too much about it until you'd read it for yourself, but I knew that if it rang true with you, that would be it.'

'Bob,' said Chic. 'I'm now a man with a mission. Let's meet and get this cracker moving.' In Chic's mind there was no doubt. He was glad now he had limited his solo television appearances to guest spots on other artists' shows—instinctively he had felt that was enough until the real stuff came along. This was it, he felt, here was solid gold.

Recording went ahead in August 1975 with a projected transmission date of 'later in the year'. These were the days when Stanley Baxter was working for months on end to do his yearly 'special'; Chic was allocated precisely one and a half days—including rehearsal time.

As one after another of the transmission dates was pushed forward, Chic expressed his concern to anyone who would listen, before in the end a definite date was set—1 January 1976 at 8 p.m. 'Christ,' said Chic. 'There'll be nobody watching. What a daft time to choose.' For whatever

Chic as the fiddlemaker in *The World of Chic Murray*.

reason—Chic was heartbreakingly right. The show was a complete flop, attracting abysmal ratings. From those who did watch it a stream of protest was forthcoming, complaining it was either unfunny, in bad taste, or both. The critics joined in, maintaining they either couldn't make head nor tail of it or that it was too clever by half.

Chic was shattered. 'I tried to do something different,' he said, 'but it seems all anybody wants is red-nosed comic stuff. Obviously it doesn't pay to be ahead of your time.' One or two discerning commentators picked up on this remark and agreed. 'It *was* ahead of its time—it's the sort of programme that will last for years,' Derek Gibbons wrote. 'The Beeb could show it again in ten years' time and it would get a rapturous reception.'

Chic already had *Secrets of a Door to Door Salesman* on release and *Ups and Downs of a Handyman* scheduled for later in 1976, but he was inconsolable—and not just for himself, but for the whole team who had worked so hard from the inspired original script. He could not pretend to be anything other than bitter over the show's failure and 'That chapter is closed,' was all he would say to one critic who wanted to get his reaction later. For the BBC it was closed also, for there was no repeat showing of the production either then—or ten years later.

Scottish comedian Jack Milroy got to know Chic well, or as well as anyone did, although they never appeared together. Jack first caught Chic's act at the Victoria Theatre in Paisley, when he and his wife, Mary, had gone backstage to introduce themselves. The next time Jack came across Chic was in the breakfast buffet line-up at the Norbreck Hotel in Blackpool. Chic was in front of Jack in the queue for breakfast—dressed as a spiv, with a ginger wig, teddy boy suit and big bovver boots, standing there with a tray in his hand, helping himself to orange juice and cornflakes.

'Oh, the television people are coming shortly to collect me,' Chic explained morosely, 'take me along to the North Pier and throw me in the water for a gag. What a way to earn a living!' So saying he went back to the business of loading his tray. 'The next time I saw him was when I was with my wife Mary,' Jack recalled. 'We were sitting in the airport at Ibiza. Chic walked in with his tartan bunnet, limping badly. He had been on one of the islands and had to make a boat journey to Ibiza to catch the plane home. He'd caught his leg on a jagged piece of steel on the boat, requiring hospital treatment and stitches. We made sure he got VIP treatment on the plane, stretched out across three seats the stewardess cleared for him. We gave him a lift home in our taxi and he asked if I thought he should sue the Spanish boat people. I said certainly and gave him my solicitor's number. Some weeks later we met again and I asked him how the claim had gone. With that odd look of his he said, "Well, Jack, we got the name of the captain, but we canny find the bloody boat!" Then he gave his distinctive laugh.'

Chic remained friends with Joe Beltrami, Glasgow's famous defence lawyer, and told him that he must on no account miss *Ups and Downs of a Handyman*. When the film arrived at the Odeon, Joe decided to go along, and take his wife to see it as well. All he expected was a 'saucy' comedy, liberally spiced with Chic Murray humour. Not a regular filmgoer, Joe and his wife turned up early at the cinema and secured seats in the circle. With the supporting film, the advertisements and trailers over with, they relaxed during the intermission, all cued up to see Chic's film. As the lights were going down there was still a girl selling ices in front of them.

Joe's well-known voice, famous for its ability to be totally audible in court even when whispering, could now be heard by the packed circle, urgently demanding of the unfortunate ice cream girl, 'Look, could you please get out of the way! I've come to see this picture specially and I don't want to miss a single *minute*.' At this the lights went out and the movie started. Even before the credit titles came on, the first scene took place on a bed. A man and a woman stripped and began making love—in what to Joe and his wife, unaccustomed as they were to mid–Seventies permissiveness, was embarrassing detail. Even more embarrassing—as the apparently endless scene went on—was Joe's distinct impression that the entire circle was looking at him. 'I've come to see this picture specially—' was that what he'd said? And, 'I don't want to miss a single minute.' Joe groaned. 'Well?' asked Chic when they met next. 'What did you think—wasn't it great?' 'Terrific,' Joe said, a stern expression on his face, before bursting out laughing and telling Chic the whole story.

Chic's circle of friends continued to widen, although there were few whom he would allow too close. 'He was like the Scarlet Pimpernel,' Ian Christie remarked. 'He was just off to London—or Edinburgh, or just back. He was on the phone to his travel agent trying to get a few snatched days in the sun, or he was just back. Jenny and I were two of his Beeb gang, then he had his STV gang and his lawyers and accountants and dozens upon dozens of other acquaintances. We were all allowed just so much of him and no more—the unfortunate thing was he could appear suddenly when you were at your busiest.'

Another friend was Israel (Issy) Kaye, a furrier in Mitchell Street, Glasgow, whom Chic first met in Aberdeen in the 1960s. Chic turned up one day in Issy's premises years after their first meeting and resumed their spiky, down-to-earth friendship. Thereafter Issy welcomed a visit from Chic, though he never made a fuss or treated him like a star. From the wrong man Chic would have found this difficult to take, because he was fairly partial to a show of deference, despite his frequent protestations to the contrary.

'He came back into my life after a couple of years away,' Israel recalled, 'and at that point I hadn't seen him since the divorce. I said, "Holy God, Chic, what the hell have you been up to? You look like a bloody tramp!" He had a worn old jacket, baggy pants and an open-necked shirt that was badly frayed at the collar. He didn't like being criticised and fobbed it off by saying that he didn't have time nowadays to bother, but did I have any suggestions? I told him I could fix him up with a good tailor who would run off half a dozen suits for him in no time at all, wholesale of course. Chic agreed, then when he got the suits he kept the guy waiting forever before he paid him. The tailor was an elderly man and I used to say to Chic, "You're such a miserable bugger. You're hoping he'll pop off, then you won't have to pay him!"

'He was such a complicated man—why he put up with me I'll never know, except he seemed to like me and there is no doubt he was a lonely soul. I used to ask him why he didn't go back to Maidie. "Oh, that's all in the past," he would maintain—but I knew damned fine it wasn't. He never got over her.

'I would say to him, "Chic Murray? You're *nothing* now. A has-been as far as Glasgow's concerned." He'd just look at me and twinkle. He knew I loved him, the big sod. When he kept cadging rolls at lunchtime at my place, I'd say, "Why don't you go to Littlewoods? They'll give you a roll—you're a *big shot*. You're *Chic Murray!*"

'Once I asked him back to my flat for a meal. My wife and I had a chicken in the oven. For a laugh I put the chicken's head on the plate beside Chic's portion. He said, "What the hell's that?" I said, "It's the head—don't tell me Chic Murray throws that away?" Ever since then he'd say to my friends, "Don't go back to his place for a meal. He serves you hens' heids!"

'We'd often go for a drink to the Gordon in Mitchell Street, just next door to my showroom. He might turn up in a nice suit, spoiled by a crummy raincoat and big boots. There he'd meet all his newspaper reporter pals, who congregated there. One would ask, "Ho, Chic, what're you up to?" He'd spin them what I always took to be a yarn—I guess I never was the star-struck type, in fact I'm sure that's why we got on. "I'm off to Saigon next week to make a movie for Thames," he said once and I thought, "and the rest!" Next thing I knew *Saigon—Year of the Cat* was on the telly—so you never could dismiss anything he said.

'He could be so nice, then so abrupt. Once in my showroom one of my customers asked, "Are you Chic Murray?" and he promptly walked out. I chased after him and said, "Here, *you*. Don't you treat my customers like that. I don't give a damn who you think you are—you'll behave yourself while you're here!" He took his telling-off. He always maintained that he didn't like to be recognised, but it was all baloney. He loved it, especially when it got him a free drink or two. Once we went into a bar and I ordered as usual. The girl behind the bar said that she recognised me and was I ever on the telly? I said no, didn't she mean the guy next door, motioning to Chic. She said, "No, I've never seen him, but I'm sure it's you I've seen on telly." Chic didn't like that.

'So he was no longer a top star—oh, I know he made dozens of appearances here, there and everywhere and featured in the odd film, but there was something sad and melancholy about him. I would say to him, "You should *sell* yourself more, Chic," but he wouldn't have it. He would do only what he wanted to do. And one of the things he would *never* do was appear in Glasgow. "*Never* without Maidie," he would maintain. "I couldn't face a Glasgow audience without her. Too many memories. Too many Metropoles, Empires and Pavilions. No."

'The extraordinary thing I found with Chic was that he would never run anybody down. As an example I remember once for some reason everyone was knocking Jimmy Logan. He was in trouble with his New Metropole and for a while everything seemed to be going badly. In more than one instance the knives were out. Chic just said, "Jimmy's OK. He'll come through." He wasn't jealous of anyone either, he didn't have a jealous bone in his body.

'The "meanness" stories? Well, he certainly helped to spread these himself, but my opinion is that it was all one big act. When somebody bought him a drink in a pub they got full value for their money, believe me, and I'm sure that's the way Chic looked at it too. He gave them himself—it was all he had to offer, and it was enough, it was plenty. When he was in town he'd come up to my place every week to do the pools. On every single occasion he'd ask me for the perm, saying he could never remember it. I used to ask him how the hell he'd ever managed to memorise his lines!'

Another friend Chic made through Scottish Television was Tom Walsh, who had contributed to many of STV's redoubtable *One o'clock Gang* shows, notching up a total of over 350 screen credits. Tom asked Chic back to his home one night for dinner and recalls, 'He stayed for over a week! The man was a gypsy! The first evening was a late one, so my wife and I suggested he just bed down for the night. He had a late breakfast in bed next morning and that was the procedure established. One night we sat chatting and it was nearly midnight. We'd had a pleasant evening talking about the business we were in. Suddenly he got to his feet. "Tom," he declared, "I'll be off then." I was completely taken aback. "Don't be daft, Chic," I said. "Where are you going to go at this time of night? It's nearly midnight." Off he went upstairs and reappeared minutes later with the two plastic bags he'd brought with him that contained his accoutrements. Nothing we could say would dissuade him and off he went. My wife and I sat there—dazed—for several minutes. After coming just for dinner and staying for more than a week, he'd suddenly departed at midnight!

'You had to get to know him to understand this, and even then you were given only clues. Chic would communicate—and at the same time remain incommunicado. The only pattern he had was no pattern at all and if any pattern threatened to develop, he'd change it. Months passed after that and all we got was the occasional telephone call. It would be,

"I've just got back from Tenerife," or "I'm just off to Majorca," or "I'm calling from my tailor's. Do you want any suits made wholesale?" Usually the charges would be reversed, as in "It's Timothy Tighthole on the phone from a call box in London. Will you accept the charge?"

'After weeks without seeing him I was busy in the studios editing a weekly STV series, *Time for Tennent*. I'd asked one of the stars appearing in the show, the American singer Dick Haymes, back to our house for a bite to eat. That day I got a call from Chic and something in his tone told me he knew that Dick Haymes would be visiting that night. He was in town and said it was high time we had a meal together—how about that night? I told him I was having Dick Haymes round and he feigned surprise. "Funny," he said, "I've always admired him and his singing. Do you think you could squeeze me in, Tom?"

'Of course I did, but I couldn't see that the two of them would have much in common. I was so wrong! They were like long-lost brothers—it turned out they'd appeared in many of the same venues all over the world, like America and Australia. They knew the best bars—even the bartenders' names—in city after city. They chatted as equals all night. My wife and I were confined mainly to listening, but nevertheless we had a marvellous evening—for once listening was enough.'

At a charity function soon after Chic heard a familiar voice as he walked in with Tom Walsh. It was Father Joe Mills, a priest from Dumbarton, doing his Chic Murray impersonation. 'How do I follow that?' Chic asked Tom in mock despair. 'Come on over and I'll introduce you,' Tom offered. Chic shook Father Joe firmly by the hand, told him he was pleased to meet him—then promptly turned his back. Joe and Tom were momentarily nonplussed until Chic spun straight round again with a broad smile on his face. 'Seriously, that's not a bad wee act you've got there,' he told Joe, who relaxed immediately.

Some months later Father Joe was on holiday in Majorca with fellow priests Larry and John. They were looking at the tariff in a car showroom window, trying to figure out if they had enough pesetas to hire a vehicle, when Joe recognised Chic walking down the hill toward them, a bathing towel rolled up under his arm. Chic was taking a break during filming in Majorca and was on his way to the beach. 'I didn't recognise you without your dog collar,' Chic remarked to Joe, obviously delighted to bump into him again. The four of them arranged to meet that night for a meal and found they had much in common, not least a liking for lashings of spaghetti bolognaise—washed down with Valpolicella. 'You should come to our Italian evenings back home in Dumbarton—we hold one every Wednesday,' Joe told Chic. 'We make a huge bowl of spaghetti and have a good gab.' Chic agreed to attend whenever he was in town.

'He kept lapsing into this American underworld jargon that kept us all in stitches,' Joe said. 'He'd be lying on his lilo on the veranda outside his

flat when I'd arrive for him. "Did Tex send you?" he'd ask. "Is everything going according to plan? Talk freely." On the beach one day, when he'd had enough sun, he got up and said in his best Philip Marlowe accent, "Suddenly it got to be four-thirty. After a big lunch and a hard afternoon sunning myself I was ready for something long, cool and sparkling—like an Alka-Seltzer!"'

When they all got back home Joe phoned Chic to remind him of the Italian evening, 'But it's in Dumbarton, isn't it?' Chic asked. 'It is, Chic.' There was a long pause, then, 'If one of you happened to be coming anywhere near Glasgow, you could pick me up.' 'I'm sure something could be arranged, Chic,' Joe said. 'Great! Leave the Valpolicella to me, then!' The evening became a fixture thereafter whenever Chic was in town, which began to occur with increasing frequency as he found himself being chased by the tax authorities.

John Tate was Chic's accountant for a number of years and well remembers when he first took over Chic's tangled financial affairs. 'Chic had neglected to produce evidence of his income to the tax authorities and was eventually summoned to appear before the General Commissioners of the Inland Revenue. After a tax inspector put forward his case with an estimated assessment, Chic was required to make a statement to three lay persons and a magistrate. He asked me along, then insisted on speaking for himself. Normally the entire proceedings are expected to take about five minutes, but Chic held forth for a full half-hour. The presiding magistrate listened agog as Chic's life story was laid out before him, while I sweated and thought of the queue outside waiting their turn. At the end of it the magistrate quickly modified his inspector's assessment—in Chic's favour—and summed up the case by stating, "I don't believe it will be necessary for Mr Murray to appear again." Chic insisted on getting up and thanking the court. On his way out he "whispered" to me in a voice that carried all over the court, "The man's a poltroon!"

'From time to time Chic would pop in to our office for a chat and a coffee. He could behave badly at times, but was usually full of penitence afterwards. He once agreed to go along to a function I was to attend, providing there was no question of his being asked to perform. The chairman of the function ignored this and after the dinner invited Chic to say "a few words". Chic was furious—and by this time he had had a skinful. He got to his feet and turned to the unfortunate chairman's wife. Glaring at her, he said, "Here's a few words then—your husband's got a mouth like a skate's arse." A stunned silence greeted this while Chic balefully swayed and surveyed the throng. He then said, "Sorry, I shouldn't have said that. I was doing a skate's arse an injustice." With that he sat down heavily and fell asleep. It was not his finest moment. Next day he was thoroughly ashamed of himself and insisted on sending the chairman's wife a bouquet of flowers. The note with it read, "A thousand apologies. Let's run away together, Chic Murray".'

Although he had promised to take Ian Christie to meet Maidie, Ian doubted somehow that the trip would ever happen. 'Then out of the blue it was on,' Ian recalled. 'I arranged to pick him up at his flat after breakfast and drive him through to Edinburgh. Unfortunately, I twisted my ankle badly on my way to the garage in the morning. For five minutes the pain was excruciating and I didn't think I'd be able to drive, but after my wife had soaked it in cold water and dressed it, I felt better.

'When Chic emerged from his front door, I saw that he too was limping badly. "Gashed my leg last night on some railings," he explained. I smiled at the coincidence, then winced at the pain from my ankle.

'When we arrived at the hotel, Chic asked the barman to let Maidie know we had arrived, then ordered drinks. A few minutes later the door into the bar from the living quarters was pushed open and Maidie emerged, while we both looked on incredulously. Her right leg was covered in plaster and she was leaning heavily on a pair of crutches—all set for a show of sympathy, rather than the hilarity which instead greeted her entrance. As we got up, Chic turned to me and remarked, "She's done it again, Christie—only this time she's topped us both!" Then we hobbled over to Maidie, who only then saw the joke.'

While Chic was in Aberdeen at a function as a guest speaker, impresario Ross Bowie asked if they could meet at the Caledonian Hotel to discuss some future dates. Chic agreed, but got the time wrong and turned up an hour early. At a loose end, he began to wander through the hotel's capacious corridors, until the sound of a meeting in progress came to his ears. It turned out to be the Annual General Meeting of the local golf club, so Chic slipped in and sat at the back, joining the 50 or so members already gathered.

The chairman seemed to be nearing the end of his speech and as Chic sat down, he declared, 'That brings us to the final matter of annual subscriptions. The proposal here is that these be raised from £75 to £80. You are all perfectly aware of the extra facilities we have laid on—the new bar in the club-house, the opening of a brand new green, and I'm sure you are all agreed that the modest increase is fully justified. Can I request formal approval of this by a show of hands?'

Chic stood up immediately. 'Just a minute,' he cried. 'I'd like to protest. Certainly we're aware of the increased facilities—but surely they will attract new members and create extra revenue—why do we need a subscription increase on top?' The chairman looked decidedly perplexed at this unexpected protest, but Chic hadn't finished. 'It's the thin end of the wedge. Someone's got to be the voice of reason. There's too much of this going on over the whole country. This club should take pride in being the odd one out, not joining in with the crowd. There's got to be a stand taken sometime and I suggest we take it now.'

'Wh-what do you have in mind?' asked the chairman, feeling thoroughly browbeaten. 'We should strike a blow!' Chic declared. 'A symbolic gesture! I suggest a reduction in subscription fees to £70!' Uproar followed as Chic sat down, while on the podium a hasty consultation took place. Finally the chairman once more called for order. 'Taking into account the points made, we now put forward a fresh proposal. Could we have a show of hands—in favour of holding the fees where they are?'

Fifty pairs of hands shot up and the proposal was unanimously carried. As Chic got up to slip away the fellow on the seat next to him gripped his arm. 'I don't remember seeing you here before. Are you a member?' Chic glared down at him, 'A member?' he echoed. 'Of this club—certainly not. I would never consider joining any club who would have me as a member!'

17

Hospital Case

'As I was waiting for a bus I asked the lady standing beside me, "Does your dog bite?" She replied that it didn't, so I patted it and it almost bit my fingers off. I said, "I thought you said your dog doesn't bite." She said, "That's not my dog." '

'I'm appearing in the new Texaco ad,' Chic informed Issy, who was singularly unimpressed as usual. 'Bit of a come-down after *Casino Royale* is it not, Chic?' He received a glare for his pains. 'Nothing,' declared Chic, 'would be a climb-down after that film. No, in this Texaco production, I play the lead role of petrol pump attendant No. Two.' 'Wow!' Israel enthused. 'And it's on tonight, so never mind your "wows", get the telly on now, make sure it's properly warmed up!' When the commercial did appear, it did set some sort of record for a mega-budget 60-second production, featuring as it did Chic, Bob Hope, Fred Emney and James Hunt.

As the commercial opened Fred Emney addresses a petrol pump attendant. 'Thank you, good day,' he says before driving his antique car out of the Texaco station.

'I'm sure that was Fred Emney,' the attendant muses.

'Did you ask him?' says Chic.

'No, I didn't like to.'

Just then James Hunt arrives, driving a snazzy open sports car, with a gorgeous leggy model in the passenger seat.

'Fill her up and check the oil, please.' The attendant puts the nozzle into the tank and checks the oil. He interrupts James, who is chatting away to the girl, to show him a can of oil.

Attendant: 'You can't buy better oil—'

James: 'Yes, I know. I'm in a bit of a hurry actually.'

The attendant disappears to put the oil in the engine. Closing the hood, he takes the payment from James, who then drives off.

Attendant: 'James Hunt! The world champion.'

Chic: '*Never*.'

Attendant: 'It was; I'm positive.'

Chic: 'Did you ask him?'

Attendant: 'I didn't like to.'

Now Bob Hope drives in, in a large Cadillac. On the seat beside him are his golf clubs. 'Thanks for the Memory' is playing on the soundtrack. The attendant recognises him and turns to Chic, pointing at Bob excitedly: 'Look! Look!'

Chic: '*Go* and *ask* him.'

The attendant goes up nervously to Bob Hope.

Attendant: 'Sir?'

Bob Hope: 'Yes?'

Attendant: 'Aren't you Bob Hope?'

With his famous grin, Bob replies, 'Has a chicken got two legs?' Chic comes over, 'Well *is* it Bob Hope?'

Attendant: 'I don't know, he didn't say!'

As the commercial ended Chic turned to a puzzled-looking Israel, 'Well, what did you think?'

'Was it *really* Bob Hope?' Israel asked.

'Does a hen *really* have two heids?' asked Chic. 'You should know, Issy, you're the expert on hens' heids!'

One day Chic took a phone call from Laurence Henson, the producer of a comedy short he had made, *The Boat*, to tell him that the film was showing as a featurette on a programme at the Salon cinema in Hillhead, Chic's local. Down Chic went and introduced himself to the manager, Willie Walker. 'I didn't know you came from round here, Mr Murray,' said Willie. 'Oh, yes,' Chic replied. 'I'm one of your constituents right enough. And call me Chic—everyone does—or "Lord", whichever takes your fancy.' He looked around him approvingly as they stood in the foyer. 'Nice cinema you've got here. How are the tickets going for this programme? I would imagine *The Boat* would be really packing them in.'

'Well, as a matter of fact, Chic, we haven't even advertised it. Just the main feature.'

'This is nothing short of infamy! Here I am—personal appearance and that, plus Paramount wants me—OK, have the lights gone down yet? I'll just slip in and hope nobody *recognises* me.'

After the show an usherette, not destined to be one of Chic's favourites, passed the open door as Chic and Willie were having a coffee in the office. 'How much did you pay them to appear in that?' she asked. Chic bristled, then turned to Willie, nodding sympathetically, 'Staff *can* be a terrible problem.' From then on the Salon and Willie's office became a regular port of call for Chic. Willie recalls Chic's enjoyment of the many films he saw there, but also his experiences at some of the extended runs the popular cinema enjoyed. 'We had *Cabaret* running for nine straight weeks, then a return visit for four. Chic nearly went demented. "My filmgoing's gone to hell," he declared. I think he regarded *Cabaret*'s extended run as some sort of Communist plot. He kept on going back to see it, though, couldn't get over Lisa Minnelli or that wee man that played the master of ceremonies.'

Chic was well aware of the rise of a new breed of Scottish comedian in the inimitable Billy Connolly, but had no conception of the influence he had exerted over him. As Billy recalled: 'I'd always wanted to get laughs and had admired the quips that the smart buggers in the yards came out with to the bosses, but the desire was unco-ordinated until I saw Chic on the telly that fateful night. That was *it*, I realised, *that* was what I wanted, and from then on Chic was the *master funnyman* as far as I was concerned. He just brought it all *together* for me.'

Years later—and shortly after Billy made it to the top—he dropped into an art gallery in Glasgow. As he moved around looking at the various pictures, he spotted the unmistakable figure of Chic, sitting silently in front of a Magritte canvas. This was Billy's first encounter with the 'master funnyman' in person and after hesitating for just a few seconds, Billy went over and introduced himself. He was pleased beyond measure to get a friendly greeting, then to discover that Chic was a great fan of his. This came out only once the formalities were out of the way, since at first, Billy remembers, they were like two dogs circling and sniffing each other out, unsure of their ground, until the ice was broken and an outpouring of mutual admiration was expressed.

After ten minutes of desultory conversation, however, the talk faltered as both men realised at one and the same time that they had much more to say to one another than merely an exchange of pleasantries. As Billy's last words seemed to be left just dangling there in mid-air, Chic abruptly declared, 'Let's have dinner and a proper talk.'

Billy could scarcely believe his ears. 'Great,' he said. 'Where?'

'Your place,' came the prompt reply.

'He came back that very night for a meal and stayed for 24 hours. Oh, we talked all right. We were like long-lost buddies. He talked about his family and his early days in Greenock, how he met Maidie, then his own influences, like Damon Runyon and W. C. Fields. Chic put on such a simple front, but then zapped you with his encyclopedic knowledge—of music, films, theatre, sport, politics—you name it, he was there. When he was on a Runyon streak—something he never did on stage—it was like a running private joke of his—he excelled in fluent Runyonese. We touched on art and his visit to the gallery, which prompted him to tell me why he felt attracted to Magritte's work. It was because he sensed in him a kindred spirit with an apt, surrealistic feel for the ridiculous.

'Later we made a point of meeting whenever we could. He was always

Billy Connolly, after the presentation of Chic's bunnet by Annabelle.

at it, pulling me along. He'd be on the phone in the hall and hear me opening the living-room door. Quick as a flash, he'd be saying something like, "Yes, ask for £300, but be prepared to accept £30. And check back with me before you sign anything. Right! Goodbye!" Then he'd slam the phone down.'

On one occasion Billy was enjoying a drink with Chic in the BBC canteen when he noticed a petite Glasgow lassie carrying in a half-gallon bottle of whisky to replace the empty one on the gantry. Chic had his back to her, but Billy was able to follow her movements as she unbuckled the empty bottle, set it down, then went to lift the replacement up to the gantry. Although she was not much bigger than the bottle herself, she laboriously manoeuvred it into position and stood back when she felt it was secured. Unfortunately it wasn't and no sooner was she in the process of admiring her handiwork than the bottle slipped a notch and began to topple, the girl promptly ducking as the bottle crashed to the floor. The deafening noise it made on impact was followed by a veritable tidal wave of the precious fluid washing along the BBC's floor.

Chic had never paused for a second between the bottle being replaced and talking to Billy at the same time, but when he heard the crash he looked around at the scene of devastation. Glaring at the petrified girl, he bellowed, '*Stop* that!' before turning back to Billy and carrying on the conversation as if nothing had happened. Billy only later heard that Chic was instrumental in having the girl kept on, telling the canteen manager, 'If you must employ small girls, forget about half-gallon bottles of whisky—get in some miniatures instead!'

Billy remembered Chic being particularly taken with the story of Franz Kafka, the Czech author, and a chance street encounter he had in pre-First World War Prague. Out for a constitutional one day, Kafka had turned a corner to find a mother comforting her five-year-old daughter, who was sobbing her heart out. When Kafka inquired what the matter was, the mother replied that the child had lost her doll, whereupon the sobs grew even louder. Kafka then asked the mother to describe the doll. 'Oh, very pretty, with blonde hair and blue eyes. Her name was Hélène,' the mother replied. 'Why,' Kafka declared, 'I just passed Hélène on the street a few moments ago!' At this the girl stopped crying and looked up at Kafka as he continued, 'Yes, she told me that she was off on holiday—to the seaside, I'm sure she said. She told me she was very sad to be leaving her young mistress even for a short time, but that she would write to her very soon.'

By this time the little girl was staring at Kafka in astonishment. 'Did you really speak to my dolly?' she asked, eyes wide. 'Most assuredly,' Kafka replied. 'She is safe and well. I'm sure you will be hearing from her soon. Give me your name and address so that if by any chance I bump into Hélène again before you do, I can let you know.' With the information duly obtained, Kafka left the child happily chattering away to her delighted mother.

It so happened that Kafka was off to a seaside resort himself that very week and as soon as he arrived he wrote the child a postcard: 'I am safe and well, but missing you very much. Love, Hélène.' He never saw the little girl and her mother again, but it became his habit thereafter, whenever he was in a new town, to dispatch postcards of a similar nature to Hélène's mistress. He continued to do this until his death in 1924 at the age of 41, when the 'little girl' was well into her teens.

'Chic was entranced with this tale,' says Billy. 'It seemed to appeal to him on a variety of levels. He liked to be reminded of it from time to time—it never failed to move him. And when I got a bit uppity, and there *were* occasions, he was just the boy to bring me back down to earth! Once I had given him my precious unlisted phone number and a stranger called up and said, "Is this Billy Connolly? Hold on, I've got Chic Murray for you." After Chic and I had talked for a minute I said, "By the way, I hope you haven't been handing my number out to everybody." "Oh, God!" Chic answered. "Hang on just a minute, Billy . . ." and off he went, leaving me holding on for at least six or seven minutes. When he finally came back, by which time I was *spitting*, he explained, "The thing is Billy—I gave your number to a Chinaman last night and he won't give it back!" It dawned on me that Chic was telling me something. "You bastard!" I yelled at him, then burst out laughing. He did too, but he'd made his point.

'The very next time I saw him he paid me a beautiful compliment. He was going through to Edinburgh to see his daughter on her birthday. We'd been talking, and before he left—this man that to me nobody could top—said, "Billy, give me a 'wee Connolly' to take to Annabelle." I was touched enough at the time, but thinking about it again later, I could have wept. He'd asked *me* for a "wee Connolly"—this guy I'd admired so much—I felt like I'd been paid the ultimate compliment. Thank God for him—and the fact we had so much in common. "Connolly's OK, me and him speak the same language," he told a friend.

'We had always tended to approach things from the wrong side of the mirror, which reminds me of Michael Caine's contribution to the ranks of Chic Murray imitators, which incidentally is uncanny. Chic goes to look for digs and a landlady asks, "Have you got a good memory for faces?" Chic replies that he has. The landlady says, "Oh, that's good, because there's no mirror in the bathroom!" Michael was another big, big fan—but that's a measure of Chic's genius. *Everybody* has a Chic Murray story.

'One day we'd had a pint and we were rabbiting away. It was a lunchtime meeting and he told me he had been to Greenock to watch Morton. Now I believe him—I thought fine, this guy's been to see the football—and I didn't know I was being led into one of his visual fantasies. And he talked in pictures, he had me by the knees. I was howling, and he was describing this match and everybody in it—when he was finished you believed he'd described everybody in the crowd.

'But the one thing that sticks out in my mind—there was this man apparently who was standing beside him who had his baby with him— this big wean—and he had this big snottery wean in his arms, and a big dummy stuck in its face. And he was in terrible misery, the man, with this horrible child that kept screamin' and greetin'. And then Chic went from that to describing the wife—"You're goin' to the match are you? Well, you'll take *this* wi' ye!"—and slammed the big wean in his arms.

'So they're standing there—and the rain is *horizontal*—blowing right into the man's face and, I suppose, into the wean's face as well. Morton were being beat 4–0 at the time according to Chic, and this guy who's standing there in the wind and rain with the wean says, "Come on, Morton, *stop the kidding!*"

'Well—by now I'm clinging to the counter of the bar, the tears running down my face, and Chic starts to describe a bunch of dockers who were there, all watching the game, saying "C'mon, Morton!" and they were all big men, like Chic himself, except for one. There's four big men and one scrawny guy with a pointed face. I can see him to this day, although Chic only described him.

'And they've got a bottle of wine—Four Crown or something—and one glass, so they're pouring themselves a glass of wine, then passing the bottle to the next in line. And the wee guy at the end can't hold as much as these monsters, who look like wine barrels standing there scoffing, so he's swaying in the wind—and *Chic*'s swaying telling me the story—and eventually the wee guy goes too far forward, loses his balance and skids away down the terracing on his face—like the Cresta run. So he's all ash and stuff, he's all scraped and two wee boys say, "Ho, mister, here"— and they help him and get him back to where his big pals are standing up against one of those barriers, they prop him up. His face is all bleeding, it's all got charcoal in it, he's standing there, and the big man next to him hands him the bottle and the glass and says, "*Behave yoursel'!*" '

By 1978 Chic was approaching a crisis. His new-found friendship with Billy Connolly had given him a tremendous boost, but Connolly's enormous popularity had ironically underlined at the same time just how far Chic had slipped in his solo career. The failure of *The World of Chic Murray* still rankled and although he was kept busy—after a fashion—it was increasingly being brought home to him how much he was out of the limelight.

What's Up Superdoc? was about to be released, but he had worked on that film for precisely four days. Years of irregular meals—and drinks *instead* of meals, combined with constant travelling—had left him feeling rootless and lethargic. A visit to his doctor, he decided, would be in order. All he needed was a tonic, surely, just something to buck him up, put some of the old snap back. His doctor was shocked at his appearance.

Reggie McKay, already an old friend, asked him to sit down. 'I knew it was bad when you said that,' Chic said afterwards.

After a thorough examination Dr McKay declared, 'It's serious, Chic. You're not an alcoholic, but you've got liver trouble caused by heavy drinking. You're anaemic and you have an iron deficiency. You've neither been eating properly nor taking any sort of care of yourself. You need an immediate blood transfusion. On top of that—you've got duodenal ulcers.'

'Oh,' said Chic. 'But apart from that, I'm fine?'

One hour later he was admitted to Stobhill Hospital, where he was subjected for the next three weeks to constant care and attention from Dr McKay and a bevy of nurses competing for his attention. He had been invited to appear on the *This Is Your Life* TV presentation for Jimmy Shand and after much coaxing, the doctor agreed that he be allowed out for this towards the end of his stay—accompanied by three nurses. Dr McKay recalls Chic's stay in Stobhill. 'Apart from his various illnesses, he needed a damned good rest. His nonchalant act was just that—an act. He was an inward worrier and never gave himself a break. His hospitalisation did him a lot of good—with Stobhill's glamorous army of nurses vying for the big man's attention. Oh, and an army of visitors we had to hold back.'

Chic was pleased and touched to see anyone who came to visit him, but none more so than Annabelle, Douglas—and Maidie. At the start of her first visit he expressed his gratitude that she had come. 'Did you think I would do any less?' she asked him tenderly.

'No,' he replied, then beckoned her closer. 'Did you know I was very popular with the nurses in here? They seem to really like me.'

'Of course they do,' Maidie replied. 'When you're on your best behaviour there's no one nicer. One of them was telling me what a model patient you've been.'

Chic eyed her astutely. 'Not like all those times with you, Maidie, I know. I remember Cyprus, Blackpool, Hawaii—I wasn't such a model then. Maybe I've mellowed.'

Maidie smiled, 'Trust me—someone else is getting the best of you!' Then her smile faded and her voice was full of concern. 'Chic, how did you get yourself into such a state?' she asked.

He stared for over a minute through the window opposite his bed before quietly answering. 'Everything just seemed to get on top of me. I've been busy enough and yet not busy—you know, hunger or bust. And generally overdoing the drinking, I dare say. On top of that, some of the charge has gone out of it. When you're not getting a very positive feedback it makes for a hard grind, Maidie. How about you—how is love's young dream?'

Maidie grinned ruefully. 'It's broken down,' she replied quietly.

'Something along the lines of out of the frying pan and into the fire just about sums it up. Love's young dream, as you call it, flew out of the window.'

'I'm sorry to hear that,' said Chic, trying to sound genuine and failing miserably.

'No, you're not,' Maidie retorted.

'OK, no, I'm not,' he agreed. 'Except—I'm sorry it didn't work out from your point of view, Maidie. From my own point of view—'

'Yes, Chic?'

'—I've heard worse news.' He leaned over to rummage in the drawer of his bedside cabinet. 'Here's a pill for your headache,' he said holding out his hand. Maidie shook her head. 'I haven't got a headache,' she said.

'No? Jump into bed, then,' came the prompt reply, accompanied by an ear-to-ear grin.

Maidie smiled fondly, 'It strikes me you're on the mend.'

'I feel better for seeing you, Maidie, but you know what they say about extramarital sex?'

Maidie did her comic's labourer. 'No, Chic, what do they say about extramarital sex?'

'That it's OK so long as it doesn't hold up the wedding. On the other hand, I'm like the guy who was asked if he got any extramarital sex and replied, "Extra! I'm not getting *any* at all, never mind *extra*!"' Now Chic looked at Maidie with his best semi-serious expression. 'So is this visit your first overture? Is this you crawling back to me?'

'Back to the frying pan?' Maidie replied with a smile. 'That *will* be right! Just assure me of one thing—that you'll take better care of yourself when you get out. Don't forget—you're nearly 60 now—'

Chic's eyebrows shot up. Quietly looking round to make sure no one had overheard, he whispered, 'Don't be daft, Maidie. According to the papers, I'm only 50—'

'Aye, and the rest,' she continued, 'So you should be more careful with your schedule, your diet and your drinking. If you do take care, Chic, your best years are still ahead of you.'

At this Chic was genuinely incredulous. 'Come on,' he protested, 'For God's sake, be honest with me. My best years are well behind me, like back in the Fifties when we were topping bills, more than 20 years ago.'

'You just have no idea,' Maidie replied. 'You're becoming a blinking legend in your own lifetime. There's never a week goes by on the telly or the radio when you're not mentioned, or someone does a Chic Murray story or impersonation. You could be bigger than ever, Chic, but no one can get a hold of you. You seem to spend most of your life in limbo— endlessly travelling back and forth on trains and buses and planes. Push yourself, Chic, get a master plan worked out and stop ricocheting about from one project to another.'

'I'll try,' Chic promised, and Maidie felt it was time to go, for the big man looked exhausted. He still had something on his mind, as it turned out. 'Maybe we could reform the double act,' was his parting shot as she got up to go.

'One Pinky and Perky's quite enough in the business,' Maidie smilingly replied, before giving him a tender, lingering kiss.

Jimmy Hepburn was another welcome face at visiting time. 'I'm going to have to ca' canny with the booze in future,' Chic admitted, 'otherwise I'll be potted heid!' Jimmy smiled at the rhyming slang. 'What I need is a holiday—how about a few weeks in Tenerife with me, Jimmy? How do you fancy it—a couple of old teetotallers?'

'If that's what you want Chic,' Jimmy replied. 'It's on.' Looking back on the trip later, his old friend recalled, 'We had a great time, lay in the sun, ate a lot, gambled some and I watched Chic get his strength back. He thought a lot about what Maidie had said and seemed to get a lot of strength from his friendship with Connolly. But one thing hadn't changed—if Chic had always been careful with his money in the past, now he seemed determined to set new records.

'We both arrived with brand new bars of soap, shaving cream, toothpaste and all that, and we placed our stuff on either side of the bathroom cabinet. Chic's remained untouched in their packets while mine disappeared rapidly. He had a habit of getting up early in the morning and soaking for hours, so one morning I hid all my stuff, leaving just his, pristine and untouched. I lay there drowsing when he got up to run his bath—15 seconds later he was shouting me awake and demanding to know where I'd hidden my soap and toothpaste!

'At the end of the holiday I'd picked up the bill for just about everything and he asked me how much I'd spent. "About £600," I replied. "How much have you spent, Chic?" "168," he replied. "Pounds?" I asked incredulously, wondering where I had been while all this was going on. "Not at all," he chided. "Pesetas, Jimmy. *Pesetas*!"'

*   *   *

Only a few months after his release from Stobhill Chic was back in hospital again, this time with complete nervous exhaustion diagnosed. Even after Maidie's assurances and the few weeks' holiday with Jimmy, he had come back to few engagements and far too much time on his hands. A *Looks Familiar* on Thames Television, a Butlin's cinema advertisement and a few 'Grousebeater' overdubs for McEwan's lager was all he had been able to come up with during this lean time. He felt dumped and deserted—years after losing touch with Billy Marsh, he was suddenly and acutely aware of his lack of direction.

The nurses and doctors lavished attention on him until gradually they could see an improvement, and he began to regain some of his old sparkle. 'I always know you're on the mend when you start cheeking back to me,' one of the young nurses told him; then later in conversation with Dr McKay, it turned out that they had a mutual acquaintance. 'Anna Young?' Chic declared. 'I remember—that night at the King's Theatre she came backstage to see me with her husband and two sons . . .' His voice tailed off at the stricken expression on Reggie McKay's face, as he realised he would now have to tell Anna's tragic story—that her husband and one of her sons had been burned to death when their house had caught fire. Her husband had run into the blazing house in an attempt to save the trapped boy, then had been overcome by the flames himself, while Anna had looked on in horror. The shock had been too much for her and she had been ill ever since, sunk in a deep, dark depression. Chic recalled Anna's sparkling demeanour and radiant charm the night they had met at the King's, and a chill went through him as he tried to imagine how she must be feeling in the aftermath of such a tragedy. Somewhat against his better judgement—for he felt that Chic had enough to cope with—Dr McKay promised to trace Anna.

'I've heard your terrible news,' Chic told her when her phone call came through, 'and I want to express my most sincere and heartfelt condolences. Now—when can we meet?'

'Oh, Chic, I don't know,' Anna began, and Chic could hear her begin to choke up with tears. 'I'm not well, Chic—and I've heard you're not exactly full of beans either—'

'Never mind me,' Chic cut in. 'I'm right as rain now, whatever that means. And I'll phone you as soon as I know I'm getting out of here. You and I can have a good long talk.'

Two days later, still indeed far from well, he insisted on being discharged from hospital and arranged the meeting with Anna, who looked back on the start of Chic's many visits as a miracle. 'Chic purely and simply pulled me through,' she said. 'I helped him in return, but he did more for me than I ever did for him. He literally nursed me through the terrible depression I was having. And he would do it without my ever being aware of it. He'd start one of his daft stories and I'd be off, out of myself, away into his fantasy world.

'There was never anything between us other than the deepest friendship. I was his "big pal". He would often phone me up and he could tell from the tone of my voice if I was slipping away again. Immediately, he'd say he was coming round and I'd watch as he walked up the hill underneath my window. He wasn't well himself and walked like an old man, but up that street he hobbled. People often describe Chic as mean. They didn't know him! Oh, he never rushed in with presents or anything. I think he bought me a bottle of wine once or twice, then there were those crazy postcards—usually free ones from the hotels he was staying in, but he was generous *of himself*—he *gave himself* unsparingly and unceasingly. He made me want to live again.'

The Links

PAVILION

CARNOUSTIE

1946
Summer Season

CHALMERS WOOD
presents

BACK IN CIVVIES

With

BILLY McLEOD

AND FULL SUPPORTING CAST.

Change of Programme
Every MONDAY and
THURSDAY.

18

Gregory's Girl

'Hillhead used to be so tough you had to put your name down to get mugged. It's so rough there they've got John Conti as an Avon lady. There were so many fiddles going on that Mantovani could have been the District Clerk.'

As Chic gradually drifted back to work he was contacted by a voice from the past—none other than Billy Marsh. 'We'd lost touch. It was one of these inexplicable things. After *Casino Royale* things had just seemed to fall away a bit,' Billy said. 'Now, almost into the Eighties, we got together again. Chic was determined to work and exploit the 'Chic Murray' image. He was astute enough to realise that the image itself was worth more than he was at the time, but we determined to put this to rights.'

Despite Chic's disappearing tricks, Billy Marsh was able to pin him down sufficiently for a steadily increasing slate of engagements, both for television and radio. One assignment was for Scottish Television, where he arrived to find the rehearsal rooms fully booked. 'You can rehearse in there, Mr Murray,' Liz Moriarty heard the producer's voice say, then the next thing she knew Chic had entered her office. He introduced himself, then sat down opposite her. The main obstacle between them was a very large typewriter which Liz was very hard at work on, turning out an urgent report in her capacity of production assistant at Scottish Television.

As she continued her typing, Chic seemed to be determined to get her attention. Try as she did to keep her head down, he kept on explaining what it was he was trying to do. 'See, I'm this ventriloquist dressed like Liberace and I've got this large invisible dummy sitting on my shoulder. I've got to try to make the audience "see it". I'll show you what I mean. I start off by saying—' Liz stopped her typing and looked across at Chic as he explained the 'business'. 'You see? Now I'm getting the message that there's something going wonky and—'

Chic as the headmaster in *Gregory's Girl*.

'Chic, I'm sorry,' said Liz. 'I've got to get on.'

'OK,' said Chic. 'No problem. I'll just sit here quietly and run through all the patter. If you see my lips move you'll know what it is.'

Over the noise of the typewriter Liz could hear Chic going through the whole act, ready for a TV shoot later that week. Ten minutes later he started jumping up and down to attract Liz's attention. 'Look, Liz,' he said. 'I'm *doing* it now.'

From then on the two of them were gradually flung together more and more until soon a mutual fondness began to develop. 'Write me off, I don't care,' Chic would often say. 'I can still spring the occasional surprise.' Liz wondered what he meant by that and in the ordinary way of things she might never have found out, but one day she mentioned casually that she was taking her six-year-old son Jamie to the circus after work. 'What kind of circus?' asked Chic.

'Just one of these totty things that tour.'

'I'll take you and Jamie,' Chic declared. 'It'll be my treat. I'll pick you up at your house.'

When Liz opened the door to Chic that evening, he indicated the waiting Rolls-Royce and chauffeur outside with a sweep of his hand, accompanied by a broad grin. 'For you, Madame,' he intoned.

'But Chic,' Liz replied, 'the circus is only round the corner on the green!' This threw Chic for just one second.

'Even so,' he said, unperturbed, 'Climb in. It's our chariot for the night.'

Five minutes later all three of them were sitting in the front row under the tiny 'big top', sawdust all around them as the mini-show got going. 'And he loved it,' Liz recalls. 'I never found out to this day where he got our "chariot" but it certainly bore out his words about the occasional surprise! Jamie's eyes nearly popped out of his head when he saw the Rolls, and Chic gave us a decent run in it after the show as well.'

Chic did his first straight acting in a Scottish Television series and the experience gave him pause to think, for although it was a small part in a local soap opera, he had enjoyed it thoroughly. 'There could be something in this,' he mused to Billy Marsh, 'although I don't know why they call it legit—does this mean I've been "illegit" all my life?'

A journalist friend, Bernard McGovern, bumped into him in Glasgow and asked him how he felt about being the source of so many impersonations. 'I'm flattered,' Chic replied. 'In a way, that is—but I just wish I got royalties on it. I heard this particular comic having a go at me in Birmingham recently. The accent was away for a Burton, but he was pretty good otherwise. In fact, it made me keen to see Chic Murray for myself, but I always seem to be working when Chic's doing his act!'

A meeting of minds took place by chance on a train journey from Glasgow to London, the minds in question being those of Scottish film director Bill Forsyth and Chic. Soon after they got talking, Bill began to envisage Chic in the small but key role of the headmaster in his soon-to-be-filmed *Gregory's Girl*—would Chic be interested? Well, yes, Chic conceded, provided he could fit it in with his many other commitments, of course. Had Bill seen him in his earlier film triumphs, he wanted to know? Forsyth had to admit he had not and was in fact more familiar with Chic's humour as purveyed by others. An acquaintance of his had told him of an encounter with Chic outside a booksellers in Hillhead. While gazing intently at the window display, Chic had sidled up to him. 'I read a book once,' he confided, shaking his head. 'Didn't like it much!'

'I did see you once on stage with Maisie,' Bill told Chic.

'*Maidie*,' Chic corrected him with a headmasterly tone, immediately confirming to Bill that he had made the correct choice. After a further few minutes of silence Bill asked if Chic had seen his recent first feature *That Sinking Feeling*. 'No, I haven't,' Chic replied, 'but I passed a cinema once where it was showing—does that count?'

When filming started the producers pleaded extreme poverty, and with some justification, since everyone was working for next to nothing. The whole production was being shot on a shoestring on location in Cumbernauld new town, in the local school and town centre. The deal they had with Chic offered only a token fee, but all his scenes were planned to take up just two days of his time. In any case, he had a feeling that the film could be important, for something about the freshness of young Forsyth's approach appealed to him. At the same time he had been advised that Bill would be an absolute stickler that the script be played exactly as written, convinced that since only he knew where particular scenes would be dovetailed in, any improvisation, no matter how small, might ruin the pace or running order of his overall concept.

Unlike many films which have an extended gestation period, *Gregory's Girl* was on the floor only weeks after the meeting between Chic and Bill, since the casting of the role of the headmaster had been left until the very last. At the end of the first day's shooting Chic ruminated on how his scenes had gone. He had played his part as straight as possible, while trying to work in a slightly sinister edge to the portrayal that was nowhere to be found in the script or in the general perception of the character.

To relax later he sat down at an old upright piano in a corner of the school gym and started to tinkle out a ditty he had conceived during an afternoon in Jenny's office at the BBC. Bill Forsyth strolled over after watching Chic for a while, still dressed in his headmaster's gown. Something about the incongruity of the headmaster and the piano struck Bill as being just right. 'That would make a great wee scene in the picture,' he observed. 'Would you mind if we worked that in tomorrow?'

'Not at all,' Chic said, getting up. 'Just one thing though, Bill. That's my own composition—would I get an extra fee for it?'

Bill's eyes widened. 'I'll need to put that to the producers, Chic. You know what a tight budget we're on. If you hang on, though, I'll see if I can reach them.'

'Oh, Christ,' thought Chic, 'I've said a dirty word. Now the ba' will be on the slates!'

Ten minutes later Bill returned with the news that the producers were prepared to offer Chic an extra £50 for his piano performance—would that do, Bill asked. 'Oh, you know me, I'll have to talk it over with my agent, but I'll get back to you tomorrow,' Chic replied, leaving a somewhat nonplussed Bill behind him.

Bob Phillips, Chic's old neighbour and frequenter of the Chic Murray Hotel in its heyday, was someone with whom Chic always kept in touch, and like most of Chic's friends he also became his unofficial adviser in certain matters. With Bob it was monetary, for a reason that he has never yet been able to fathom. Now the call came, 'I'm in Edinburgh tonight. Fancy a drink? And there's something I'd like your advice on!'

As soon as the first round was set up, Chic got down to business. 'Bob, I'm making a film just now called *Gregory's Girl*. Everyone concerned with it is broke to the breek-arse and I'm doing it for very little money. So after we finish shooting today in this school in Cumbernauld I discover a piano in the gym. I haven't been tinkling away at the old ivories for more than a few minutes when this bright young bugger of a director comes over and says, "That's a nice tune you're diddling away at, Chic, maybe we could use that in the movie and add an extra bit of business." So I'm the headmaster of the school, right, but what I do after hours is my own business, get it? I point out to the wee pauper that the tune I'm knocking out on the old joanna is my own, that I'll expect an extra remuneration—money, that is—for so doing, if you get my meaning. So this gadje Bill Forsyth, whose sister wrote *Day of the Jackal* I believe—says oh, we can't afford any extra, Chic. He then goes into a huddle on the phone with his Swiss banker and comes back and offers me £50. Bob, the question is—should I take it?'

Bob sat quietly for a moment. Knowing Chic, he felt it was pointless to query the reference to Freddie Forsyth: the hard-up director's name was Forsyth and he obviously was making the film for peanuts. 'Did you say you wrote the tune yourself, Chic?'

'Correct.'

'Well, then you're entitled to royalties. I'm not up on these things, only being a property dabbler myself, but I think you could chance your arm a bit. Tell them you'll settle for five per cent of the world gross takings—that seems fair—*and* a flat sum of £500. That'll put the wind up them.'

Chic looked pained. 'Well, I don't know about them, but it's certainly put the wind up me! Don't you think that's a bit much, Bob?'

'Try it, what have you got to lose?' the bold Bob asked.

An excited Chic phoned Bob the very next day. 'I owe you a drink the next time I see you.' (Bob smiled at this.) 'I got on to that miserable tight-fisted bugger Forsyth and told him what my financial adviser had advisered, whereupon the whole production was just about shut down! When he heard the five per cent gross demand, he just about came down with artistic dementia, which as you know is almost invariably fatal. Bob, in the end they've agreed to pay me an extra £1000 flat providing I forget about a percentage!'

Chic considered he had done his bit for the production, following Bill's direction almost to the letter—while adding his own unique touches—but anarchy, never far away from the surface, reared its head as he and actor Alex Norton lined up for the last scene to be shot. As take after take proceeded, something went wrong on each occasion. The whole unit was tired and wanted to break for the night, but Bill Forsyth knew that Chic's last scene had to be finished before they could all go home. The take was a tricky one, starting as Chic was walking through the school corridors with Alex Norton, playing a teacher. Alex was supposed to say, 'Miss Muirhead's off again today, headmaster,' then Chic was to reply, 'Oh dear—that means we'll have to put class A in with class B for geometry, then the boys' afternoon games will have to be merged with the girls'—' Alex was then to chip in brightly, 'Don't worry, headmaster, I'll fix it up for you!' By this time he was due to be standing with his back to his classroom door, with one hand on the handle. 'Fine,' Chic was to say, 'I'm *depending* on you then!' before turning and walking away. As he did this, Alex's door was to ease open to reveal inside the entire class giving them both the 'V-sign' behind their backs. End of scene.

As they stood around for what was to be positively their last attempt to get this in the can, Chic took Alex to one side. 'Alex,' he explained, 'you know when you're standing there with your back to the classroom door, and I've said to you "I'm *depending* on you, then!" I want you to say to me, "By the way headmaster, did you know Miss Muirhead's been quite ill recently?"'

Alex blanched. 'Chic, what *for*? Bill will go *batty*, for God's sake.'

Chic was insistent. 'Just *do* it, Alex. I assure you it'll be perfectly all right,' he cajoled, giving Alex a most unreassuring wink.

As shooting re-started the scene went smoothly while Alex prepared himself for the departure from Bill Forsyth's carefully arranged scene. 'Don't worry, headmaster, I'll fix it up for you,' Alex said on cue. Chic stared at him. 'I'm *depending* on you, then!' he said. Alex almost froze, then managed to get Chic's line out. 'By the way, headmaster, did you know Miss Muirhead's been quite ill recently?' He then stared at Chic, who quick as a flash produced a large green apple from his voluminous robes. '*Has* she?' he asked. 'Give her this then, it'll make her feel better!' Alex stared at the apple disbelievingly, before breaking into helpless laughter, drowned out by the rest of the unit—with one exception. When the laughter began to subside, Chic strolled over to the impassive figure of Bill Forsyth. 'Very good, Chic,' said Bill, 'Now could we do it the other way?'

So it was done again—Bill's 'other way', and they all went home rejoicing after getting it perfect on the very next take. Alex later rationalised—after managing to avoid Bill Forsyth for a while—'Maybe sometimes you need a little bit of anarchy on the set as a break from all the tension—but Chic certainly gave me palpitations. I still break out in a cold sweat when I think of it!' Unfortunately for posterity, neither Chic nor Bill's version was included in the final cut of the film.

A few months after *Gregory's Girl* was completed Chic was asked out

for a meal by journalist John Gibson. The waiter produced a wine list
and suggested Pouilly Fuissé. 'I'm not fond of birds or cats,' Chic
retorted, 'let's settle for a nice Beaune.' He then explained that he had
taken a wine course during the filming of *Casino Royale*, adding, 'At
least some good came out of the picture. I can't remember much about
the course now, but I once heard about a guy who claimed he was a
connoisseur of fine wine. His method was quite simple—he just ordered
the dearest.'

Gibson got the subject on to films and Chic waxed lyrical about
Gregory's Girl, which was already being talked about inside the business.
'I think it'll be a right cracker,' he declared, 'and establish young Bill
Forsyth as a major film-maker. And me as an international superstar, of
course.' Gibson suggested there was something of the 'charming
heidbanger' about Chic, whose reaction was one of mock indignation.
'The public can appreciate the finer arts,' Chic pointed out, 'like the ease
with which a comic can deliver. They know there's an art in timing.
Mind, I don't like to see a comic sweat—unless he's an acrobatic comic.
Same with singers. You never see Sinatra sweat. He'll loosen his tie, yes.
I tried to do that once myself on stage, just like he does.' At this Chic
fell silent.

'What happened?' Gibson wanted to know.

'I couldn't get it loose,' Chic replied, shrugging his shoulders. 'I don't
mind comics who *mutter*. Elmer Prettywillie used to do it all the time,
probably to cover up the fact he'd forgotten his lines, which we all do
from time to time. I mutter myself quite a lot. Maybe you've noticed. I
believe I've muttered today already!'

He was still muttering later when he met the comedy all-rounder
Johnnie Beattie, whom he had known off and on for some years, without
ever actually spending any length of time with him. After enthusing over
Gregory's Girl for the second time that day, notes were compared on the
continuing Connolly phenomenon. Johnnie had met Billy when he was
on the point of leaving the Humblebums group Billy had formed with
Gerry Rafferty. Billy had written some jokes for Johnnie and confided
that what he really wanted to do was become a performing comedian
himself. 'Within a year,' Johnnie related to Chic with a laugh, 'he had
streaked past the whole bloody lot of us!' This started off an evening of
show-business talk and reminiscences which ended with the world being
put right at 5 a.m. the following morning. Along the way Johnnie
showed Chic a copy of 'Desiderata', which Chic fell in love with
immediately. Johnnie promised to get hold of a copy for him before the
two men, previously 'hail fellow, well met' acquaintances, now firm
friends, parted to go their separate ways once again.

Johnnie remembers the night fondly. 'When you met Chic you knew
that something unusual was happening. You were amused, intrigued,

Chic, Tommy Cooper and Eric Sykes in mid-sketch.

often slightly puzzled and generally bewildered. Still and all it was a pleasant experience that left you believing the world was a better place— the big man had just proved it.'

Shortly after this, Jimmy Logan would have disputed Johnnie's words. As the producer of the *Stars for Spastics* charity bill at the King's Theatre in Edinburgh he found himself with an all-star cast that was running well over time. 'Chic, you've got to do something,' he told him. 'You're one of nine comedians on the bill and all you're allocated is 12 minutes.' He awaited Chic's reply anxiously, but could see from the set expression on his face that he was in for a hard time. Already Jimmy had chopped his own spot and persuaded several of the other comics to perform in groups—now the very last bastion was Chic, whose act was currently running at 18 minutes. Jimmy pressed on manfully, 'Chic, I'm only asking you to cut back to what we originally agreed, no more than that.' 'I'll do what I can,' said Chic, 'I can't say fairer than that.' 'Chic, you've *got* to,' Jimmy urged, 'otherwise the second house won't be out till midnight!'

With the show further tightened up Jimmy felt reasonably certain that he was on top of things—until Chic's first house act went on and on.

From Chic's point of view it was the old adrenalin—he was back on a stage performing live and from the beginning received a rapturous welcome. Thus emboldened, he remained on stage for a record-breaking 22 minutes, while all Jimmy Logan could do was fume impotently in the wings, then watch in amazement as Chic swept past him afterwards, exiting to a storm of applause. 'Chic, for God's sake—' Jimmy began, but he sensed it was pointless. '—the bloody place being run by people with stopwatches,' he heard Chic mutter. Jimmy was not to know this was an old wound reopened.

The house manager rushed up to Jimmy. 'Did you mention his overrunning?' he wanted to know. 'I did,' Jimmy wearily replied, 'but I might as well have spoken to the wall. I don't know what's got into Chic.' 'I'll just run after him and see what he says,' the house manager said. 'He's got to listen to reason.' A moment later he returned, a sadder and wiser man. 'What did he say?' asked Jimmy, although one look at the man's face told him all he needed to know. 'He told me to take it up with his agent,' came the reply. 'That's *it*!' Jimmy hissed through clenched teeth, striding over to speak into the dressing-room tannoy. 'The second house will go ahead exactly as the first except that Mr Chic Murray will *not* be taking part.'

After making the announcement Jimmy strode into his office and banged the door behind him. He did not have long to wait, Chic making sure that his entrance was dramatic as he opened with, 'You realise that you're *sacking* me, Jimmy! And in my *home town*!' Jimmy turned to face him. 'That's right, Chic,' he said. 'I'm sorry, but that's right. The show's a team effort—maybe you're too much of a loner to play as part of the team.'

A few weeks later the two men met at a party. Jimmy felt a tap on the shoulder and turned round to find himself looking up at Chic. 'Hallo, heid the ba',' was Chic's greeting. 'Hallo, big man,' Jimmy replied.

'Produced any good shows recently?'

'As a matter of fact I'm working myself just now for a rather exacting producer,' Jimmy replied. 'I *am* sorry to hear that,' said Chic. 'Now are we going to stand here like a pair of prannies all night or what?'

'Maybe I was a bit intransigent—' Jimmy conceded, looking deep into his glass. 'I was definitely uppity—' Chic admitted eyeing his fingernails. 'You definitely were,' Jimmy assured him. 'Hey,' said Chic, 'how about forming a double act? Intransigent and Uppity—it's got a certain ring to it!' The two men shook hands on this and from then on the charity show was never referred to again.

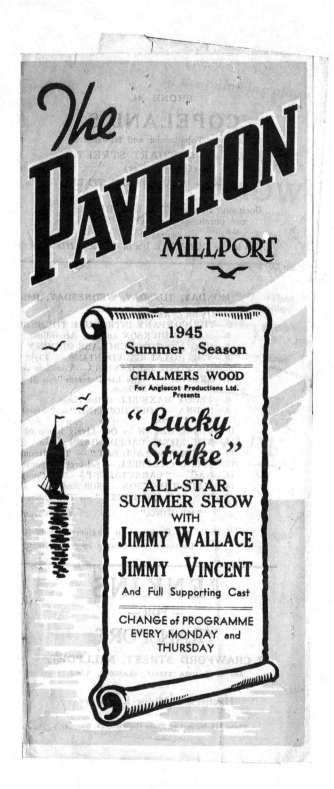

The PAVILION

MILLPORT

1945
Summer Season

CHALMERS WOOD
For Angloscot Productions Ltd.
Presents

"*Lucky Strike*"

ALL-STAR
SUMMER SHOW
WITH
JIMMY WALLACE
JIMMY VINCENT

And Full Supporting Cast

CHANGE of PROGRAMME
EVERY MONDAY and
THURSDAY

19

Saigon—Year of the Cat

'Yes, I'm making a film,' Chic told a reporter. 'Well, actually someone else is making it, I'm just appearing in it. The first fellow I met was the producer. He produces everything except cigarettes—seems to prefer using mine. Then there's another man hanging around; they call him the associate producer—I think that's because he's the only one who'll associate with the producer. Another important man is the floor manager, he manages the floor apparently. I expect he's got a flair for it!'

As the show-business buzz continued to build around *Gregory's Girl*, Chic was being kept unaccustomedly busy—a weekly series on BBC's Radio Scotland, *Chic's Chat*, was planned, for which Chic was to write all the scripts and choose the records; Ian Christie had plans for a television special which would be shot in the Mediterranean; and Chic had received further intimations of movie roles in the offing from Billy Marsh.

Journalist Gordon Hyslop, a well-known and faithful chronicler of Chic's movements over the years, was leaving the Scottish Television studios one afternoon as Chic arrived. 'Just the person I want to talk to,' Chic declared. 'I can't stop now, but I'll phone you in an hour.' Eight weeks later a postcard arrived for Hyslop from Valencia. Chic had 'dashed off' there for a working holiday and wrote that he hoped to see him on his return. This time he did phone and an appointment was made. 'What happened, Chic?' Hyslop asked, 'I'd given up hope after eight weeks. I thought you were going to ring in an hour.' Chic looked mysterious. 'Let's go for a drink,' he suggested. Hyslop led him towards a bar he knew, but Chic demurred. 'Not this one, Gordon—the barmaid always *questions* me,' he explained.

The next bar Hyslop suggested Chic said he didn't like the look of from the outside, and again they moved on. A third suggestion met with his approval and once they had sat down he asked for a soda water and lime, explaining that he was meeting an executive from the BBC later in the day and wanted to be fully compos mentis. 'Not that it's for a *Mastermind* or anything,' he added, 'but you know what they can be like, Gordon.'

He then began to explain his failure to phone and subsequent disappearance. 'A few minutes after I left you I got a call to fly to the Sahara to discuss a film with producer John Heyman. He'd made a picture with Elizabeth Taylor called *Boom* and I think he had a remake in mind with yours truly co-starring, this time re-named *Boom Boom* or some such tarradiddle. He said the part was that of a killer, cool, calculating and sardonic, a heavy part, but with a touch of humour. I don't know when it's due to start, but my bags are packed ready for the off. Right enough, they're always packed, but this time I've included my suntan lotion, so you know it's serious stuff.'

'Are you ever entirely serious about anything, Chic?' Hyslop wanted to know.

Chic considered this for a moment, then looked at the columnist bemusedly. 'Would you like to rephrase that question now, or shall we be off to Alan Rough's bar in Firhill to obtain another of these delightful concoctions?'

As they entered Rough's bar the footballer greeted them warmly. 'Chic,' he asked, 'where have you been? I haven't seen you for weeks. Ever since you gave me that tip on a horse that went down.'

'Business, business,' Chic muttered. 'By the way, Alan, that was a great one-handed save last Saturday. You were waving to the crowd with the other when you made it!'

Hyslop sat on after Chic left to keep his BBC appointment. He had heard the buzz on *Gregory's Girl* and knew what it might do for Chic—the question was, would Chic capitalise on it this time, or fritter it away as he had done before? There was something about big Chic that you just couldn't pin down, he mused, something that avoided the serious commitment necessary to follow through on the breaks. Ah well, maybe this time would be different . . .

When the first *Chic's Chat* went ahead the listening public were treated to a new kind of record programme. Apart from boasting some excellent records—more often than not selected with Annabelle's help—Chic's scripts were stamped with his own unmistakable style.

He went on to film the comic travelogue, *Chic Ahoy*, next for producer Ian Christie at the BBC. Ian's idea was to shoot the programme in seven episodes around the Mediterranean, starting in Genoa and sailing on to Cannes, Barcelona, Palma, Tunis, Palermo and Naples. It was arranged that the eight-strong film crew would travel aboard the *Victoria*, the agreement of the Greek line Chandros having been obtained to join the already packed charter. As a result of this the unit found considerable

restrictions placed on their time and were obliged to adhere rigorously to
the charter's tight schedule—if four hours were all the time the boat was
docked in Palma, then this was the precise amount of time they had. If
they failed to report to the ship before it embarked again on the next leg
of their trip, they would be left behind like any other passenger.

Ian quickly reached the conclusion that two circuits of the ports
would be required, one to sort out locations and the other for the actual
shoot. He vividly remembers the many hilarious—and alarming—
moments he and Chic shared, which culminated on the first circuit as
they were boarded at Tunis by heavily-armed policemen. No one was
allowed to leave the boat until all passports had been inspected. Alarmed
by this potential incursion into his precious reconnaissance time, Ian
undertook to collect the documents from all his personnel. As he set off
on this task, he left the Tunisians brandishing their sub-machine guns
and scowling ominously.

He called on Chic first, who replied through the closed door of his
cabin that he would produce the passport presently. 'OK,' said Ian, 'but
don't delay, Chic. I'll collect everyone else's and come back for yours
when I've finished.' Five minutes later he returned to Chic's cabin,
clutching his pile of passports in one hand. With the other he tried to
open the door to Chic's cabin—only to find it locked.

'I'll be right with you,' Chic shouted. 'I'm just finishing dressing.'

'Oh, hurry up, Chic, for God's sake,' Ian replied. 'This is cutting
down our time on shore.'

Five long minutes passed as Ian watched a steady stream of passengers
leaving the boat—still there was no sign of Chic emerging. 'Chic!' Ian
yelled. 'I need your passport. *Now*!'

'Won't be long,' Chic replied infuriatingly. 'Just finishing.'

At the back of his mind Ian had a fair idea what Chic was playing at.
Having gone along with various newspaper reports that had given his age
as between 50 and 55, he clearly had no wish to have his cover blown for
all time by a handful of armed Tunisians. Nevertheless, it seemed to Ian
as he fumed and sweated that this was hardly a reason to prevent the
whole crew going ashore in Tunis. As he saw the last of the
passengers—except his personnel—leave the ship, he roared at Chic
through the door. 'Chic! Hand over your passport *now*! I don't care if
you're a *hundred* and flaming sixty! I want it *right now* or I'll order these
Tunisians to *shoot you*!'

Seconds later the door opened a few inches and the passport was
handed over. As Ian rushed off he heard Chic mutter, 'No need for that
sort of talk!'

The harassed producer found the Tunisians busy taking his camera
equipment apart piece by piece and recording the serial numbers, a
process to be repeated later. While on shore Ian engaged an interpreter

and hired transport to meet them on the dock on the second tour. 'Any ideas what props you might need when we return here?' he asked Chic.

'A camel,' Chic replied.

Ian communicated this to the interpreter, who nodded enthusiastically, assuring him there would be no problem. 'You got your passport back again OK, Chic?' Ian asked later.

'I did,' Chic replied, fixing him with a beady eye. 'A passport is a very personal document,' he lamented. 'The next thing you'll be wanting to know is what size of shoe I take.'

Ian felt it pointless to explain that neither Chic's age—nor his shoe size—aroused even one iota of curiosity in his breast, and wisely changed the subject, choosing instead to mend fences. 'Your idea for a sketch involving a camel sounds really interesting Chic,' he told him. 'What have you in mind?'

'Oh, it just came to me in a flash while you stood there yapping away at that so-called interpreter of yours. I'll let it do the rounds of the old cranium—it'll be ready for our return to Tunis, don't you worry.'

Ian felt exhilarated—things were falling into place and Chic, around whom the whole trip was built, was working well.

When filming began on the second tour Ian felt even better. They had some marvellous footage from everywhere they had been, with Barcelona providing the only problem. As Chic had tried to describe an ancient monument in the town square, he had been constantly interrupted by barking dogs. Despite numerous takes, they had been unable to get usable footage and Ian had more or less made up his mind to scrap this and show Chic on the boat with some background material he had shot separately.

When they finally arrived back in Tunis they were told they had precisely five hours on shore. The interpreter turned up at the docks with two jeeps, into which the crew and equipment was loaded. 'Everything fixed?' Ian asked eagerly. 'You have found camel?'

'I take you,' came the reply.

'How far?' Ian asked. 'Not much time.'

'Soon,' he was assured, and off they set.

Chic sat next to Ian in the front seat of the jeep, looking for all the world like a visionary as he surveyed the endless miles of sand stretching before them. As the journey progressed it seemed impossible to obtain from the interpreter any idea of how long it would take before they arrived at the whereabouts of the beast. After a full hour had passed, Ian added the hour on it would take them to get back and started to worry, especially when their convoy was forced to stop suddenly behind a lorry blocking the road. It transpired that they had joined a queue for a ferry and as the waiting continued all Ian could think was, 'Have I come all the way to Tunis to sit and stare at the back of a lorry? I could be sitting in Byres Road in Glasgow doing this!'

Just as Ian began to contemplate grabbing the interpreter by the throat and choking the life out of him—while Chic gazed disdainfully in front of him into the middle distance—the convoy started to move and to Ian's intense relief they just managed to squeeze on the ferry.

'Five more minutes only on other side,' Ian's interpreter assured him, then a full 15 minutes later the weary party, grimy and hot after the uncomfortable and sticky journey, discerned a green patch ahead. Was it a mirage? No, it was a small village, in the centre of which was a palm-fronted hotel. Even more incredible—the long-promised camel was securely tethered outside. 'Oh, boy, we're in business,' Ian chuckled. 'It is *our* camel, isn't it?' he asked the interpreter, who assured him that it was. It was a feature of the hotel, whose guests could be photographed sitting on it and even led a few paces on its back.

Ian supervised the unloading of the jeeps and smiled beatifically as he saw Chic walk towards the camel, then stop a few paces away from it. 'Everything OK, Chic?' he asked.

Chic turned to face Ian, a perturbed look on his face. 'No, it's not,' he replied. 'Ian, this is not a *correct* camel. This—' here Chic paused, as if for full effect, 'is a *tourist* camel.'

'But Chic,' Ian protested, 'it's all we've got. A camel's a camel, surely. What's the difference?'

'No, it won't *do*, Ian,' Chic insisted. 'You know I had pictured an oasis-type scene in the middle of the desert.'

Ian breathed a sigh of relief. 'Oh, if that's the problem I can get over that. We'll keep the hotel out of the picture.'

Chic was adamant. 'It's no *use*, Ian. I can't do it—not with an *incorrect* camel.'

Ian felt his heart sink to his boots—first Barcelona and the barking dogs, now it was Tunis and an incorrect camel! He tried again to coax Chic to go ahead anyway, but got nowhere, while all around them the film crew stood about awaiting instructions. Finally Ian glared at Chic in desperation before turning to address his crew.

'We've got a problem,' he told them. 'It seems that in Chic's eyes the camel's incorrect. Yes, *incorrect*! He looks OK to *me*—he probably looks OK to *you*, but he's out as far as *Chic* is concerned, so that's that. Shoot some background stuff, then we'll load up and get back to the ship.'

When they were safely back on board Ian was able to rationalise the day's events and get them into perspective. Chic was an artiste after all, not a plumber being asked to fix a tap. No one could say how comedy 'worked' and if something in the set-up made the comic uneasy then it had to be respected—all the same, it had not been an easy day. When Ian met Chic for dinner he slapped him on the shoulder and said, 'Come on Chic, let me buy you a drink.' Chic looked surprised, as this was hardly the reaction he had been expecting, but he was clearly pleased and the matter of the 'incorrect camel' was not referred to again.

When Ian was busy editing the programme, he reconsidered his view of replacing the Barcelona footage with stock shots, for Chic's fluffs as he was constantly put off by the dogs barking off screen, were hilarious in their own right. Naturally, he felt that Chic must be consulted first and his agreement sought, so he called him up and explained.

Chic's reaction was one of horror. 'You can't do that,' he declared. 'It's not professional.'

'Will you come over and have a look at them for yourself, Chic, before you finally decide?' Ian asked.

'Of course I will,' Chic said, 'but I'm telling you now . . .'

Within the hour Ian had played the tapes through to Chic. He watched Chic start to smile as he played the takes, spliced together one after the other. 'I don't know,' Chic said after the first viewing. 'Let's have another run through, Ian.' The clips were run again and this time Chic had no hesitation. 'Great,' he declared. 'Christie strikes again! I'll bet this turns out to be the funniest part of the whole show.'

'You mean you approve?' Ian asked, incredulously.

'Approve?' Chic echoed. 'I'll sue you if you don't include it!'

Ian smiled and shook his head. He could have hugged Chic, but more importantly—for the first time the camel episode suddenly clicked into place and Ian was given an insight into Chic's mind.

'What's the matter?' asked Chic, solicitously. 'Have a nippy sweetie by the way, Ian.'

'Nothing's the matter,' Ian replied, accepting Chic's rare gift. 'I think we've got a terrific programme here.'

'That's what it's all about, Ian,' Chic replied breezily.

*   *   *

The triumph of *Gregory's Girl*, which everyone looks back on now as an instant *fait accompli*, was something less than that. Its distributors, Lew Grade's ITC, felt that they had a hit on their hands after years of flops, but knew that it might be difficult to get the message out to the public. To spread the word Alan Kean of ITC arranged for the young cast, including John Gordon Sinclair, together with Chic and Bill Forsyth, to attend a sneak preview of the picture at Glasgow's Odeon cinema.

Bill chose to sit on his own at the back of the circle while the unspooling took place, before seeking refuge in the projectionist's booth when he could stand it no longer. 'Don't worry, Bill, it's playing well,' he was assured by the couthy operator who had seen them all. Later they had to meet the press, where Chic held forth to various scribes. 'D. W. Griffith will be turning in his grave,' he declared. 'Billy Wilder will resign from screen comedy. And the Bowery Boys will re-group. I see the picture as Cecil B. De Mille meets the Three Stooges, or Tom and Jerry in *The Incredible Voyage*—see what I mean?'

Despite Chic's optimism the film went on to run for only a few weeks at the smallest cinema in the Odeon's three-screen complex, but ITC were not too discouraged, calculating that the film would take on a new lease of life when it subsequently opened in London. In this they could not have been more correct, for on its release in the metropolis excellent takings began to be realised as the English critics went overboard in their praise for the film. *Gregory's Girl* was soon outgrossing films that had cost many times its minuscule budget—so it was back to Scotland, where the film was re-booked at Glasgow's La Scala cinema in Sauchiehall Street—now, alas, no longer with us. Here it ran to packed houses for months on end. In Edinburgh the story was the same at the unique Dominion cinema, where the film enjoyed an unprecedented run of almost two years.

Nor was the film finished even then, for the marketing boys had other plans. Independent British film producer David Puttnam—who had, ironically enough, been offered *Gregory's Girl* first by Bill Forsyth and turned it down—brought off a triumph of his own with *Chariots of Fire*, directed by Hugh Hudson. The film told the story of two British athletes, one of them a Scot, Eric Liddell, and their triumph at the 1924 Paris Olympics. It had swept the board at the Hollywood Oscars ceremony, where Puttnam had personally collected the 'Best Film' award, and had enjoyed a tremendous run at the box-office, not least in the US, where it became the biggest ever British grosser.

With the run of both *Gregory's Girl* and *Chariots of Fire* apparently ended, Puttnam had an inspired idea—why not reissue them together in a double bill? When this was done the programme went on to earn more than any other feature on release, to the astonishment of the film world. Nor was there any question of either film hitching a ride on the other, for preferences varied from area to area, and not always in the way that might have been predicted. Bill Forsyth's name was made—and in an ironical twist, he was signed to make his next movie for none other than David Puttnam. For Chic, the feedback was tremendous, for his scenes were among the funniest in a delightful film. If the whole venture ended up being somewhat overpraised, as many felt, who was to demur as the money poured in through the box-office tills? The Samuel Goldwyn Company signed to release the film in the States, where it repeated its success with both the critics and the paying public—albeit in a completely re-dubbed version! If the public had needed a reminder that Chic Murray was alive and kicking—here it was, with a vengeance.

With the John Heyman film shelved for financial reasons, Chic was none the less on the crest of a wave, receiving not one but two further offers for movies. One was to be a big-budget television project,

Saigon—Year of the Cat and the other was a home-grown venture from the idiosyncratic Murray Grigor, *Scotch Myths*.

He looked back on Maidie's words to him during his hospitalisation not so long ago. 'If you do take care, Chic, your best years are still ahead of you.' He had given this little credence at the time, but now how could he deny it? Not that he had ever been short of a crust—never that, but he had undoubtedly lost his place, and in an odd way that was where the Chic 'cult' probably began. Most show-business stars have actually to expire before passing into legend, probably because of the impossibility of any new material with their demise. Without planning it, Chic had rationed his exposure to the point many people thought he *was* gone—and in his 'absence' been aided by the innumerable impersonations that kept him constantly in the public eye. Now he was back with a bang—as Maidie had predicted.

While Chic was still in Bangkok filming *Saigon*, Murray Grigor anxiously awaited news of his promised arrival back in Scotland to work on *Scotch Myths*. The *Saigon* team had wanted him to stay on beyond his scheduled time in case retakes proved necessary, but they were aware of his prior commitment and agreed that he leave. 'I could have had a couple more weeks by the pool,' said Chic later, somewhat ruefully, 'but a promise is a promise and I didn't want to bring about the downfall of the entire Scottish film industry!'

It was doubly a wrench to leave the *Saigon* unit as Chic had managed to forge friendships with the entire cast, including the stars, Frederic Forrest and Judi Dench, and director Stephen Frears, so it was with a sense of considerable culture shock that he found himself swathed in tartan for *Scotch Myths*. 'There was one Scottish connection in Bangkok while I was there,' he recalled, 'apart from myself, that is. *Gregory's Girl* was being shown locally and the whole unit trooped down to see it. The cinema was not air-conditioned, which lent a distinctly Eastern atmosphere to the entire proceedings.' When asked what the locals made of it, Chic replied, looking bemused, 'I think they made a curry with it. Anyway it seemed to go down quite well.'

Murray Grigor was soon to discover, as Bill Forsyth had before him, that gentle anarchy was liable to break out on the set while Chic was around. No one could be quite sure when he was entirely kidding or not, and after one unfortunate actor accidentally trod on his hand during one scene, he rounded on him with a cry of, 'You've stepped on my fingers! You know, in America you would be sued for that! Yes! I know it sounds funny—permanent loss of pressure in the pinky, but today it's a palpitating pinky—tomorrow it could be a malfunctioning pinky!'

Chic's unerring sense of the surreal surfaced again one night when he was invited to stay for dinner with Murray and Barbara Grigor. They had been discussing an article in *Scottish Field* which mentioned Chic and featured a photograph spread on him. As they sat down to dine a friend of the Grigors appeared at the front door. His unexpected arrival and the fact that he was sailing three sheets to the wind notwithstanding, the Grigors invited him to join them for dinner. After the meal the newcomer spied the open edition of *Scottish Field* with Chic's photographs splashed over two pages. 'See that man!', he exclaimed. 'He's absolutely the greatest comedian of them all!' Chic, sat opposite him, immediately piped up, 'Oh, I *certainly* don't agree with that.' The Grigors were then treated to the spectacle for the next half-hour of Chic arguing vociferously against himself to the guest, who remained all the while blissfully unaware that his judgement was being questioned by the very recipient of his praise.

After dinner, with their friend departed, Murray Grigor explained to Chic that he and Barbara had been asked to auction off some items from Hugh MacDiarmid's estate at the request of his wife, Valda, the proceeds of which were to go towards funds to commission a memorial sculpture to the late poet. When he heard of one of the rarest items—a pipe which

MacDiarmid had been given by Sir Harry Lauder—Chic offered to auction this himself. 'And I'll have a bit of fun at the same time as getting you a record price,' he promised them.

So he did, as over an hour was spent by him outrageously increasing the bids. Chic's eyes sparkled as he spotted Jimmy Logan among the sea of faces, for he knew that Jimmy was a keen collector of Lauder memorabilia. 'You can have it, Jimmy,' he chuckled to himself, 'but by the wee man, you're going to have to go some!'

'Do you realise,' he asked the bidders, 'that whoever buys this will walk away with a little piece of Scots history? Sir Harry was a famous man—but this was also a famous pipe. And as you can see,' he gestured round the saleroom, 'it's already proved a big draw!' As the price went up and up, Chic kept them all hanging on. 'I can picture him now,' he declared, 'strolling along Sauchiehall Street, kilt swingin' in the breeze and this grand old pipe belching forth fire and smoke. He took it everywhere with him and the greatest in the land had to put up with it. When Sir Winston Churchill lit up one of his cigars, Sir Harry was there with his pipe. At meetings with the Prince of Wales, Henry Ford and Andrew Carnegie, they had to like it or lump it. Think where it's been!' As the bidding resumed Chic was ready for his final salvo. 'One of Sir Harry's last requests as he lay dying was for this self-same beloved pipe of his to be wheeled in. Now whoever gets it today can look forward to doing the same!'

'You make a great auctioneer,' Jimmy Logan ruefully told Chic later, as he was about to leave—empty-handed.

'At what point did you drop out of the bidding, Jimmy?' Chic asked.

'When we passed the point of no return and it was obvious you were going to start charging us all bed and breakfast,' Jimmy replied.

Murray Grigor recalls a premonition he had that something would come of the confrontation between Chic and the maverick Hollywood film director Sam Fuller. Sam had agreed to do a day's shooting on *Scotch Myths* for Grigor as a favour for an old friend, having met him in his previous capacity as director of the Edinburgh Film Festival, when Grigor had mounted a retrospective of Fuller's classic movies, such as *House of Bamboo, Pick up on South Street, Underworld USA, Naked Kiss* and *Shock Corridor*.

Unfortunately their schedules did not coincide and it was only later, when the finished *Scotch Myths* was unveiled, that Grigor's premonition proved correct. After talking quietly in a corner to each other for half an hour, Fuller announced that Chic was perfect for the part of one of the characters in his new movie, *Quint's Game*. The film was postponed for the moment, he explained, the result of a lack of cash, 'but when it does roll,' he proclaimed, 'I want Chic Murray in Paris for the shoot.'

Now came rumours of an even more spectacular kind. As a result of meeting Frederic Forrest on *Saigon—Year of the Cat*, Forrest had

Johnny Beattie the perennial favourite.

spread the word on Chic to none other than Francis Ford Coppola, Forrest's director on *Apocalypse Now*. It seemed that Coppola was looking for someone to play the part of the likeable night-club owner, Orrie Kelly, in *The Cotton Club*—the role that subsequently went to Bob Hoskins.

Chic was bemused at his change in circumstances, for he had come back from his lowest ebb. *Gregory's Girl* was on reissue with *Chariots of Fire* and doing tremendous business. There was already advance praise for his straight role as the dour, brave Scottish bank manager in *Saigon—Year of the Cat*. *Scotch Myths* was in the can and looking good.

Now all sorts of possibilities began to open up. Murray Grigor had a 'porridge Western' in mind to feature Chic and Billy Connolly, with a Don Camillo flavour—only in reverse. Chic saw himself as the 'heavy', an anarchic gun-toting priest who kept a revolver inside his Bible, while Billy would be the 'goodie' mayor with whom he would constantly be at odds. Things had never looked brighter since Chic's solo career began—now there was only one thing missing in his life.

EMPIRE

⋯THEATRE⋯
GREENOCK.

6.30——TWICE NIGHTLY——8.30

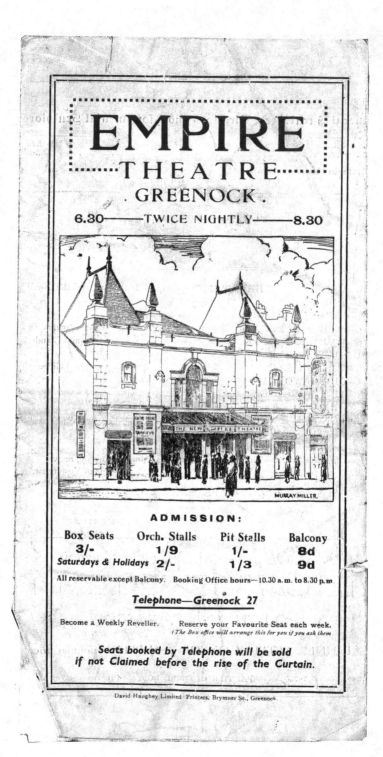

MURRAY MILLER.

ADMISSION:

Box Seats	Orch. Stalls	Pit Stalls	Balcony
3/-	**1/9**	**1/-**	**8d**
Saturdays & Holidays **2/-**		**1/3**	**9d**

All reservable except Balcony.   Booking Office hours—10.30 a.m. to 8.30 p.m

Telephone—Greenock 27

Become a Weekly Reveller.   Reserve your Favourite Seat each week.
(The Box office will arrange this for you if you ask them

Seats booked by Telephone will be sold if not Claimed before the rise of the Curtain.

David Haughey Limited Printers, Brymner St., Greenock.

Chic MURRAY

20

You'll Never Walk Alone

'I was standing at the bus stop the other day when a man came up to me and said, "Have you got a light, mac?" I said, "No, but I've got a dark brown overcoat." '

If someone had told Maidie she would ever tread the boards again, she would have laughed out loud—but the call did come, for a charity affair to be held at the Usher Hall, Edinburgh. When one of the acts had taken ill and the organisers were desperately trying to think of someone to fill the vacant spot, Maidie's name came up. The engagement was for Maidie the soubrette—an act she had not performed for years, but for old times' sake she accepted.

Chic would never have heard of it but for a chance meeting he had in Glasgow with Tom and Jack, the Alexander Brothers. 'Maidie on stage?' he asked incredulously. 'You're kidding me on!' Eventually he was convinced they were not and that furthermore Tom and Jack themselves were also on the bill. 'In that case give me a hurl through to Edinburgh with you—but don't let on to Maidie I'm in the audience.'

Maidie had rehearsed five numbers, including a Scots selection to start, with the old accordion dug out of the mothballs it had lain in for years and pressed back into service. Chic sat well back in the stalls as the announcement was made. 'Ladies and gentlemen, you'll remember Maidie Dickson as one half of the wonderful Chic and Maidie partnership—or maybe even before that as Maidie Dickson, soubrette. She's agreed to come back tonight specially for you. Give a big hand for the little lady—Dainty Maidie Dickson.'

Chic felt a lump in his throat as the tabs opened ('The tabs, Chic.' 'Tabs?' 'The curtains!') and Maidie came on, her diminutive figure resplendent in the spotlight. Chic felt himself transported back to his first sight of her in Isabella's parlour, then her appearances at the dear old Greenock Empire. What a cracker she had been then—and still was.

A grateful patient dispensing largesse to his nurses.

He was able to choke back the tears only until her second number, 'A Little Bitty Tear', then the memories were just too sweet and too strong.

When Tom and Jack picked Chic up later they both pleaded with him to go backstage to see Maidie. 'I can't,' he declared, gruffly. 'I've got the father and mother of a cold coming on. Come on and get me back home like good boys.'

'Not a word was said going back in the car,' Tom recalls. 'Just the odd sniffle from Chic in the back—and it wasn't a cold he had either.'

Chic found himself back in hospital again soon after and on the receiving end of another cautionary warning from Dr McKay. He knew that he would ignore these warnings at his peril, but was exuberant at the boost his career had received. He had never been in greater demand and as long as Billy Marsh kept the offers coming, why should he put the brakes on? There was still plenty of him to go around, even though there was less recently than there had been, with his weight now down from 14 to 12 stone. 'And a good thing, too,' he told himself. 'I've got to keep light on my feet.' He surveyed himself in the mirror—a bit grizzled, sure, but otherwise not much to contradict a newspaper article that placed him in the 'mid-fifties'.

On a recent visit to Maidie's he had struck up a real friendship with his young grandson, Douglas. 'A right wee ripper,' he called him, and still even then he led Maidie on. 'I'd like a bath,' he announced one night. 'OK,' said Maidie. 'I'll go and run it for you now, Chic.' Chic flicked away at the television remote controls, until Deanna and Douglas were both up in arms. 'Grandad! We're wanting to see *Top of the Pops*,' they protested. 'If you want that noise, go and watch it in black and white in the kitchen,' Chic told them.

Off they went, then Maidie returned. 'Where are the kids?' she asked. 'They're off to watch *Top of the Pops* in the kitchen. They prefer it in black and white apparently,' Chic blithely replied. Maidie shook her head; she knew that once Chic was in charge of the remote control he monopolised the viewing. 'Your bath's ready now, anyway,' she announced. Chic looked up absently. 'Oh, Maidie. Would you mind? I'd rather have it once the news is finished. Wee Douglas could have it now, then I could have it after him.'

'He'll not be very keen during *Top of the Pops*, but I'll ask him,' said Maidie.

'There's just one thing.'

'Yes, Chic.'

'Well—it's a wee bit delicate. Now I think of it—he's not likely to *pee* in the bath water, is he?' Maidie's eyes widened in indignation.

'Certainly not,' she exclaimed. 'He's a wee boy who's been better brought up than that.'

'But he did pee in the bed as a wee boy, Maidie,' Chic persisted. 'Oh, Chic! Lots of wee boys pee in the bed,' said Maidie. Chic looked up at her with an old-fashioned expression on his face. 'I *know* they do, Maidie,' he replied, 'but not from the top of the wardrobe!'

Maidie realised Chic had done it again, leading her on like an idiot and winding her up. As far as he was concerned the double act had never split! 'I'll have that bath now,' he chuckled.

*   *   *

When 1984 was only a few weeks old Chic heard from Billy Marsh about an offer from the Everyman Theatre in Liverpool. 'Money-wise it's no big deal,' Billy told him. 'Forget the money,' Chic replied, 'I'm doing it.' The company wanted him to play the lead in a musical play called *You'll Never Walk Alone*, the subject being Liverpool FC's late manager, Bill Shankly. 'Did someone call *me* a legend?' Chic was heard to say. 'If it's true, then one legend's about to play another.'

For the entire run of the play Chic stayed in Liverpool, for he loved the city and its people, well remembering how the Scouses had always turned out in their thousands to see Chic and Maidie—although he hadn't realised then that the crowds had regularly included Shankly himself, a big fan. Now he was playing the hero, who also happened to be *his* hero—the whole enterprise had such a feeling of rightness about it. 'I would have done it for nothing,' he told Maidie. 'He's like a God still in Liverpool, but, though his ghost is supposed to walk through the play, I'm going to play him as a living, breathing person. I would never have taken part if it had been trying to make fun of him or rip him apart, I think too much of the man for that.'

Chic's first task was to get the famous Shankly voice right and many of the staff at Anfield were taken aback when they first heard him. 'It's uncanny,' they told him. 'That's just how he spoke.'

'The accent wasn't too difficult,' claimed Chic. 'Ayrshire bordering on Lanarkshire, because he came from a wee fitba'-daft community where he played for the Glenbuck Cherrypickers—a marvellous name that, and absolutely true. The trick is to get the Shankly delivery. With him, everything was definite. He spat everything out and didn't waste a word. "Him up there may have blown the final whistle," he'd say, "but I'm playing extra time."'

'I loved Shankly's style and I loved the stories about him,' Chic declared. 'Like the apocryphal story of when he first arrived at Anfield and tested the team by placing 11 barrels on the pitch and having them play against them. "By half-time," Shankly reported, "the barrels were winning 3–1!" Another time he was told that a Jewish signing, because of his religion, might not be able to play on a Saturday and commented, "There are ten others doing the same!"

'Like me, Shankly was a loner who went his own way and didn't listen too much to other people. He went to one coaching course and said afterwards, "I do the opposite of what they do and do well. They know *nothing* about football." Bill's secret was that he had the common touch. He's a national institution because he was a character. By the time the play's off I'll know all there is to know about fitba'—and since I've got the Shanklyisms off pat, I'll be the man to motivate the players. When the run finishes it'll just be the start of the season in Scotland. Who knows, maybe my next engagement will be in the Premier League!'

In a jubilant mood when he got back to Edinburgh after the show's extended run in Liverpool, Chic stopped off to visit Annabelle, now in her own flat, before spending the night with Maidie. Billy Connolly was being interviewed on television that night and as father and daughter watched, he was asked about his own favourite comedians. He unequivocally replied: 'Chic Murray, in my opinion, is the best comedian in the world. I think he's the funniest man on earth and I aspire to be what he is. As he gets older he gets more outrageous, which is a lovely thing, and more absurd. Sometimes I meet Chic and he tells me a joke— and I don't know it's a joke until he's three quarters of the way through. The man's a genius. I hope as time goes on I can hone my material as fine as Chic. He goes into his tales like a story and *becomes* all the characters. That's what I ideally aspire to as a comedian—to be as good as him. I'd like to get more off the wall as I get older, the way he has done.'

Chic was taken aback by this generous tribute from one artiste to another. 'No wonder they call him the Big Yin,' he said, 'it *takes* a big man to come out with that.' When Maidie excitedly asked if he had seen the show when he arrived at her place later, he replied, 'Aye, I did, and it was nice of Billy, but I think maybe he's got mixed up with *Ruby* Murray!'

When Chic was introduced by another long-time fan, Jimmy Tarbuck, on his TV show *Tarbie and Friends*, Chic was his usual bemused self—and soon slaying the audience. 'I was staying in a hotel here in London,' he started off, 'and I'm not a complainer, but I went downstairs and I could see the manager looking at me. He said, "What is it?" I said, "I would like a *door* in my room." He said, "You're funny, aren't you?" I said, "I *prefer* a door in my room. I'm *used* to a door in my room." "Oh well," he said, "in that case we must get a door for you somewhere." So after some time a door arrived—not on its own of course, two fellows brought it up. And one of them said, "I'm the carpenter—would you like a handle on the door?" I said, "Well, it seems like a good idea"—just to give him confidence, as it were. So once the door was fixed I made my way out, because I wanted to get out, you see, and turned the handle. There was one on the other side, I noticed that on the way out, really useful, otherwise you'd need to put your arm round the door.

'So I went down and the manager said, "Have you got the door?" I said, "Yes, the door's in the room." He said, "You've no sooner got the door in than you start going out. When you made your way in here, I thought, here's *trouble*." I said, "Well, I don't think I'm causing a great deal of trouble. I just wanted a door in my room." "Well, you've *got* one," he said. I said, "Yes, yes, I have." "You're going out for a while," he added. I said, "Yes." He said, "Why?" "Because I don't want to stay in, that's why," I told him. So I made my way downstairs. The stairs led down to the street—they led all the way up too, of course—saves them having two stairways really.

'As I was perambulating along the sidewalk, this fellow approached me. I knew him otherwise I'd never have allowed him near me. And he stopped. So *I* stopped—just to let him see I could do it. And he was surprised. He didn't say he was surprised, but I knew he was surprised—I could see it by his eyes. He'd found someone as good as him! "Oh," he said, "It's you." I said, "Yes." I couldn't deny it *standing there*. He said, "I thought it was you." "Oh," I said, "it's me all right"—I could remember coming out. I said, "You've got a nice dog with you"—he had a dog with him *otherwise* I'd never have mentioned it. He had it on a lead—he didn't seem to be too sure of it. He said, "Yes, it *is* a nice dog." It wasn't, it was a *dreadful* creature. It wasn't trained properly—you just had to stand there and hope for the best. I always think if they can teach them to beg—they could surely teach them to look up and see your lips, just an extra kick would do it, you know.

'He said, "Do you know the Battersea Dogs' Home?" I said, "I never knew it had been away." So he said, "This dog—this may interest you—this dog can *talk*. *Speak!*" he commanded. "*Speak!*" then, "I don't know what's come over it," he said. "It would happen. I'll give it a touch of the hobnails, that livens it up." So he had a quick look round and gave it a good kick. Again he said, "*Speak! Speak!*" The dog looked up. "What'll I say?" it asked. "Och," he said, "anyway it doesn't make any difference, I'm getting it destroyed." I said, "Why, is it mad?" "Well," he said, "it's not *pleased!*"'

In conversation with Tarbie after his monologue, Chic kept deadpan as he was asked question after question. After, Jimmy recalled Chic's 'A woman opened the door in her dressing gown. I thought—funny place to keep a door!' The audience laughed approvingly and Chic broke his silence, cracking, 'That *used* to go down well, Jimmy!'

*   *   *

The whole family was present for the great day, Chic's 65th birthday, as Gran Dickson, Douglas and Annabelle, young Douglas and Deanna all joined Maidie in the celebration, watching as Chic opened each card and present. He was on his very best behaviour as he declared, 'That's a great one!' or 'Hey, this one's a stoater!'

'Oh, Chic,' Maidie thought. 'Why can't you always be such a hero? You can be so good at it when you want to.' It was the very last time the family would be together.

21

Final Curtain

'I've always been a bit of a philosopher and I've come to the conclusion that nothing succeeds like a toothless budgie. And a good thing to remember is that you can drag a horse to water, but a pencil must be lead. I'm often asked if that joke closed Finsbury Park Empire. Well, it certainly helped!'

Before Chic had left for Liverpool and the triumph of *You'll Never Walk Alone*, he recorded a *Halls of Fame* television programme at His Majesty's Theatre, Aberdeen. He was in superb form, as his old friend and sparring partner Jimmy Logan noted, 'It was like vintage champagne all the way.' Soon after Chic recorded a pilot for Independent Television, *Smellie Broon*, then decided a week abroad would be a tonic, for he was feeling decidedly run down. He showed little sign of strain as he went along to the BBC to say farewell to Ian and Jenny.

'OK, Christie, what have you been up to?' Chic asked as he accosted him in the canteen. 'What new delights are you about to inflict on the long-suffering licence-payers? Have you noticed the vogue for sequels in the cinema? In the old days it would have been *Chic Ahoy Got Married* or *Son of Chic Ahoy*—now it would just be *Chic Ahoy II*.'

Ian winced inwardly. *The Terror of Chic Ahoy* would be more appropriate he was thinking, as he recalled the camel episode and the endless journey into the desert following the passport débâcle.

Jenny was Chic's next stop, her desk piled high with music sheets. Chic picked one off the top. 'Don't get them out of order,' pleaded Jenny. 'It's taken me hours to sort those out.'

'My good woman, you are talking to someone for whom disorder is anathema!' he declared, grabbing another couple of sheets. 'With my microscopic memory you are in safe hands!'

He looked at the top sheet—it was the music for Joe 'Mr Piano' Henderson's 'Trudie'. 'Ah, what memories this one recalls!' he exclaimed. 'The days of yore, of Chic and Maidie, Harold Fielding's *Music for the*

Millions, the Granite City, a wee slip of a girl called Petula Clark—where are they now, that's what I want to know!'

'Put them back,' said Jenny distractedly.

'I see you're in no mood for my gay repartee,' Chic said.

'I am,' Jenny replied, 'but give me just a minute and I'll have all this shuffled off. We need to talk, as it happens.'

'Indeed?' said Chic, eyebrows raised, winking at Jenny's secretary. 'Nothing *untoward*, I trust?'—'Untoward' coming out like 'Bech-u-a-na-land.'

With the music sheets safely stored away, Jenny turned to Chic. 'You left an old bag of rubbish when you were last here,' she stated.

'I'm sorry, Jenny. I meant to put it in the bucket.' 'It's as well you didn't,' Jenny scolded. 'We were going to do the same, then decided to check first. Three of the crumpled-up bits of paper were uncashed cheques from the BBC.'

Chic studied his fingernails. 'And?' he asked.

'Oh,' said Jenny. 'Pardon *me*, Chic, I didn't know you were working for nothing nowadays—you have your reputation to think of. All those meanness stories would fall a trifle flat if this got around. Anyway, they were out of date so I got accounts to cancel them and have new ones issued. Here they are, you big baby—'

Chic looked perplexedly at his old friend, then a little smile broke out. 'Thanks, pal,' he said. 'Now give us a kiss!' Before leaving he slapped his cheeks, grinned broadly and looked at Jenny. 'How'm I looking?' he asked. 'Good?'

Jenny thought he looked a bit tired. 'You're looking good,' she told him, 'but look *after* yourself, Chic.' Neither she nor Ian would ever see Chic again.

His last appearance on television—in a BBC Hogmanay show live from the Gleneagles Hotel—was a disaster, as it was for most of the cast who appeared, the main problem being the decision to move the production overnight lock, stock and barrel from the BBC studios, with its attendant technical facilities. Chic was seen on camera declaring. 'This is chaos!' and asking distractedly, 'What do you want me to do?', which had one observer wryly commenting that for a comedian who had made a career out of hilarious confusion and chaos, it was a not inappropriate exit.

Early in the New Year Chic declared it was time for a renewal of a friendship he had kept up for some years with publican Bernie Alderton. 'There's a—Lord Carnarvon to see you, Mr Alderton,' the girl on the switchboard announced. Since making the arrangement to meet Chic for lunch, Bernie had received an urgent call from group headquarters that a full report had to be knocked out and in the post that very night. Bernie had been working flat out since he heard the news and was about to involve his secretary in it as well before the 'Lord Carnarvon' announcement floored him.

Chic breezed in as usual and suggested a drink before lunch from Bernie's office cabinet. Bernie explained it would have to be a quick one as he was really pushed for time, then when Chic suggested a second drink, he knew he had to level with him. As he was explaining about the report and waving at a pile of papers on his desk, he knew what he had to do. His secretary thought the world of Chic and would jump at the chance of a lunch with him. 'How about taking Mary?' he asked Chic. 'And it's on me.'

'I'll bet that's the first sensible decision you've taken all day,' Chic declared. 'But how do you get to the restaurant?'

Bernie replied that he would have his chauffeur run them there, then wait and bring them back. 'But please,' he cautioned Mary, 'be back in an hour and a half at the latest. I need your help to get this report away tonight.'

'Don't worry,' he was assured—by Chic—as off they trooped.

Three hours later there was no sign of the party. It was almost 4 p.m. and Bernie knew there was now only the slenderest chance of his report making the evening post in legible form. In desperation he rang the restaurant and asked to speak to the manager. 'Is Chic Murray there?' he asked. 'Yes, he is,' replied the manager wearily. 'In fact, may I describe the scene for you? He is holding court with your secretary, your chauffeur and my assistant manager. Your secretary told me earlier that she had to get back, but I can only assume he has convinced her that there is no real urgency. Similarly he has persuaded your chauffeur that drinking and driving isn't *really* all that dangerous. In the same vein I think my assistant manager has thrown in his lot with them and departed—at least temporarily, though it could well turn out to be permanently—from my employ.'

'But what's he *doing*?' Bernie demanded to know. 'Doing?' the manager echoed. 'I think he must be a mesmerist. He's got them absolutely spellbound—all their cares and responsibilities have melted clean away. I shouldn't complain—they've also gone through vast quantities of my finest brandy.' By the time the party did eventually decant itself, Bernie knew his dream of getting the report off that night was over. 'It was a splendid lunch,' Chic assured him grandly. 'You have *nothing* to reproach yourself for!'

During the last week of January, Maidie took a call from Chic in London. 'I'm coming up to stay for a few days,' he advised her. 'Maybe more than a few days, Maidie, for I need a right good rest. I'm hoping to get up there tonight, but if I miss the last plane it'll be tomorrow morning.'

'Are you all right, Chic?' Maidie asked, for he sounded hoarse and distant.

'I'll be fine when I'm there with you,' he replied.

'Sounds to me like you're planning to move in for the duration,' Maidie said gently.

There was a long pause, then, 'I've done dafter things in my life.'

By early afternoon Chic was getting ready to leave central London when he discovered that a colleague would soon be driving up to Edinburgh. A lift was promptly arranged and an hour later the two of them set off. Chic was fast asleep before they reached the motorway and slept soundly until they arrived at Carter Bar, when he woke up, and looked out into the darkness and realised where he was. He closed his eyes again, and pictured Maidie emerging from the kitchen in Dundee, bearing a steaming pan of custard. What a temptress! 'My God, that was some pan of custard,' he said out loud, licking his lips. 'What's that, Chic?' his driver asked. 'Nothing,' said Chic. 'I was just saying I could go a pan of custard right now.' 'Will we stop and get a bite?' 'No, no. I'm only kidding. Drive on, Macduff. You're doing a grand job.'

'Drop me on the corner, here,' Chic said as they drove up to the park near Maidie's. 'And here's saxpence for your trouble,' he joked as he went on his way, swinging his shopping bag. Walking towards the house he could see that the lights were off. He looked at his watch under the street lamp—11.45 p.m; no wonder there was no sign of life. Oh well, he thought, Bob Phillips next door will put me up for the night. He saw that his light was on and rang the bell until Bob's wife Eleanor appeared. 'It's yourself !' she cried. 'Come on in, Chic. Are you all right, man? You look tired out. Bob! Come and see who's turned up—'

'Oh, I'm half asleep, just,' said Chic, as Bob appeared. 'I've missed Maidie—she's off to bed. Could you put me up for the night?'

'Of course, big man,' Bob replied. 'Come awa' in and we'll get you a nice toddy, then it's off to bed with you. You can sleep in my mother's old room, the one just through the wall from Maidie—why you can even shout through to her if you want.'

After the drink with his friends, Chic took a second toddy to his room and sat up in bed for a while contemplating Tretchikoff's *Chinese Girl* print on the wall opposite. Before Bob turned in himself he looked in first on Chic to make sure he was comfortable. 'I'm fine, just awful, awful tired,' Chic remarked, then, 'Very nice,' he added, with a nod to the painting, 'but on the whole I prefer blondes myself.'

'I know you do—and one blonde in particular,' Bob added. 'Not a million miles from here.'

Chic put his empty glass down on the bedside table and eased himself into the pillows. 'That's right,' he said as Bob left. 'One blonde in particular.' Chic sat up in bed and reached for his spectacle case. From it he took his glasses and a crumpled sheet of paper, then smoothing it out, he crooned the words softly to himself:

That feeling keeps returning,
It makes me yearn the whole day through,
To hold you close and find
That feeling is shared by you.
That feeling lures me to you
Dreamborne it seems I travel on.
People seem pale and distant
Only that feeling is strong.
The road's been long but nears its end,
Soon, very soon, we'll meet once more,
Moments from now I'll reach for you
With all the joy I knew before.
That feeling has rejoined us
Now I will know as I hold you
Whether you share that feeling
I've felt so long for you.

Finished reading, he replaced his spectacles in their case and, leaving the sheet of paper lying beside it, switched the bedside lamp off.

Maidie woke at 6 a.m. to find the bed covered in pictures of the double act. Unable to sleep the night before after waiting up for Chic, she had dug out some of the hundreds of old photographs she had kept over the years before finally dropping off to sleep. She dreamt fitfully, as she often did, of those early days, the mysterious Mrs Pollock, the pay-poke correspondence, Nellie Sutherland, the mental homes tour . . .

Deciding that a pot of tea would be in order, Maidie got up and was making her way downstairs in her dressing gown when the phone rang. It was Bob Phillips with the news that Chic had died in his sleep.

To this day Maidie has no idea what prompted her to ask which room he had been sleeping in. 'My mother's room, the one next to yours,' Bob told her, making her tremble at the thought of Chic on the other side of the wall while she had been poring over the old photographs.

Maidie dressed automatically, then braced herself and went next door. Although he had died as a result of a perforated duodenal ulcer, as the doctor explained, Maidie was relieved beyond measure to see how peaceful Chic looked, as if in a deep and dreamless sleep. It was a moment or two before she noticed the sheet of paper he had left on the bedside table, and the title, 'That Feeling'.

*　　　*　　　*

The funeral was organised by Annabelle in the distinctive Chic Murray tradition of nonconformity, with the service in the capable hands of not one but two ministers—the 'Reverends' Johnnie Beattie and Billy Connolly. When both had delivered eulogies, Billy led the mourners in

the well-known hymn 'You'll Never Walk Alone', while Chic's coffin sat
there, his tartan bunnet perched on top.

As the coffin disappeared Johnnie swears that the tartan bunnet
waggled from side to side. This could, reasonably, have been caused by
the motion of the coffin itself, but since this was Chic's last exit a far
more likely explanation offered itself—he thoroughly approved of the
service and wanted to show it in a last farewell gesture.

As the coffin lid between the curtains, the mourners burst into
spontaneous applause. It seemed an appropriate way to say farewell
and pay tribute to this unique, complex and unforgettable character.

Someone once asked Chic which career he might have taken up if not
that of a comic. 'That's easy,' he replied.'I'd liked to have become a brain
specialist, a philosopher, a psychiatrist, a beachcomber, a mental homes
inspector–' he paused and shrugged '–but I couldn't think of a better
way to combine all these things!' Or–he might have added–a better
way to walk.

Index